The Culture of Mean

Sharon R. Mazzarella
General Editor

Vol. 30

The Mediated Youth series is part of the Peter Lang Media and Communication list.
Every volume is peer reviewed and meets
the highest quality standards for content and production.

PETER LANG
New York • Bern • Frankfurt • Berlin
Brussels • Vienna • Oxford • Warsaw

Emily D. Ryalls

The Culture of Mean

Representing Bullies and Victims in Popular Culture

PETER LANG
New York • Bern • Frankfurt • Berlin
Brussels • Vienna • Oxford • Warsaw

Library of Congress Cataloging-in-Publication Data

Names: Ryalls, Emily D., author.
Title: The culture of mean: representing bullies and victims in popular
culture / Emily D. Ryalls.
Description: New York: Peter Lang, 2018.
Series: Mediated youth; Volume 30
ISSN 1555-1814 (print) | ISSN 2378-2935 (online)
Includes bibliographical references and index.
Identifiers: LCCN 2017038561 | ISBN 978-1-4331-4618-3 (pbk.: alk. paper)
ISBN 978-1-4331-4619-0 (hardback: alk. paper) | ISBN 978-1-4331-4620-6 (ebook pdf)
ISBN 978-1-4331-4621-3 (epub) | ISBN 978-1-4331-4622-0 (mobi)
Subjects: LCSH: Bullies in mass media.
Bullies—United States.
Bullying in schools—United States.
Bullying—Social aspects—United States.
Teenagers in mass media.
Classification: LCC P96.B852 U679 | DDC 302.34/3—dc23
LC record available at https://lccn.loc.gov/ 2017038561
DOI 10.3726/b12950

Bibliographic information published by **Die Deutsche Nationalbibliothek.**
Die Deutsche Nationalbibliothek lists this publication in the "Deutsche
Nationalbibliografie"; detailed bibliographic data are available
on the Internet at http://dnb.d-nb.de/.

The paper in this book meets the guidelines for permanence and durability
of the Committee on Production Guidelines for Book Longevity
of the Council of Library Resources.

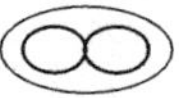

Printed in the United States of America

For Mom

TABLE OF CONTENTS

ACKNOWLEDGMENTS

During my doctoral program at the University of South Florida, a professor questioned how we found ourselves in a class doing media criticism. "No one dreams of being a film critic," he opined, but he was wrong. I did. My earliest passion was popular culture. On Saturday mornings, when my peers were watching cartoons, I was glued to the TV watching *Siskel & Ebert.* I am grateful to them for showing me at a young age that nerding out over popular culture could potentially be a career choice. I try to always remind myself how fortunate I am to live a life in which I love and critique popular culture and get to share that passion with my students who consistently turn me on to new shows and movies that I would certainly miss if left to my own devices.

While my family undoubtedly thought it strange that I spent my days off from school walking to the local video store, they have shown me unconditional love. I thank my father who I am slowly but surely turning in to, and Aunt Lorraine who I always hoped I would become. I thank my brother for never hesitating to make fun of me and, in doing so, reminding me to not take myself too seriously. I thank my godmother for continuing to beg me to not become too liberal (it's too late, Aunt Donna), and Aunt Debbie for being always willing to see a movie with me, without asking questions, even though she knows that odds are she won't "get" it or it will make her uncomfortable.

Although often exasperated by my political leanings, my family never misses a chance to tell me how proud they are of me for which I am forever grateful.

I spent a few years between my MA and PhD programs adrift, but when I got to Clemson University as a Lecturer, I met Sharon Mazzarella who helped me find my place in academia. Sharon has been my teacher, colleague, and mentor. She has shown unending support for my academic prowess (way before I trusted I was even competent). Perhaps, most importantly, Sharon mirrored for me that studying girls and girls' media was an important terrain of critical research. Publishing this book in her Youth and Media series brings me full circle.

The students and professors I met during my time in the Communication PhD program at the University of South Florida are my friends to this day; many are cited in or served as editors for this work. I remember fondly writing with Rachel and Steve on his lanai, recognizing even then how rare those moments would be as I forged my career. Jillian was one of the first faces I met at USF; it seems apropos the next leg of my career has me following her to California. Alisha was one of the last friends I made at USF. Her extreme chattiness and willingness to share a cheese plate and a bottle of champagne are a large part of what got me through the dissertation process. I thank David Payne for stretching my brain in the classes I took with him. I thank Elizabeth Bell whose ability to balance excellent teaching, prolific research, and outstanding leadership is something I one day hope to emulate. Thanks also to Lori, Eric, Tony, Amanda, Robin, Antoine, and Linda, who all offered wisdom or a hug when it was most needed.

I wrote parts of this book as an Assistant Professor at Mississippi State University. During that time, Danny, JoAnn, Taffi, Kimberly, and Chuck Bass kept me sane. I am so thankful to The Bachelor Crew for continuing to show me love and support even after its members moved on to bigger and better things, and I offer a huge thanks to Taffi who became my travel buddy and allowed me to escape to warm beaches when things got too crazy. Watching Kimberly fight for the Gender Studies program on a conservative campus taught me so much about the kind of academic and person I want to be. More importantly, if not for her, I would not have adopted Chuck Bass who has changed my life in the loveliest ways (he wears bowties, y'all).

The final parts of this book were written at Cal Poly. I am genuinely grateful and appreciative of my amazing colleagues in the Communication Studies Department who have shown nothing but support and generosity in the time I have been here.

I am eternally indebted to Rachel Dubrofsky who, on most occasions, has shown more faith in my ability to succeed than I have. In the nearly six years since I have graduated, Rachel has continued to be my closest mentor. She gives selflessly and exorbitantly of her time, and I know with utmost certainty that she has played a role in all of my academic successes.

I dedicate this work to my mother who raised me with a feminist sensibility and who has shown unwavering support for my academic ambitions. Keeping this book a secret from you was one of the most difficult things I've done. I hope the surprise was worth it! I love you.

INTRODUCTION

Mean Girls, Cyberbullying, and Bullycide:
An Introduction to Bullying Culture

On April 20, 1999, high school students Eric Harris and Dylan Klebold went on a shooting rampage, killing 13 and wounding many more before turning their guns on themselves. Mainstream news outlets reported a number of potential causes for Harris and Klebold's killing spree, including the music of Marilyn Manson, violent video games, and Internet technology (Serazio, 2010), but the most commonly cited cause of their anger was the alleged bullying they faced from popular "jocks." The Columbine shootings "solidified the logical connection between schools and anti-violence initiatives" and placed bullying at the forefront of discussions about youth problems (Chesney-Lind & Irwin, 2008, p. 93). Following the Columbine massacre, The Secret Service and the U.S. Department of Education released a report that claimed almost three quarters of school shooters "felt persecuted, bullied, threatened, attacked or injured by others prior to the incident" (Vossekuil, Fein, Reddy, Borum, & Modzeleski, 2002). Importantly, the report did not make claims about "what caused these shootings. Despite this, journalists, legislators, school districts, and school administrators made note of the fact that so many of the school shooters felt bullied" (Chesney-Lind & Irwin, 2008, p. 94), implicitly connecting bullying to school shootings and setting the stage for an increased focus on the presumed damage caused by bullies in schools.

In 2002, the publication of two books compounded the concerns about bullying raised in the aftermath of Columbine. Rachel Simmons's *Odd Girl Out* and Rosalind Wiseman's *Queen Bees & Wannabes* brought girls into the discourse about bullying by claiming to document a hidden culture of girls' aggression where "mean girls"[1] run rampant. Basing their research largely on social scientific scholarship regarding the ways in which girls aggress, Simmons and Wiseman explained that girls use indirect aggression, which is a form of social manipulation. This covert form of aggression, also referred to as "relational" or "social" aggression, includes a series of actions aimed at destroying other girls' relationships, causing their victims to feel marginalized (Crothers, Field, & Kolbert, 2005). The books were best sellers, and the authors, who garnered a reputation as experts, were often interviewed for newspapers and magazines and on television programs. Additionally, both books served as the basis for fictional films about girls who bully—*Odd Girl Out* (2005) and *Mean Girls* (2004). Suddenly, the image of the mean girl who manipulates other girls in order to strengthen her power and increase her privilege took hold. While the books focused on themes of cliques, cultural ideals of femininity, and girls' vulnerability, the larger cultural narrative picked up and reframed these issues as "bullying."

It is the contention of *The Culture of Mean* that, in the 15 years since the publication of these books, the United States has seen an explosion of discourse on youth bullying. Concerns about bullying are widespread, reflected in several sites of contemporary culture. For instance, all 50 states (and Washington, D.C.) have anti-bullying laws (prior to 1999, no states had laws clearly addressing bullying). In 2006, October was designated National Bullying Prevention Awareness Month; in 2010, the Department of Education implemented a $38.8 million Safe and Supportive Schools grant program and held the first federal school bullying summit; in 2011, President Obama convened a day-long White House Conference on Preventing Bullying; and, during the 2016 Presidential campaign, future first lady, Melania Trump said she would like to begin an initiative to put an end to cyberbullying. Anti-bullying websites abound, such as stopbullying.gov, a federal government website managed by the U.S. Department of Health & Human Services, and, perhaps most famously, ItGetsBetter.org, which features Public Service Announcements made by politicians and celebrities to communicate to lesbian, gay, bisexual, transgender, and queer (LGBTQ) youth that life gets better after high school when, presumably, the bullying ends. *The Huffington Post* and *The New*

York Times offer sections dedicated entirely to "bullying," "cyberbullying," and "school bullying," which include blogs, commentary, and archived articles.

This book offers a feminist critical exploration of mediated representations of youth bullying, bringing into conversation scholarship on feminism, media, new communication technologies, surveillance, gender, race, sexuality, and class. I look at popular mainstream discourses about bullying, and examine the movement of bullying from mean girls to youth bullying to cyberbullying. Through critical research that employs a feminist lens, I explore how media has contributed to the U.S. bullying discourse. An investigation of the construction of the mean girl who uses verbal communication provides access to how conceptualizations of bullying have shifted over time from acts of physical violence to verbal aggression, and recently to a more intense focus on bullycide (suicide said to result from bullying) and cyberbullying (bullying carried out using newer forms of media such as text messaging and social media). *The Culture of Mean* explores this trajectory, considering the ways these shifts are inextricably tied up with gender (girl use words, which is seen as more damaging than boys' physical violence), race (a narrow focus on white youth), and sexuality (concern with the bullying of gay boys).

While it seems common sense to view bullying as always wrong and dangerous, not all aggression is bullying and it is problematic to assume so, because it becomes very difficult to differentiate between healthy conflict and unhealthy (potentially violent) torment. Mediated stories focus on constructing victims of bullying as decidedly weak and vulnerable, and bullies as markedly cruel and violent. In nearly all cases, images of bullies and their victims are white and middle-class. Most often (although not always), victims are boys who self-identify as or are presumed to be gay or girls. Thus, discourses about bullying align with established discourses about young girls, whiteness, and homosexuality but update them for the new current concern: bullying.

Surveilling and Disciplining Teens

I place the contemporary bullying discourse within a "moral panic" paradigm. Moral panics are the interplay of (over)reactions from the media, the public, politicians, and agents of social control to youthful deviance. Moral panics frame the activities of youth as immoral and, in so doing, suggest that in contemporary times we see a "moral decline, in which people—especially the young—can no longer tell the difference between right and wrong" (Thompson, 1998, p. 4).

Although McRobbie and Thornton (1995) argue that the moral panic paradigm needs to be reconsidered since moral panics no longer instigate a singular popular reaction, what is noteworthy about the bullying discourse, particularly as it relates to cyberbullying and bullycide, is just how standardized the public reaction is. My analysis suggests the bullying moral panic is monolithic in its unnecessarily extreme reaction, which is damaging and ineffective. As the ideas framed in the bullying discourse about youth, gender, and aggression become common sense, they structure the way authorities think about and react to the risks of bullying. Many of the taken-for-granted ideas that circulate within the bullying discourse have led to unproductive responses, such as increased surveillance of students on and off school grounds.

In the wake of the Columbine massacre, schools began implementing bullying prevention programs that expanded surveillance over students' lives. "Implicit to most understandings of surveillance is the idea of real people being watched, often unknowingly" (Dubrofsky & Magnet, 2015, p. 2). Foucault (1995) stressed that surveillance is productive—it aides the state in producing docile bodies, individuals who come to police themselves. "This form of internalized surveillance is often captured by the spatial landscape of the Panopticon" (Dubrofsky & Magnet, 2015, p. 2). The power of the Panopticon is "evident in contemporary society with its pervasive mechanisms of surveillance ranging from identity cards and passports at borders to the security and traffic cameras populating urban landscapes" (Jiwani, 2015, p. 82). Giroux (2003) maintains that surveillance is just one example of schools' "turn toward state repression and social containment" through "the growth of domestic militarization policies in which practices that are endemic to the penal system" are normalized (p. 49). According to Giroux (2003), "The distinction between the school and the prison has been blurred" through the "growing presence of metal detectors, guards patrolling the corridors, use of surveillance cameras, and harsh zero-tolerance policies" (p. 49). Indeed, "in the 1999–2000 school year, only 19% of public schools reported using security cameras. By 2011–2012, it was up to 64%. By 2013–2014, it had risen to 75%" (Klein, 2016). In an examination of high schools in Chicago, Shedd (2015) argues, "A carceral apparatus consisting of security guards, cameras, and metal detectors…" forces students to become accustomed to "being viewed from a 'criminal gaze' that operates not by force" (p. 95; 99). Thus, in the way that Foucault described surveillance culture as working, adolescents have internalized this sense of watchfulness, so they learn to "behave as if they are always under surveillance, since they can never know whether or not they are being scrutinized" (Dubrofsky & Magnet, 2015, p. 2).

In line with increasing surveillance of students in school are calls for school officials to monitor students' social media, potentially infringing on students' right to free speech. For instance, a middle school in Georgia suspended two dozen students for sharing or commenting on a Facebook post that encouraged students to break the school's dress code by wearing red the next day. The students were suspended regardless of whether they actually followed through and wore red, because the principal labeled the action of responding to Facebook a "terroristic threat" (Stampler, 2014). In another example, in 2009, two tenth graders at Churubusco High School were suspended from extracurricular activities for the school year when they posted pictures of themselves school administrators contended could "discredit" or "dishonor" the school. The court disagreed, arguing the girls' pictures were "raunchy" and "juvenile" but also "protected speech" (Sengupta, 2013).

Many of these punishments are over-reaches that align with zero-tolerance policies, which suspend or even expel students for, in some cases, relatively minor offenses. For example, in 2014, a 17-year-old girl in Michigan was expelled when she was caught with a pocketknife in her backpack at a school football game. Atiya Haynes, an Advanced Placement student with a 3.0 grade point average, explains she forgot she had the pocketknife, which her grandfather gave her the previous summer as protection for when she biked alone through some of Dearborn Heights' rougher neighborhoods on the way to her job as a lifeguard (Gross, 2014). In April of 2012, Nathan, a 9-year-old boy was suspended from his elementary school when, after weeks of being bullied, Nathan fought back when the bully once again kicked and punched him. Despite clearly being the victim to a bully, Nathan was expelled because the school had a zero-tolerance policy for violence (The Independent Florida Alligator, 2012). These cases highlight some of the problems with zero tolerance. Although neither student was arrested, their suspensions, like those of other victims of overzealous zero-tolerance policies, will almost certainly cause them to fall behind in their education. Additionally, zero-tolerance policies have sent far too many "kids into the juvenile justice system, and have been tied to the 'school-to-prison' pipeline contributing to mass incarceration in the U.S." (Zoukis, 2016). Moreover, zero-tolerance policies disproportionately target students of color, LGBTQ students, and those with disabilities (Flannery, 2015).

Embedded within the militarization practices outlined by Giroux (2003) are problematic and troublingly vague policies aimed at putting an end to bullying. Surveilling students' online communication in the guise of fighting cyberbullying and expelling students found guilty of bullying only contributes to the police state that has become common in many educational environments. Moreover, since the label "bullying" often does not differentiate between teasing, conflict, and violence, increasingly the most common way of dealing with youth accused of bullying is to criminalize their actions. For instance, in 2013, Sheriff Grady Judd of Polk County arrested two girls (one 14, the other 12) for cyberbullying when 12-year-old Rebecca Ann Sedwick committed suicide. When the Polk County state attorney's office decided to drop the felony charges against the girls, citing a lack of evidence, Polk claimed he had no regrets since he had "raised awareness" (Alvarez, 2013). Lawrence Walters, a first amendment attorney, argued, "That is a misuse of the criminal justice system. You don't bring felony charges against a 12-year-old to raise awareness of a society issue" (Alvarez, 2013).

While the popular discourse champions the escalation of punitive treatment of teens, I argue the cultural response is an overreaction that is actually counterproductive, missing entirely structural systemic issues of oppression, instead reducing sexism, racism, classism, and homophobia to individual bullying behaviors. *The Culture of Mean* illustrates how constructions of bullies as purely evil provide the foundation for the growing reliance on legal retribution in cases of bullying. This discourse takes for granted that bullying is a serious, menacing problem and that victims of bullying experience intense and long-term negative outcomes. These common sense notions defy the need for specificity—who would dare suggest that bullies are three-dimensional and more than just terrible people? Constructions of bullying in film, television programming, and news media create an overly simplistic binary of good and bad people, individualizing the problem of bullying and disallowing a more complex understanding of the structural issues at work in the discourse by suggesting that putting an end to bullying simply requires incarcerating those evil teens who are prone to bullying behaviors.

Technological Determinism

Technological determinism, as explained by Winner (1980), is the naïve "idea that technology develops as the sole result of an internal dynamic, and then, unmediated by any other influence, molds society to fit its patterns" (p. 122). This view of technology, whether utopian or dystopian, assumes "technologies possess intrinsic powers that affect *all* people in *all* situations the same way" (boyd, 2014, p. 15). When new communication and media technologies are introduced (for example, the telegraph, comic books, movies, and the Internet), they are often met with corresponding optimism and anxiety about their potential effects on society (Hasinoff, 2015). An optimistic utopian view of technology heralds technology as having the ability to transform society in such a way as to solve major world problems (boyd, 2014). As explained by Winner (1980), "Scarcely a new innovation comes along that someone does not proclaim it the salvation of a free society" (p. 122). Contrastingly, anxiety ridden dystopian visions concentrate on the mythical negative effects of new technologies, suggesting their adoption will lead to the social, intellectual, and moral decline of society (boyd, 2014).

Moral panics that revolve around youth and technology are generally episodic (boyd, 2014). Many of the moral panics of the last century have been framed around young people's tendency to be early adopters of technology (Wartella & Mazzarella, 1990). For instance, in the 1950s, television, comic books, and rock 'n' roll were all linked to juvenile delinquency (Mazzarella, 2007). "Popular music has long been a favoured candidate for a 'moral panic'" (Springhall, 1998, p. 148). In the mid-1980s, the Parents' Music Resource Center (PMRC), which was headed by Tipper Gore, led a campaign against heavy-metal rock. The PMRC, without any scientific or controlled evidence, claimed a link between heavy-metal rock and "adolescent drinking, drug use, sexual promiscuity, rape, and suicide" (Mazzarella, 2007, p. 52). Then, the 1990s saw a public outcry over rap when C. Dolores Tucker of the National Political Congress of Black Women argued gangsta rap was *the* reason Black children were out of control and more Black men were in prison than college (Mazzarella, 2007). As discussed earlier, blame for the mass shooting at Columbine High School was also placed on popular culture, including music. In the hundreds of articles that were published following the massacre, journalists listed the cause of the tragedy as popular music (Marilyn Manson), the goth subculture of which Manson was a symbol, "movies (for example, *The Matrix* and *The Basketball Diaries*), video games (*Doom* and *Quake*), (and) the Internet" (Mazzarella, 2007, p. 54).

As was the case with the Columbine shootings, media and the general public (especially, in the case of moral panics) are quick to subscribe to the dystopian view of technology as "determining" kids' behaviors, espousing a cultural anxiety that even good kids can be led astray by technology. Such is the case with discourses of cyberbullying, which frame teens as using technology, including "cell phones, computers, and tablets as well as communication tools including social media sites, text messages, chat, and websites" to bully (U. S. Department of Health & Human Services, n.d.). According to the Department of Health & Human Services (n.d.), which manages the federal government website stopbullying.gov, "Examples of cyberbullying include mean text messages or emails, rumors sent by email or posted on social networking sites, and embarrassing pictures, videos, websites, or fake profiles." Teen sexting, which is often framed as part of a cyberbullying epidemic, is "the practice of sending or posting sexually suggestive text messages and images, including nude or seminude photographs, via cell phones or over the Internet" (Klein, 2012, p. 227). Sexting becomes bullying when the photographs are distributed, without consent, by others attempting to embarrass, shame, or otherwise hurt the individual in the picture. Concerns about sexting illustrate the notion of technological determinism, as media coverage suggests that "teens' use of technology encourages and supports sexual encounters that, without technology, might not take place" (Draper, 2012, p. 225). However, as explained by Hasinoff (2015), "Viewing technology as the root cause of sexting may not be the most accurate or productive position" (p. 10).

These extreme visions of technology as utopian or dystopian "are equally unhelpful in understanding what actually happens when new technologies are broadly adopted. Reality is nuanced and messy" (boyd, 2014, p. 16). "One hallmark of moral panics is that they focus attention and direct resources toward simple solutions to complex problems and often serve as smokescreens enabling us as a society to ignore larger, more troubling problems" (Mazzarella, 2007, p. 56). As explained by boyd (2014), the focus on technology appears straightforward because technical changes are easier to see than broader systemic issues. For example, the dystopian notion that teens are addicted to social media overlooks the fact that new forms of communication technologies fulfill teens' "fundamental desire for social connection" (boyd, 2014, p. 17). Moreover, with regard to moral panics, the dystopic view of technology is often generational, as new technologies are framed as dangerous *only* to young people. For example, when adults engage in sexting, "it is often considered free speech and even encouraged" (Klein, 2012, p. 227). However, because child pornography laws are vague, they are increasingly being used against sexting teenagers, which "makes sexting seem more dangerous and deviant" (Hasinoff, 2015, p. 14). Similarly, with regard to cyberbullying, as Bazelon (2012) explains (in reference to the Tyler Clementi case, discussed in Chapter 2), "civil rights statutes are being stretched to go after teenagers who acted meanly, but not violently." Cultural anxiety over the intersection of communication technologies with bullying has led to the demonization of teenagers, as opposed to a focus on systemic issues (such as racism, classism, sexism, and homophobia) at the heart of much bullying.

Feminist Girls' Media Studies

The Culture of Mean explores books, films, television programming, newspapers, and magazines, situating the work in what Projansky (2014) calls feminist girls' media studies. An understanding of feminist girls' media studies must begin with a brief look at the broad history of the academic discipline of girls' studies. In the late 1970s, feminist cultural studies scholar Angela McRobbie noted the absence of girls in youth subcultural work. "Combining critical analysis of media representations with a nuanced understanding of girls' negotiations with media culture, McRobbie insisted that girls and girl cultures matter" (Projansky, 2014, p. 14). McRobbie's work "paved the way for a growing cadre of feminist cultural studies scholars focusing on the culture of girls" (Mazzarella & Pecora, 1999, p. 1).

In 1982, Carol Gilligan published *In a Different Voice,* in which she noted the different approaches used by men and women when thinking and speaking about relationships. Scholars in psychology and education followed Gilligan with investigations into the ways in which adolescent girls' development was distinctive from that of boys (Mazzarella & Pecora, 1999). The primarily sociological and psychological studies that ensued focused on the troubling effects of being raised a girl in patriarchal society. These examinations of girls' vulnerability highlighted the social and development issues girls face when they enter adolescence, including a drop in IQ, math, and science scores, along with a loss in resiliency, optimism, curiosity, and risk-taking (Pipher, 1994). The studies emerging at this time noted a series of trends regarding girls' development in a misogynistic culture. As they enter into adolescence, girls observe when and where women speak and how they are silenced. Girls further recognize that being "good" is celebrated, and that being good means taking care of others at the expense of one's self (Mazzarella & Pecora, 2007b). As they become aware of the ways in which women are positioned unequally in relation to men, girls learn that "proper" girls are "heterosexual, chaste, submissive, attentive to their 'looks,' family-oriented, professionally unambitious and compliant" (Aapola, Gonick, & Harris, 2005, p. 6).

As a part of this first wave of girls' studies, "scholars studying girls' cultural artifacts in the United States focused primarily on representations of, and messages sent to, girls in and by the mass-produced products of the culture industries. These representations and messages were often linked to perceived negative effects on young female audiences" (Mazzarella & Pecora, 2007b, p. 110). The literature coming out of girls' studies at this time "galvanized a powerful public response, particularly from adult women. Several of the publications identified connections between women and girls as a key means for promoting girls' healthy and safe adolescent development" (Ward & Benjamin, 2004, p. 17). The construction of girls as vulnerable was important because it brought attention to the ways in which girls internalize structural inequalities. Despite the many gains of the feminist movement, the barriers to full equality persist, and, as these scholars noted, these inequalities manifest on girls' bodies and psyches (Aapola *et al.*, 2005).

Although this research was incredibly important, it also upheld many demeaning stereotypes by representing girls as victims, cultural dupes, and hysterical. Further, in much of this early scholarship, girlhood was considered a physical and emotional stage of development that all young women, despite their individualized experiences, suffer through in more or less the same way, ignoring the systemic issues girls face such as racism, classism, and homophobia. More recently, girls' studies scholars have begun to consider other ways of seeing girlhood. This research grapples with the diversity of girls' experiences and, in so doing, considers constructions of girls' identities from an intersectional approach (a framework for investigating the constitutive structural identities of race, class, gender, and sexuality). "American popular culture has produced a seemingly ever increasing focus on girls since the late 1980s, arguably marking the present and recent past as a particularly intense and sustained moment of cultural obsession with them" (Projanksy, 2007, p. 41). As such, it is not surprising that feminist girls' media scholars are exploring images of girls in a wide range of media sites as a way to access the cultural desires and anxieties about girls that these images animate. Scholars in feminist girls' media studies explore films (Driver, 2007; Dubrofsky & Ryalls, 2014; Gateward & Pomerance, 2002; Hains, 2012; Hentges, 2006; Projansky, 2014), television (Banet-Weiser, 2004, 2007; Ono, 2000; Projansky & Vande Berg, 2000; Ryalls, 2016), newer forms of media technologies (Almjeld, 2015; Hasinoff, 2015; Mazzarella, 2008, 2010b), as well as magazines, newspapers, and advertising (Mazzarella, 1999, 2010a; Mazzarella & Pecora, 2007a; McRobbie, 1991; Projansky 2007; Ryalls, 2012; Walkerdine, 1997).

Analyses of representations of girls in popular culture consider what these representations have to say about the social and political world that modern girls inhabit.

Exploring Bullying Media Culture

The Culture of Mean asks: how is the contemporary discourse about youth bullying constructed in television, film, and print media with regard to gender, race, class, and sexuality? What anxieties and desires undergird these narratives? What gets lost in the transition from a discourse of mean girls to one of generalized youth bullying? What can media tell us about how contemporary U.S. culture thinks about teens, aggression, and bullying? Do media sites featuring cyberbullying reflect cultural concerns about youth and emerging forms of media? How do images of girl bullies reflect cultural concerns about female empowerment, feminized aggression, and girls' success?

The book offers a series of case studies of media sites that are important in defining what it means to be a bully and a victim. The popular media I explore are "symptomatic texts" (Walters, 1995), texts that serve as "symptoms" of the larger culture in which they exist, providing insight about that culture. My analysis focuses on media discourses produced after 2002 (when Simmons and Wiseman's books were published) that contain the themes that are discussed most often in the bullying narrative (i.e., social aggression, cyberbullying, bullycide, and mean girls). I do not attempt a comprehensive reading of all the images of bullying in popular culture; instead, I concentrate on a range of media artifacts that provides access to how images of bullying have been constructed in various media formats and genres.

In examining films, television, books, and journalism, I take a holistic view of mediated representations of bullying, because, as explained by Negra (2009), "In a synergistic media environment, analysis of a single medium holds less explanatory power for any account that seeks to explain the complex relations between social life and media representation" (p. 9). The media sites I analyze form what Dow (1996) calls a "media culture" that has a great deal to say about bullying and its impact on our lives. Each is noteworthy for its contribution to cultural ideas about bullying and for its place within the trajectories of popular media, feminist media studies, and the evolution of representations of youth bullying. *The Culture of Mean* utilizes a critical girls' media studies perspective in order to gain insight into how girls' aggression, bullying, and youth violence are culturally understood. The book's chapters engage feminist media studies methodologies to explore the raced, gendered, classed, and heterosexualized implications of the contemporary bullying discourse. The textual examples I explore are illustrative and not meant as "proof" of a bullying crisis but rather to open up a discussion of a pattern of representation of bullies and victims.

Scholarship on Mean Girl Culture

Research on school bullying has been overwhelmingly undertaken by psychologists interested in bullying as a developmental psychological problem among children (Ringrose, 2008). There are two books that consider representations of bullying in popular culture. Patrice Oppliger's (2013) *Bullies and Mean Girls in Popular Culture* explores the influence of mediated representations of bullying on adolescents' attitudes and behaviors. Taking for granted that (a) bullying is a substantial problem and (b) that media has a significant effect on adolescents' aggressive behavior, Oppliger brings together images of bullying in television and film aimed at children, adolescents, and adults in order to highlight patterns of representation. *Bullying in Popular Culture: Essays on Film, Television and Novels* (2015) is a mixed-method edited collection that examines decades of bullying in media sites. Analyses in the collection consider many different types of bullying relationships (i.e., parents who bully, workplace bullying) in a variety of social groups and participants. These books are an excellent beginning. *The Culture of Mean* extends this work through a sustained feminist critical exploration of the *contemporary* (beginning in 2002) discourse about youth bullying, cyberbullying, and bullycide through a range of media that includes books, television, film, and news media.

Scholarly attention to girl bullying and media has noted that boys are largely absent from the mean girl narrative. Kelly and Pomerantz (2009) argue the film *Mean Girls* constructs the problem of girl bullying as an issue of female aggression, erasing entirely boys and men. In a previously published article, I (2012) explored the media coverage of the death of Phoebe Prince, arguing the media ignored, popular football player, Sean Mulveyhill in order to frame alleged girl bullies as causing Phoebe to commit suicide. Text messages sent to Phoebe's mom from Phoebe (that were released in court) framed Sean as the Queen Bee, a role so enmeshed with femininity it was difficult to conceive of a narrative in which he could take on the characteristics of a mean girl. Building on these arguments about the erasure of boys in the mean girl narrative, this book explores how and why boys *are* implicated in accounts of girl bullying. I argue the construction of boys in stories of girl bullying enables particular gendered constructions of girls' actions, framing girls' use of social aggression as more dangerous and threatening than boys' physical violence. This troubling sleight of hand contributes to increasing calls for punitive disciplinary action in response to the communicative behaviors of girls.

In *Spectacular Girls*, Projansky (2014) queers *Mean Girls*, arguing the film "holds heterosexuality responsible for meanness and articulates queer girlhoods" (p. 126). I extend Projansky's work by exploring constructions of queer boys who use social aggression (i.e., "mean boys"), including Damien from *Mean Girls*. *The Culture of Mean* shows that, historically, we have seen popular boys ("jocks") portrayed as using social aggression; however, these images have been erased from contemporary movies and television shows featuring bullies, suggesting boys only bully boys, typically through physically violent means, which is framed as an appropriate solution to conflict. In today's narrative about youth bullying, boys who use social aggression are generally queered in some way. This framing provides boys access to, what is culturally seen as, a normatively feminine way of expressing aggression by troublingly fusing notions of homosexuality with femininity.

Scholarship on popular media has also explored bullying, girls, and success. In a quantitative media effects analysis of teen movies (including *Mean Girls*), Behm-Morawitz and Mastro (2008) found that exposure to these films sends the message that female success can only be garnered through duplicitous means. Projansky (2007) similarly explores representations of girls' success in the film, claiming the mean girl is represented as a girl who makes unwise decisions, so her lack of success is her fault. In an article on *Gossip Girl*, I (2016) argue the show suggests girls' success can only be achieved through a reliance on men for economic and moral protection. *The Culture of Mean* continues these explorations of representations of girls' success (or lack thereof) by arguing that girl bullies are framed as "naturally" aggressive, as though their bullying tactics are an inborn aspect of their femininity and not a response to a culture that stifles female aggression while normalizing the physical violence of men and boys. This discourse about female aggression forefronts concerns about girls' integrity and moral character, suggesting that aggressive girls are doomed to failure.

The literature on cyberbullying derives largely from the social and behavioral sciences and focuses primarily on prevention and recovery. Similarly, scholarship on bullycide is aimed toward prevention and stems from the medical and law fields (Marr & Field, 2001). As opposed to focusing on prevention, *The Culture of Mean* asks about the ramifications of a cultural focus on the dangers of cyberbullying. boyd and Palfrey (2013) argue that because cyberbullying "feels 'new' or 'different,' schools, parents, and lawmakers are spending tremendous time focusing on what's new and different about the internet rather than addressing the holistic issue of bullying." I explore the tendency of media to present cyberbullying as the *cause* of suicide, which damningly formulates communication technologies as weapons and frames the teens who use them to bully as murderers.

This book extends scholarly discussions about the contemporary youth bullying culture by being the first to explore the intersection of film, television, books, and journalistic accounts of bullying to illustrate contemporary understandings of youth (with regard to race, class, and sexuality), violence, and bullying. I will speak to historical and contemporary discourses of bullying, as well as their similarities and telling contrasts (i.e., a shift from physical violence to cyber violence). A critical feminist analysis of media featuring representations of youth bullying provides knowledge about issues affecting the current U.S. social context and ongoing debates, such as those regarding zero tolerance and the Tyler Clementi Higher Education Anti-Harassment Act (which would require colleges that receive federal aid to enact an anti-harassment policy).

Chapter Outlines

Chapter 1 orients the reader to the Mean Girl discourse. Although U.S. culture seemingly "discovered" the mean girl in 2002, I argue the Mean Girl discourse is a continuation of the conversations about girls we have been engaging in for decades. This chapter takes a genealogical approach to the analysis of girlhood discourses in order to discover how contemporary culture came to the taken-for-granted truth that girls are mean bullies or vulnerable victims. I consider how three dominant discourses about girls—Reviving Ophelia, Girl Power, and Mean Girl—confirm and redeploy ideas about girlhood, empowerment, and aggression. Through an analysis of popular media sites, academic studies, and anti-bullying programs, I highlight that, as opposed to being a "new" discourse about girls, Mean Girl is constructed in and through *Reviving Ophelia* and *Girl Power*. Tropes of girls as vulnerable popularized in *Reviving Ophelia* are heightened by representations of girls as victims to mean girl bullies who have taken *Girl Power* too far and are not just empowered but aggressive. I contend the Mean Girl discourse proscribes advice to teens and their parents that is bound with postfeminist notions of empowerment, obscuring power differentials across race and gender.

In Chapter 2, I explore the media coverage of the suicides of Phoebe Prince and Tyler Clementi. In January 2010, Prince hanged herself because, according to news reports, she was being bullied by "real life mean girls." Less than a year later, Clementi jumped off the George Washington Bridge, as the mainstream media narrative goes, after learning that his roommate had streamed video online of him alone in their dorm room with a man. Although the two cases are different, media coverage drew a series of parallels that articulate a cultural discourse about youth bullying. The young people accused of bullying Tyler and Phoebe to their deaths were charged with felonies (i.e., invasion of privacy, violation of civil rights). Media coverage of both cases ignores the fact that suicide rarely results from a single incident, instead exacerbating concern about teens using new communication technologies (i.e., text messaging and social media sites) to bully. I argue the emphasis in the discourse on punishing and exiling bullies in order to protect the public reduces sexism and homophobia to a problem of mean individuals and obfuscates an examination of the structural issues that play a role in teen suicide.

Media sites featuring mean girls typically show boys as completely unaware of what is happening within the girls' friendship networks, which situates relational aggression as a normatively feminine form of aggression. Chapter 3 interrogates the cultural insistence that only girls use covert forms of aggression to bully, a claim that functions to demonize girls who are seen as "naturally" mean and damningly ignores boys' use of indirect aggression to bully girls. Through an exploration of "mean boys" in the television show *Gossip Girl* and the film *Mean Girls*, I argue male characters who access social aggression are queered, troublingly aligning queerness with femininity. Mean boys are shown to be gay or queer, so the association of covert forms of aggression with femininity is cemented. Additionally, the mean boy is not demonized to the extent that the mean girl is, despite using the same behaviors. This chapter is the first exploration of the similarities and differences in constructions of mean girls and mean boys.

The 2011 documentary *Bully* follows three victims of bullying over the course of a school year, as well as features the stories of two boys the film constructs as having killed themselves in response to school bullying. In Chapter 4, I examine *Bully* as a lens into how the U.S. bullying discourse is raced and gendered. The film is symptomatic of a popular mainstream discourse that suggests a cultural desire to fight bullying, a seemingly admirable aim, but the ways in which this discourse functions is problematic. I argue the film is deceptively simple and uses melodrama to contribute to a cultural discourse that constructs a causal link between bullying and suicide ("bullycide"). Although the film's concern is theoretically placed with victims of bullying, there are victims who "matter more"—white, middle-class girls and boys. Even when articulating concern over children and adolescents, *Bully* (and the discourse to which it contributes) fails to be progressive since it hierarchizes appropriate victims as male, white, and passive.

The FOX television show *Scream Queens* (2015–2017), a hour-long amalgam of horror and black comedy, represents contemporary mean girls as using cruelty and violence when targeting their victims——girls who are less popular, queer, or differently abled. Through references to mean sorority girls in the 1990s, the cult mean girl classic *Heathers* (1988), and Cleopatra, *Scream Queens* poignantly reveals that the mean girl is hardly a "new" image of girlhood. However, the show presents millennial mean girls to be even more pathological, antisocial, and narcissistic than their predecessors, suggesting millennials' obsession with new communication technologies causes the girls to lack compassion and empathy for others. This chapter considers what anxieties about youth, race, technology, and morality are revealed in *Scream Queens'* postracial (the myth that racism and race are not relevant in contemporary times) millennial context. I argue the show contributes to the bullying discourse by situating millennial mean girls as racist, selfish, and dangerous, highlighting cultural concern regarding millennials' supposed excessive connection with new communication technologies.

Gossip Girl, an hour-long drama that follows middle- and upper-class teens in the Upper East Side of Manhattan, takes as its central narrative class-based relations, so the show allows for a nuanced examination of the upper-class Queen Bee/middle-class Wannabe relationship. In Chapter 6, I argue *Gossip Girl* presents middle-class girls' attempts to be popular in order to improve their social standing as altering them from authentically "good" to dangerously "bad." The show suggests that middle-class girls are doomed to failure when attempting to be mean (a quality the show situates as authentic only to upper-class femininity), so they inevitably become bad, highlighting the cultural presumption of a slippage from meanness (covert aggression) to badness (violence). *Gossip Girl* positions economic capital (being rich) as a necessary component of being mean. In contrast to many other representations of mean girls, the show demonstrates that upper-class girls of color can also be mean; however, they are never considered for the role of Queen Bee, situating whiteness as a necessary requirement to be leader of the clique. This narrative turn polices racial boundaries by reproducing a social hierarchy in which girls of color are limited to subordinate positions as minions who serve to protect and enforce the power of the Queen Bee.

In being critical of the bullying discourse, I aim to highlight the overly simplistic manner in which media culture has structured bullies and victims. On the surface, many of the myths I emphasize are completely illogical (for instance, the insistence that boys do not use indirect forms of aggression and only bully other boys), yet they circulate unchallenged throughout media sites and in policy decisions. It is important to question the myths about bullying perpetuated in the dominant discourse because these myths have created an atmosphere in which concern is misplaced on issues such as mean girls, cyberbullying, and bullycide, as opposed to looking broadly at the systemic oppressive structures that factor in to teen anger, violence, and suicide.

Note

1. I use quotation marks here to note the impreciseness and constructed nature of the mean girl image. That is, I do not assume a true, essential, or "authentic" mean girl exists. After this, I will not put the phrase "mean girl" in quotation marks, but it should be understood as such in order to indicate the fictional notion of a girl who uses social aggression to terrorize her classmates and maintain her popularity.

References

Aapola, S., Gonick, M., & Harris, A. (2005). *Young femininity; Girlhood, power, and social change*. New York: Palgrave Macmillan.

Adelson, O. (Producer). (2005, April 4). *Odd girl out* [Television broadcast]. United States: Lifetime TV.

Almjeld, J. (2015). Collecting girlhood: Pintrest cyber collections archive available female identities. *Girlhood Studies, 21*(2), 6–22.

Alvarez, L. (2013, November 21). Charges dropped in cyberbullying death, but Sheriff isn't backing down. *The New York Times*. Retrieved from http://www.nytimes.com/2013/11/22/us/charges-dropped-against-florida-girls-accused-in-cyberbullying-death.html

Banet-Weiser, S. (2004). Girls rule!: Gender, feminism, and Nickelodeon. *Critical Studies in Media Communication, 21*(2), 119–139.

Banet-Weiser, S. (2007). What's your flava? Race and postfeminism in media culture. In Y. Tasker & D. Negra (Eds.), *Interrogating postfeminism: Gender and the politics of popular culture* (pp. 201–226). Durham, NC: Duke University Press.

Bazelon, E. (2012, March 29). The problem with *Bully*. *Slate Magazine*. Retrieved from http://www.slate.com/articles/news_and_politics/bulle/2012/03/bully_documentary_lee_hirsch_s_film_dangerously_oversimplifies_the_connection_between_bullying_and_suicide_.html

Behm-Morawitz, E., & Mastro, D. E. (2008). Mean girls? The influence of gender portrayals in teen movies on emerging adults' gender-based attitudes and beliefs. *J & MC Quarterly, 85*(1), 131–146.

boyd, d. (2014). *it's complicated: the social lives of networked teens*. New Haven, CT: Yale University Press.

boyd, d., & Palfrey, J. (2013). What you must know to help combat youth bullying, meanness, and cruelty. *Kinder & Braver World Project* (Vol. 2013–5). Cambridge, MA: The Berkman Center for Internet & Society.

Chesney-Lind, M., Irwin, K. (2008). *Beyond bad girls: Gender, violence and hype*. New York: Routledge.

Crothers, L. M., Field, J. E., & Kolbert, J. B. (2005). Navigating power, control and being nice: Aggression in adolescent girls' friendships. *Journal of Counseling and Development, 83*(3), 349–355.

Dow, B. J. (1996). *Prime-time feminism: Television, media culture, and the women's movement since 1970*. Philadelphia, University of Pennsylvania Press.

Draper, N. R. A. (2012). Is your teen at risk? Discourses of adolescent sexting in United States television news. *Journal of Children and Media, 6*(2), 221–236).

Driver, S. (2007). *Queer girls and popular culture: Reading, resisting, and creating media*. New York: Peter Lang.

Dubrofsky, R. E., & Magnet, S. A. (2015). Introduction: Feminist surveillance studies: Critical interventions. In R. E. Dubrofsky and S. A. Magnet (Eds.), *Feminist surveillance studies* (pp. 1–17). Durham, NC: Duke University Press.

Dubrofsky, R. E., & Ryalls, E. D. (2014). *The Hunger Games*: Performing not-performing to authenticate femininity and whiteness. *Critical Studies in Media Communication, 31*(5), 395–409.

Flannery, M. E. (2015, January 5). The school-to-prison pipeline: Time to shut it down. *neaToday*. Retrieved from http://neatoday.org/2015/01/05/school-prison-pipeline-time-to-shut/

Foucault, M. (1995). *Discipline & punish: The birth of the prison*. New York: Vintage Books.

Gateward, F., & Pomerance, M. (Eds.). (2002). *Sugar, spice, and everything nice: Cinemas of girlhood*. Detroit, MI: Wayne State University Press.

Giroux, H. A. (2003). *The abandoned generation: Democracy beyond the culture of fear*. New York: Palgrave Macmillan.

Gross, A. (2014, October 13). The zero-tolerance trap. *Slate*. Retrieved from http://www.slate.com/articles/life/education/2014/10/atiya_haynes_case_zero_tolerance_school_choice_and_one_detroit_student_s.html

Hains, R. (2012). *Growing up with girl power: Girlhood on-screen and in everyday life*. New York: Peter Lang.

Hasinoff, A. A. (2015). *Sexting panic: Rethinking criminalization, privacy, and consent*. Urbana, IL: University of Illinois Press.

Hentges, S. (2006). *Pictures of girlhood: Modern female adolescence on film*. Jefferson, NC: McFarland & Company.

Jiwani, Y. (2015). Violating in/visibilities: Honor killings and interlocking surveillance(s). In R. E. Dubrofsky & S. A. Magnet (Eds.), *Feminist Surveillance Studies* (pp. 79–92). Durham, NC: Duke University Press.

Kelly, D. M., & Pomerantz, S. (2009). Mean, wild, and alienated: Girls and the state of feminism in popular culture. *Girlhood Studies, 2*(1), 1–19.

Klein, J. (2012). *The bully society: School shooting and the crisis of bullying in America's schools*. New York University Press.

Klein, R. (2015, May 4). In a lot of ways, schools are safer than ever. *The Huffington Post*. Retrieved from http://www.huffingtonpost.com/entry/school-safety-2015_us_5728cf31e4b016f37893a4fb

Marr, N., & Field, T. (2001). *Bullycide: Death at Playtime* (1ˢᵗ ed.). Oxfordshire, UK: Success Unlimited.

Mazzarella, S. (1999). The 'Superbowl of all dates': Teenage magazines and the commodification of the perfect prom. In S. R. Mazzarella & N. O. Pecora (Eds.), *Growing up girls: Popular culture and the construction of identity* (pp. 97–111). New York: Peter Lang.

Mazzarella, S. R. (2007). Why is everybody always pickin' on youth? Moral panics about youth, media, and culture. In S. R. Mazzarella (Ed.), *20 Questions about youth & the media* (pp. 46–60). New York: Peter Lang.

Mazzarella, S. R. (2008). Coming of age with Proctor & Gamble: Beinggirl.com and the commodification of puberty. *Girlhood Studies, 1*(2), 29–50.

Mazzarella, S. R. (2010a). Coming of age too soon: Journalistic practice in US newspaper coverage of 'early puberty' in girls. *Communication Quarterly, 58*(1), 36–58.

Mazzarella, S. R. (Ed.). (2010b). *Girl wide web 2.0: Girls, the Internet, and the negotiation of identity*. New York: Peter Lang.

Mazzarella, S. R., & Pecora, N. O. (1999). *Growing up girl: Pop culture and the construction of identity*. New York: Peter Lang.

Mazzarella, S. R., & Pecora, N. O. (2007a). Girls in crisis: Newspaper coverage of adolescent girls. *Journal of Communication Inquiry, 31*(1), 6–27.

Mazzarella, S. R., & Pecora, N. O. (2007b). Revisiting girls' studies: Girls creating sites for connection and action. *Journal of Children and Media, 1*(2), 105–125.

McRobbie, A. (1991). *Feminism and youth culture: From 'Jackie' to 'Just Seventeen.'* Boston: Unwin Hyman.

McRobbie, A., & Thornton, S. L. (1995). Rethinking 'moral panic' for multi-mediated social worlds. *The British Journal of Sociology, 46*(4), 559–574.

Messick, J. (Producer), & Waters, M. (Director). (2004). *Mean girls* [Motion picture]. United States: Paramount Pictures.

Murphy, R. (Producer). (2015). *Scream queens* [Television series]. Los Angeles, CA: FOX Broadcasting Company.

Negra, D. (2009). *What a girl wants?: Fantasizing the reclamation of self in postfeminism.* London: Routledge.

Ono, K. A. (2000). To be a vampire on *Buffy the Vampire Slayer*: Race and ("other") socially marginalizing positions on horror TV. In E. R. Helford (Ed.), *Fantasy girls: Gender in the new universe of science fiction and fantasy television* (pp. 163–186). New York: Rowman &Littlefield Publishers.

Oppliger, P. (2013). *Bullies and mean girls in popular culture.* Jefferson, NC: McFarland & Co, Inc.

Pipher, M. (1994). *Reviving Ophelia: Saving the selves of adolescent girls.* New York: Riverhead Books.

Projansky, S. (2007). Mass magazine cover girls: Some reflections on postfeminist girls and postfeminism's daughters. In Y. Tasker & D. Negra (Eds.), *Interrogating postfeminism: Gender and the politics of popular culture* (pp. 40–72). Durham, NC: Duke University Press.

Projansky, S. (2014). *Spectacular girls: Media fascination & celebrity culture.* New York: NYU Press.

Projansky, S., & Vande Berg, L. R. (2000). Sabrina, the teenage…?: Girls, witches, mortals, and the limitations of prime-time feminism. In E. R. Helford (Ed.), *Fantasy girls: Gender in the new universe of science fiction and fantasy television* (pp. 13–40). New York: Rowman & Littlefield Publishers.

Ringrose, J. (2006). A new universal mean girl: Examining the discursive construction and social regulation of a new feminine pathology. *Feminism & Psychology, 16*(4), 405–424.

Ryalls, E. D. (2012). Demonizing "mean girls" in the news: Was Phoebe Prince "bullied to death?" *Communication, Culture, & Critique, 5,* 463–481.

Ryalls, E. D. (2016). Ambivalent aspirationalism in millennial postfeminist culture on *Gossip Girl. Communication and Critical/Cultural Studies, 5,* 463–481.

Scheg, A. G. (Ed.). (2015). *Bullying in popular culture: Essays on film, television and novels.* Jefferson, NC: McFarland & Co.

Schwartz, J. (2007–2012). *Gossip girl* [Television series]. Burbank, CA: Warner Brothers Television.

Sengupta, S. (2013, October 28). Warily, schools watch students on the Internet. *The New York Times.* Retrieved from http://www.nytimes.com/2013/10/29/technology/some-schools-extend-surveillance-of-students-beyond-campus.html

Serazio, M. (2010). Shooting for fame: Spectacular youth, web 2.0 dystopia, and the celebrity of anarchy of generation mash-up. *Communication, Culture, & Critique, 3,* 416–434.

Shedd, C. (2015). *Unequal city: Race, schools, and perceptions of injustice.* New York: Russell Sage Foundation.

Simmons, R. (2002). *Odd girl out: The hidden culture of aggression in girls.* New York: Harcourt.

Springhall, J. (1998). *Youth, popular culture and moral panics: Penny Gaffs to Gangsta-rap, 1830–1996*. New York: St. Martin's Press.

Stampler, L. (2014, June 5). This Facebook post got 2 dozen middle schoolers suspended. *Time*. Retrieved from http://time.com/2826547/facebook-middle-school-suspended/

The Independent Florida Alligator. (2012, August 6). Playground bully. *The Huffington Post*. Retrieved from http://www.huffingtonpost.com/the-independent-florida-alligator/bullying-schools_b_1575699.html

Thompson, K. (1998). *Moral panics*. New York: Routledge.

U. S. Department of Health & Human Services. (n.d.). What is cyberbullying? *stopbullying.gov*. Retrieved from https://www.stopbullying.gov/cyberbullying/what-is-it/index.html

Vossekuil, B., Fein, R. A., Reddy, M., Borum, R., & Modzeleski, W. (2002). The final report and findings of the safe school initiative: Implications for the prevention of school attacks in the United States. Washington, DC: United States Secret Service and United States Department of Education.

Waitt, C. (Producer), & Hirsch, L. (Director). (2011). *Bully* [Motion picture]. United States: The Weinstein Company.

Walkerdine, V. (1997). *Daddy's girl: Young girls and popular culture*. Cambridge, MA: Harvard University Press.

Walters, S. D. (1995). *Material girls: Making sense of feminist cultural theory*. Berkeley: University of California Press.

Ward, J. V., & Benjamin, B. C. (2004). Women, girls, and the unfinished work of connection: A critical review of American Girls' Studies. In A. Harris (Ed.), *All about the girl: Culture, power, and identity* (pp. 15–27). New York: Routledge.

Wartella, E., & Mazzarella, S. (1990). A historical comparison of children's use of leisure time. In R. Butsch (Ed.), *For fun and profit: The transformation of leisure into consumption* (pp. 173–194). Philadelphia: Temple University Press.

Winner, L. (1980). Do artifacts have politics? *Daedalus, 109*(1), 121–136.

Wiseman, R. (2002). *Queen bees & wannabes*. New York: Three Rivers Press.

Zoukis, C. (2016, November 29). New guidelines target ending 'zero tolerance' policies, aim to stem school-to-prison pipeline. *The Huffington Post*. Retrieved from http://www.huffingtonpost.com/christopher-zoukis/new-guidelines-target-end_b_13206800.html?utm_hp_ref=school-to-prison-pipeline

· 1 ·

EMPOWERING OPHELIA

Postfeminist Empowerment in the Mean Girl Discourse

There is a hidden culture of girls' aggression in which bullying is epidemic, distinctive, and destructive…Behind a façade of female intimacy lies a terrain traveled in secret, marked with anguish, and nourished by silence. (Simmons, 2002, p. 3)
For the girl whose popularity is based on fear and control, think of a combination of the Queen of Hearts in *Alice in Wonderland* and Barbie. I call her the Queen Bee.

Through a combination of charisma, force, money, looks, will, and manipulation, this girl reigns supreme over the other girls and weakens their friendships with others, thereby strengthening her own power and influence. (Wiseman, 2002, p. 25)

The 2002 publication of Rosalind Wiseman's *Queen Bees & Wannabes* and Rachel Simmons's *Odd Girl Out*, both of which claimed to document a hidden aspect of girl culture where bullying and female aggression run rampant and unchecked, cemented the Mean Girl discourse (Mean Girl) in the U.S. public consciousness. As discussed earlier, these books and their authors received significant mainstream attention. Wiseman's *Queen Bees & Wannabes* landed on the *New York Times* best-seller list; she has been interviewed several times on *The Today Show* and is featured in the 2008 *Nightline* special "Queen Bee's and Wanna Be's" in which Ted Koppel claims girls "have elevated social nastiness into an art form." In a March 2011 *Dateline NBC* special, "My Kid would Never…Bully," host Anne Curry refers to *Queen Bees & Wannabes* as "the book of record" on bullying. Simmons's *Odd Girl Out* also climbed the *New York Times* best-seller list. Like Wiseman, Simmons has appeared on *The Today Show*, and she was featured on *The Oprah Winfrey Show* twice.

Additionally, each book served as the basis for a fictional film retelling. *Odd Girl Out* (Adelson, 2005) and *Mean Girls* (Messick, 2004) are based on Simmons and Wiseman's books respectively. The films provide access to the ways in which notions about girls' aggression and bullying transformed or were reinforced in the movement from print to visual media. In *Mean Girls*, screenwriter Tina Fey uses parody and humor to express ideas about mean girls, bullying, and aggression. The film follows Cady Heron as she is indoctrinated into the cruel politics of Girl World when her family returns to the U.S. after living in Africa, and she enters public school for the first time. In its initial airing, *Odd Girl Out* was featured as part of Lifetime's "The Truth about Teens" weekend. As a result, the fictional account of girls' meanness in the film is represented as the "truth" about the ways girls bully. In *Odd Girl Out*, middle school students Nikki and Stacey bully their onetime best friend Nessa, until their torment leads Nessa to attempt to commit suicide. The films' contrasting approaches to representing the Mean Girl discourse offer insight into popular ideas about girls, anger, and empowerment. Both are indicative of the ways in which the ideas featured in these best-selling books are transformed into fictional accounts about girls.

The image of the mean girl developed in these popular books, the films based upon them, television shows (such as *Gossip Girl* and *Scream Queens*), documentaries (for instance, *Bully*), as well as newspaper and magazine articles centers on the idea that popular girls are protecting and cultivating the power associated with their elite status in increasingly duplicitous and cruel ways. Conscious of popularity's attendant rewards (boyfriends, parties, awe, and fear in others), mean girls are shown to employ devious and manipulative tactics to maintain their social position (Kelly & Pomerantz, 2009). Specifically, mean girls are framed as using indirect aggression, which is defined in the social scientific scholarship as a form of social manipulation (Bjorkqvist, Lagerspetz, & Kaukiainen, 1992; Crothers, Field, & Kolbert, 2005; Galen & Underwood, 1997; Hadley, 2003; Remillard & Lamb, 2005; Underwood, 2003). Mean girls are situated as using covert bullying tactics that destroy other girls' relationships and marginalize their victims (Crothers *et al.*, 2005). The bullying tactics associated with indirect aggression include gossip, social exclusion, stealing friends, not talking to someone, and threatening to withdraw friendship (Crothers *et al.*, 2005). As explained by Simmons (2002), girls attack within close friendship networks or cliques. The leader of the clique, the Queen Bee, is framed as being "able to command a fleet of loyal subjects willing to do her bidding" (Kelly & Pomerantz, 2009, p. 5), so her aggression is hidden; she escapes detention while inflicting long-term pain on other girls.

In this chapter, I ask how we arrived in this mean girl moment by tracing the movement of three dominant girlhood discourses—Reviving Ophelia, Girl Power, and Mean Girl—and I consider the ways in which the discourses confirm and redeploy ideas about girlhood. In evaluating how one image builds on the next and what is at stake in these changes, I take a genealogical approach, which, as explained by Foucault (1984a), allows for an analysis that traces the development of society through knowledges and discourses. Foucault (1972) argues that, as opposed to being repressive, discourse is productive in the sense that it produces reality, seemingly confirming ideas that come to be culturally understood as the "truth." My goal is to interrogate the taken-for-granted truths about girls that have formed as a result of these three discourses.

Foucault's hypothesis is that the production of discourse is at once controlled, selected, organized, and redistributed according to a culture's institutions. As opposed to being embodied by an individual, power circulates widely and is produced through various societal apparatuses. What is at issue in this analysis is the way in which claims about girl bullying and female empowerment are "put into discourse" (Foucault, 1978, p. 11) through popular media sites, academic studies, and anti-bullying programs. In exploring these three girlhood discourses, I perform a genealogy, which does not search for the origin or linear development of knowledge (Foucault, 1984b), but, instead, "shifts the focus to competing, fractured, and discontinuous discourses culturally embedded in particular historical periods" (Diedrich, 2005, p. 755). "A genealogy will not discover new forms of girlhood, but it will discuss how knowledge about girls has shaped what it means to be a girl" (Driscoll, 2002, p. 4). It is important to note that these discourses and the tropes about girls embedded within them are not linear. Indeed, at times, as I will show, they occur alongside one another, substantiating and redeploying widely held cultural ideas about contemporary girls.

As opposed to searching for the origin of the mean girl moment, I investigate the discourses through which our cultural understandings of girls as passive victims, empowered agents, and dangerous aggressors came into existence. I explore how Reviving Ophelia, Girl Power, and Mean Girl speak to one another and, in so doing, construct notions about girlhood, postfeminism, and empowerment. This is not a study of "real" girls; instead, I am interested in girlhood discourses that provide contemporary public understandings of girls. Truth claims come into being through talk, text, and representation (Foucault, 1972). Discourses are "dynamic and partial" (Ashcraft & Flores, 2003, p. 3) and are best analyzed through varied texts. In examining the Mean Girl discourse, I look broadly at academic studies about girls' aggression, anti-bullying programs and curriculum aimed at putting an end to bullying, Wiseman and Simmons's books, and the films based on them, *Odd Girl Out* and *Mean Girls*.

Scholars have previously explored the seemingly opposing discourses of Reviving Ophelia and Girl Power (Aapola, Gonick, & Harris, 2005; Gonick, 2006); however, in investigating how these discourses produced and participate in the contemporary Mean Girl discourse, I am the first to bring the three together. I contend that, as opposed to being a "new" discourse about girls, Mean Girl is constructed in and through Reviving Ophelia and Girl Power. Tropes of girls as vulnerable popularized in Reviving Ophelia are heightened by representations of girls as victims to mean girls who have taken Girl Power too far and are not just empowered but aggressive. I argue the Mean Girl discourse obscures power differentials across race, class, gender, and sexuality by proscribing advice to teens and their parents that is bound with postfeminist notions of empowerment.

Postfeminism and Girlhood

Postfeminist narratives, disseminated through popular media sites, assume that feminism is a phenomenon of the past (Tasker & Negra, 2007). Postfeminism celebrates the success of the feminist movement in its endeavor to gain gender equality (Banet-Weiser, 2007; Dow, 1996; Dubrofsky, 2002; McRobbie 2004a; Projansky, 2001; Walters, 1995); however, it is reactionary in that it presumes that gender equality has been achieved, so feminism is no longer needed. Discourses about postfeminism both celebrate and express disdain for the feminist movement and its participants (Projansky, 2001). Postfeminism suggests that feminism has been successful in its endeavors to gain equality, while at the same time maintaining that it is because of the gains of feminism that women are unhappy (Dow, 1996; Dubrofsky, 2002; McRobbie, 2004b; Projansky, 2001, 2007; Tasker & Negra, 2007; Vavrus, 2010; Walters, 1995).

For Tasker & Negra (2007), this "limited vision of gender equality as achieved and yet still unsatisfactory underlies the class, age, and racial exclusions that define postfeminism" (p. 2). Scholarship on postfeminism in popular culture suggests iconic images of postfeminism are white[1] (Dow, 1996; Dubrofsky, 2002; Gerhard, 2005; Helford, 2000; McRobbie, 2004b; Ouellette, 2002; Projansky, 2001; Springer, 2007). Postfeminism is characterized by an assumption of economic freedom for women (marking it as white and middle-class) and a femininity that emphasizes girlness (even for adult women) (Tasker & Negra, 2007). According to Projansky (2007), "Postfeminist discourse has produced the conditions for the emergence of girl discourse and *girl discourse contributes to and sustains postfeminism*" (p. 44, original emphasis). As such, it is not surprising that like postfeminism, the Reviving Ophelia, Girl Power, and Mean Girl discourses are about white middle-class girls (Aapola *et al.*, 2005; Chesney-Lind & Irwin, 2008; Mazzarella & Pecora, 2008; Ringrose, 2006). Projansky (2007) argues that contemporary times draw "on a long-standing tradition of focusing cultural attention on girls as problems, as victims of social ills, as symbols of ideal citizenship, and as all-around fascinating figures" (p. 42). These three discourses—Reviving Ophelia, Girl Power, and Mean Girl—are indicative of this tradition.

Reviving Ophelia and Girl Power

In the early 1990s, academic and popular texts combined to highlight an alleged "crisis" in girlhood, focusing on issues such as girls' negative body image, plummeting self-esteem, and poor performance in math and science (Mazzarella & Pecora, 2008). The most popular of these was Mary Pipher's (1994) *Reviving Ophelia: Saving the Selves of Adolescent Girls*, which "spent three years on the *New York Times* non-fiction best-seller list, and has sold over 1.5 million copies" (Ward & Benjamin, 2004, p. 17). In *Reviving Ophelia*, Pipher argues that when girls enter adolescence, due to pressure from U.S. culture, they leave behind their healthy, confident, and "authentic" selves and silence their voices, feelings, and thoughts (Brown & Gilligan, 1992). This argument was picked up and built on in academic studies, newspapers, magazines, and books, all contributing to a Reviving Ophelia discourse that argues girls' self-esteem crisis is the result of a girl-hostile culture that stifles girls' expressions of their authentic selves (Aapola *et al.*, 2005). On the surface, Reviving Ophelia is critical of the image of the "nice girl," suggesting that, in response to cultural demands for proper femininity, girls begin to hide their true selves in order to present as a nice girl who "controls her emotions, is sweet and friendly, suc-

ceeds at school, and obeys her parents" (Aapola *et al.*, 2005, p. 118). Through
Reviving Ophelia, girls' vulnerability became part of authentic notions of girlhood, colliding with dominant versions of white femininity as passive (Ringrose, 2006).

Aapola, Gonick, and Harris (2005) recognize Girl Power as Reviving
Ophelia's "competing" discourse (p. 18). Like Reviving Ophelia, the Girl
Power discourse emerged in academic and popular contexts during the early
1990s but set up an opposing definition of femininity (Gonick, 2006). Originally associated with the Riot Grrrls, an underground feminist punk movement, "which was the first powerful youth movement or political subculture to
be organized entirely around young women's concerns" (Harris, 2004, p. 17),
the rhetoric of Girl Power defined girls through empowerment and agency as
opposed to helplessness and dependency (Banet-Weiser, 2004). The Riot Grrrls' critiques addressed young women's raced, classed, and heterosexist lived
experiences. Girl Power actively worked against the passivity, voicelessness,
and vulnerability associated with Reviving Ophelia (Aapola *et al.*, 2005). In
this sense, Girl Power was also a critique of cultural expectations of "nice"
femininity.

It was not long before the Riot Grrrls' explicitly feminist Girl Power was
transformed into a catchphrase for a girlhood attitude that was "a sexy, brash,
and individualized expression of ambition, power, and success" (Harris, 2004,
p. 17). As the term proliferated, the meanings of Girl Power diverged rather
explicitly from the political intentions of the Riot Grrrls (Gonick, 2006). For
instance, many point to the all-girl pop group, the Spice Girls, as popularizing
an apolitical version of Girl Power focused on fun and sassiness, as opposed
to feminist principles. Girl Power, in this new formulation, has played a significant role in the creation of contemporary images of young women as "independent, successful, and self-inventing" (Harris, 2004, p. 16). This version
of Girl Power is specifically postfeminist, because, as Taft (2004) argues, it is
an alternative to feminism that is non-political and nonthreatening. Postfeminism, considered a backlash to the feminist movement, tends to emerge
when women are perceived as gaining equality. The backlash to Girl Power
constructs girls as not simply powerful but dominant, suggesting girls have too
much power (Taft, 2004). Through postfeminist Girl Power, girls are constructed as "self-assured, living lives lightly inflected but by no means driven
by feminism...assuming they can have (or at least buy) it all" (Harris, 2004,
p. 17).

Mean Girl

It was 2002 when popular media seemingly "discovered" the mean girl; however, as Chesney-Lind and Irwin (2008) point out, images of girls (and women) being mean to one another are hardly new. Indeed, there is nothing new about the Mean Girl discourse; instead, I argue that, although Reviving Ophelia and Girl Power emerged simultaneously in the early 1990s, a decade later they converged in the Mean Girl discourse. Aapola, Gonick, and Harris (2005) contend the mean girl has eclipsed the vulnerable girl in the public attention and in the media; however, I suggest cultural focus has absolutely remained on the vulnerable girl as part of this discourse—she is the victim of the mean girl. Harris (2004) maintains that girls learn that while Girl Power "is about being confident and assertive, it should not be taken too far" (p. 29). As cultural anxiety grew that girls had taken Girl Power too far—to a place of dominance—girls were labeled "mean." The Mean Girl discourse produced an image of "an active mean girl who contributes to the daily trauma of other vulnerable girls" (Projansky, 2007, p. 56). Thus, Girl Power converges with Reviving Ophelia by situating girls as either powerful bullies or vulnerable victims. The postfeminist backlash to Girl Power resulted in "a repositioning of girls within familiar binaries of 'good' and 'bad' girls" (Aapola *et al.*, 2005, p. 39).

The cultural anxiety surrounding the mean girl suggests that girls have taken Girl Power too far and are now just as aggressive as (if not more than) boys. The covertly aggressive bullying tactics reportedly used by mean girls are often compared to the overtly violent bullying associated with boys and are postulated as having worse outcomes for both the victim and the aggressor. For instance, journalists represent girl bullying as occurring more often and in more insidious ways than that of boys (Asthana, 2008; Hill & Helmore, 2002; McVeigh, 2002; Siad, 2008). This theme is repeated in the first scene of *Odd Girl Out* when Stacey, Nessa, and Nikki, who are still friends, witness a fight between two boys in the school's gymnasium. As adults pull the boys apart, one says, "We're cool," and the boys slap hands. The boys' physical aggression is constituted as a positive outlet for aggression with few repercussions. Later, Stacey's father repeats this lesson: "Girls are brutal. They hurt each other and tear each other to bits over any little thing. Guys smack each other and go get a beer." In her book, upon which this movie is based, Simmons (2002) similarly suggests that direct physical bullying is "the province of boys," while girls' covert aggression is harder to identify, "intensifying the damage to the victims" (p. 3). The Mean Girl discourse signals girls' aggression as more brutal than that of boys and with implications that are "further-reaching" than the teen years (Wiseman, 2002), while the reason girls experience anger is simultaneously minimized. The message emanating from this discourse is that mean girls are as bad/mean as boys, maybe even more so (Chesney-Lind & Irwin, 2008). Postfeminism represents equality as women doing what men traditionally do (Dow, 1996), in this case bullying and aggression. The public anxiety that surrounds the mean girl phenomenon is a postfeminist reaction to girls who have not only become aggressive but who are conceived of as better at aggression than boys. Of course, this preposterous claim only makes sense when a very specific, indirect, covert, and seemingly feminine form of aggression is considered.

When anxiety about youth takes hold, industry steps in to offer "solutions" at a financial cost. Baumgardner and Richards (2000) suggest the Reviving Ophelia movement became a "veritable cottage industry" (p. 179), producing magazines, organizations, initiatives, books, and movies all aimed toward increasing girls' self-esteem. For instance, just three years after the publication of Pipher's book, Susan Wellman was inspired to found The Ophelia Project (The Ophelia Project, n.d.). According to its website, "From the start, The Ophelia Project recognized the truths of Pipher's recognition of a dysfunctional culture; a disconnect between youth and parents in an ever changing social context." The slippage from Reviving Ophelia into Mean Girl can be seen in the transition in The Ophelia Project to a focus on girl bullying. A year after its founding, The Ophelia Project began to address relational aggression, claiming, "Well before the term relational aggression was embedded in our national lexicon, The Ophelia Project was on top of this issue." The Ophelia Project developed the first program in the country to focus specifically on girl-on-girl bullying, illustrating the transition from a view that a "dysfunctional culture" creates vulnerable girls to one in which girls themselves are to blame.

Like Reviving Ophelia, the Mean Girl discourse has also seen the sale of a wide range of products all aimed at helping vulnerable victims of bullying. Just a sampling of books on girls' aggression and bullying includes Lamb's (2002) *The secret lives of girls: What good girls really do—Sex play, aggression, and their guilt*; Anthony and Lindert's (2010) *Little girls can be mean: Four steps to bully-proof girls in the early grades*; Kilpatrich and Joiner's (2012) *The drama years: Real girls talk about surviving middle school*; and Criswell's (2013) *Friendship troubles: Dealing with fights, being left out & the whole popularity thing*. Additionally, as schools came to see social aggression as a "certified social problem," an industry grew to meet the demand (Talbot, 2002). Programs aimed at dealing with relational aggression include the Early Childhood Friendship Project; You Can't Say You Can't Play; I Can Problem Solve; Walk Away, Ignore, Talk, Seek Help; Second Step; Friend to Friend; and Social Aggression Prevention Program (Leff, Waasdorp, & Crick, 2010).

Wiseman cofounded and served as president of The Empower Program, which "developed a curriculum called 'Owning Up' that teaches young people between the ages of twelve and twenty-one the skills to understand and proactively address the impact of Girl World"[2] (Wiseman, 2002, p. 11). With its focus on empowering young girls, The Empower Program, a national, nonprofit educational foundation founded in 1992, is imbricated within postfeminist Girl Power. As the name suggests, the foundation seeks "to empower young people and adults to create safe schools and communities by providing effective prevention strategies to address bullying and other forms of peer aggression" (National Education Association, 2000–2015). In 2008, The Empower Program lost its funding; however, the "Owning Up" curriculum continues to operate in Wiseman's new project—Cultures of Dignity. Cultures of Dignity works with teachers to implement the Owning Up curriculum through onsite trainings (Cultures of Dignity, 2016). The curriculum, which claims to guide young people to understand "themselves better in relation to group behavior; the influence of social media on their conflicts; (and) the dynamics that lead to discrimination and bigotry," can be purchased online for $39.95 (Cultures of Dignity, 2016). As is the case with Reviving Ophelia, the solutions put forth in the Owning Up curriculum are individualized. As opposed to fighting structural inequalities at the heart of much bullying (i.e., sexism, racism, classism, and homophobia), Owning Up claims that "a safe school climate depends on teaching students the skills to manage their emotions and critically think through solutions to social conflicts." The "truth" that overly empowered mean girls are responsible for victimizing others girls was cemented as the Mean Girl discourse circulated through anti-bullying programs, such as The Empower Program and Owning Up, books, films, and newspapers.

Postfeminist Empowerment

Mean Girl functions to demonize some girls (mean girls who have taken Girl Power too far) in the name of empowering others (vulnerable girl victims). It is common for postfeminist culture to incorporate and naturalize particular aspects of feminism, such as women and girls' empowerment (Tasker & Negra, 2007). This focus on empowerment is immediately recognizable in the name of The *Empower* Program. Similarly, the mission of The Ophelia Project is to "*empower* all members of a community to recognize and address relational aggression." Postfeminism appropriates feminism through expressions of agency and power (Jackson & Lyons, 2013), while simultaneously erasing feminist politics (Tasker & Negra, 2007). Thus, empowerment becomes an individualized experience (Gill, 2012), divorced from the need for any structural critique. Postfeminist empowerment operates in seemingly opposite ways in Mean Girl. On the one hand, the discourse looks to empower vulnerable victims (in line with Reviving Ophelia), on the other is the suggestion that girls are too empowered (have taken Girl Power too far); however, in both cases, the need for structural critiques of sexism, racism, classism, and heterosexism is absent.

On the surface, Mean Girl is seemingly about saving vulnerable girls from mean bullies. The image of the mean girl's victim is in line with constructions of vulnerable girls in media sites. In an analysis of the covers of *Time* and *Newsweek*, Projansky (2007) suggests the magazines figure a particular type of girl as most in need of saving:

> The most vulnerable girl is young and white, with blue, green, or hazel eyes and blond (or occasionally light brown) hair. She has an impassive face and stares directly into the camera…The predominant youthfulness of the cover girl makes her vulnerability uncontested. She is young enough that she could not possibly be at fault for the woes she symbolizes. She is thus a passive figure in need of protection. (pp. 50–51)

On the cover of *Queen Bees & Wannabes*, a young white girl with brown hair stares blankly out at the reader. Three blonde girls are positioned in the background whispering and laughing, presumably at our cover girl. The cover of Simmons's book features a young white girl with brown hair sitting on a bench. She is hunched over, her hands between her thighs, fingers lightly touching. She looks morosely down at her feet, her eyes hidden from the viewer. In images of bullying, the popular mean girl is often blonde, so it is not surprising that victims are shown to have brown hair, securing their contrasting positions and the good/bad girl dichotomy. The victims on the covers of these books are situated much like the cover girls Projansky studies. These images are persuasive in producing cultural concern by presenting vulnerable, passive victims in need of saving (Projansky, 2007).

While the concern of Mean Girl is seemingly with saving girl victims, I argue the anxiety is more concretely placed on those girls who, influenced by the gains of feminism, are too empowered and too dominant. As explained by Simmons (2002), "Aggression endangers relationships, imperiling a girl's ability to be caring and 'nice'" (p. 18). Thus, the aggressive girl is incapable of meeting cultural demands for femininity as passive, sweet, and nice. This trope is illuminated in *Mean Girls*. The film's relationship with (post)feminism is ambivalent in that feminism is shown to have been successful (for instance, when girls are shown as empowered to fight misogyny), yet the gains of feminism are blamed for creating girls who, as opposed to lacking self-esteem, are overconfident and arrogant. A scene from Cady's first day at Northshore High School illuminates this ambivalence. In the cafeteria, a male classmate, Jason, approaches and asks Cady if she likes her "muffin buttered." The sexual innuendo confuses naïve and innocent Cady, but the Queen Bee of the Plastics (the most popular clique in Northshore High School), Regina George, steps in and quickly turns the tables, asking Jason why he is "being such a skeeze." Although Jason claims he is being "friendly," Regina responds, "Jason, you do not come to a party at my house with (fellow Plastics member) Gretchen and then scam on some poor girl right in front of us three days later. She's not interested…You can go shave your back now." Although Jason refers to Regina as a "bitch" as he walks away, he does so under his breath, humiliated. Moreover, it appears as though Regina barely registers the taunt. She protects new girl Cady from Jason's sexual advances, and she defends her friend Gretchen whom Jason treated poorly.

What could be viewed as a positive aspect of Regina's personality (her ability to stand against sexism) is reframed as problematic when she is shown as manipulating others for self-serving purposes. The film makes clear that Regina is not a nice girl who treats her friends well and protects them from sexism; instead, she is a mean girl who is aggressive and calculating. Regina appears to have complete control over her mother (who considers herself a "cool mom" and offers Regina condoms when she finds her making out with a boy) and her father (who watches in silent dismay while Regina poses for photographs in an extremely revealing Halloween costume). Regina also manipulates her school's administration, faculty, and staff. For instance, when Regina worries that Cady is usurping her popularity, she devises an ingenious plan to get her suspended. Before turning The Plastics' "Burn Book" (in which the girls have written scathing captions beneath pictures of their female classmates) to her principal, Regina includes a picture of herself with the label "fugly slut." She then leads the principal to Cady and the other Plastics' members when she indicates, "There are only three girls in the entire school not in the book." In shining the spotlight on the other girls, Regina deceives the principal in order to obtain what she desires (she gets Cady in trouble, retains her popularity, and avoids punishment). Later during a school assembly, a teacher asks, "How many of you have ever felt personally victimized by Regina George?" In response, each person in the gymnasium raises her/his hand, including the principal. The film shows feminism as successful because Regina is smart, powerful, and vulnerable to no one, but Regina has taken the power feminism bestowed upon her too far and her primary characterization is as a victimizer of other girls, boys, and adults.

Although the film clearly situates Regina as a bully, she is shown as attempting to present as a victim. Despite being framed as empowered, Regina appears to knowingly perform the Reviving Ophelia discourse. When Regina expresses that she wants to lose three pounds, she stares expectantly at her friends until they reply, "Oh my God, you're so skinny." Reviving Ophelia constructs girls as developing poor self-esteem due to patriarchal socialization. Conversely, *Mean Girls* suggests that girls impersonate low self-esteem because they understand it is expected of a nice girl. This point is driven home in the film when Ms. Norbury (the math teacher) explains, "It's not a self esteem problem. I think they're all pretty pleased with themselves." Regina is framed as more powerful than anyone she encounters, yet she actively presents as vulnerable and embraces claims of victimage. For example, in her ongoing bid to refuse culpability, Regina denies the existence of any cliques and labels herself a "victim." This postfeminist construction of girls' popularity can be seen as a backlash to Second-Wave feminism, which is often accused of creating a "cult of victimization." Framing girls as pretending to be victims dismisses the ongoing realities of the many issues contemporary girls face (i.e., rape, sex trafficking, and substance abuse).

According to Olweus (1991), the bullying literature ascribes a pitifully negative image to victims of bullying; they "are more anxious and insecure than students in general…They often look upon themselves as failures and feel stupid, ashamed, and unattractive. Further, the victims are lonely and abandoned at school" (p. 423). Despite this unflattering description, the Mean Girl discourse ascribes a particular cachet to being a victim. Indeed, part of the reason that Wiseman and Simmons are considered "experts" on the topic of girl bullying is that they verify the truth of their claims about *all* girls based on their personal experiences. For instance, Simmons (2002)

shares that when she "was eight years old, (she) was bullied by another girl…
the sorrow was overwhelming" (pp. 1–2). Wiseman explains that she began
The Empower Program because she was in an abusive heterosexual romantic
relationship in high school, a relationship she suggests she was vulnerable to
because, in the multiple private schools she attended, girls were "catty and
mean-spirited" (p. 12). These girls, she claims, caused her to lose "any remaining self-confidence" (p. 12). Note this troubling sleight of hand—Wiseman
quickly dismisses the relational violence she suffered from her male partner
in one sentence; she then spends an entire paragraph blaming girls for driving her toward this relationship. Wiseman, and the Mean Girl discourse to
which her ideas contribute, negates the structural reasons a girl may stay in an
abusive relationship, instead placing the blame for her abuse not on her male
abuser, but on the girls who bullied her.

By definition, a bully intimidates or harms those who are less powerful.
The Mean Girl discourse creates a narrative in which the pretty and popular
mean girl terrorizes girls who are less popular than she is in order to maintain
her elite position. Troublingly, contemporary culture has produced a trend in
which those in power tap in to the cachet of victimhood by claiming they,
too, are victims. For instance, North Carolina's HB2 law, which requires that
people use the bathroom that corresponds to the sex on their birth certifi-
cate, is seen by many as a tactic aimed at bullying transgender individuals;
however, when Bruce Springsteen canceled a concert to protest the state's
law, U.S. Republican Representative Mark Walker claimed that "Springsteen's boycott was a 'bully tactic'" (Havrilesky, 2016). The irony of a white,
cis-gendered, middle-class member of congress claiming victim is clear. As
explained by Jardine (2011), "In the celebrity world, a touch of bullying is
almost a requirement on the CV." Meagan Fox, Rihanna, Jennifer Lawrence,
Taylor Swift, and Kate Middleton all claim to have been victims to mean girls
at some point during their youth. After the 2016 Rio Olympics, gymnast Gabby Douglas spoke out against the cyberbullying she faced. Douglas claimed the
bullying was so upsetting that "the joy of winning a gold medal was lost on
her" (McNamara, 2016). I am not suggesting that the bullying these young
women allegedly endured did not happen; however, in this cultural climate,
it is increasingly difficult to manage the potentially difficult and long term
effects of bullying since the bullying discourse obfuscates power differentials.
Moreover, there is little clarity of what constitutes bullying; rolling eyes, calling a girl a "slut," slamming a student into lockers, sexually harassing a girl
online have all been labeled "bullying" at one point.

The seemingly admirable aim of empowering young girls in Mean Girl is problematic in that the girls are empowered to fight back against other girls. Whereas Reviving Ophelia worked to empower girls to resist the patriarchal culture that was blamed for creating vulnerable girls, Mean Girl erases patriarchy, instead blaming girls themselves. For instance, Wiseman (2002) argues, "Girls have strict social hierarchies based on what culture tells us about what constitutes ideal femininity…But who is the prime enforcer of these standards? The movies? The teen magazines? Nope, it's the girls themselves" (p. 10). While Reviving Ophelia articulated the cause of girls' self-silencing as the culture within which they exist, Mean Girl suggests "the power of cliques silences" girls (Wiseman, 2002, p. 23). Similarly, *Mean Girls* makes clear that sexism is not performed by boys, but by girls when they call one another "sluts and whores" (Kelly & Pomerantz, 2009). As opposed to seeing empowerment as necessary for girls to succeed and thrive in a patriarchal, misogynistic culture, Mean Girl puts forth empowerment as necessary for girl victims to fight back against girls who are too empowered and as a result mean.

Making (White) Mean Girls Nice

As discussed above, Reviving Ophelia and Girl Power were critical of normative expectations of femininity as nice. Contrastingly, Mean Girl reproduces the rhetoric of postfeminism by insisting girls reclaim an essentialized and idealized femininity. The discourse centers on images of girls who are mean, selfish, and out of control. In turn, girls are empowered to transform into the ideal archetype of girlhood—the nice girl who is kind, selfless, and demure (Aapola *et al.*, 2005). Negra (2009) utilizes the term "retreatism" to describe the postfeminist insistence that working women give up paid work to return to their proper roles as wives and mothers, which she argues is one of the master narratives of postfeminism (p. 5). I extend this idea of "retreatism" by suggesting that the postfeminist Mean Girl narrative works similarly to encourage girls to return to normative ideals of "good" girlhood, in essence preparing them for their future roles as wives and mothers. Postfeminism proposes that girls can be strong and agentic, but they must balance this empowerment with heterosexual desirability (Jackson & Lyons, 2013). U.S. culture conceives of girls who are aggressive as unfeminine and unattractive.

The goal of the Mean Girl discourse is to maintain "nice" femininity, marking the phenomenon as largely white and middle-class (Aapola *et al.*,

2005; Chesney-Lind & Irwin, 2004, 2008; Gonick, 2004; Ringrose, 2006; Ryalls, 2012). The nice girl is the culturally assumed "authentic" identity for white girls. In much popular culture, girls of color are seen as "naturally" more violent and less capable of managing their emotions (Grindstaff & West, 2010), so they remain incompatible with dominant views of appropriate femininity. Because U.S. culture conceives of Black girls as overtly violent and as contrary to nice girls, they are largely ignored by the Mean Girl discourse. Generally, in psychological studies on social aggression, race is either not mentioned (Bjorkqvist *et al.*, 1988; Olweus, 1991) or studies have been performed on largely white populations (Galen & Underwood, 1997). For instance, in a study of 491 third through sixth-grade children, Crick and Grotpeter (1995) note that 37% of the sample was African American; however, they do not factor race into their findings, only gender. In their longitudinal study, Orpinas, McNicholas, and Nahapetyan (2014) do take race into account. Suggesting a cultural bias that Black girls do not use covert forms of aggression, the researchers found that "more African American students *than expected*" were part of the "High declining relational aggression trajectory"—a group that showed high use of relational aggression in Grade 6 but that steadily declined by Grade 12 (p. 6, my emphasis).

Race is very rarely mentioned in the Mean Girl discourse, and, when it is, it is taken up in troubling ways. For instance, in the book *Bullied*, Berry (2016) "conveys and analyzes five compelling stories of bullying written by students" (p. x). Of the five women who contributed to the book, one is Black. In her narrative, Iman writes, "Most of my harassment started in middle school…I started noticing that kids of *my own race* started rejecting me. I was been (*sic*) picked on for not being 'black enough'" (p. 29, my emphasis). In his analysis of Iman's story, Berry suggests Iman's Black body "provides bullies with fodder for bullying," concluding "bullying speaks to an underlying logic that seeks to create and maintain fixed racial categories" (p. 37). Presumably, this logic is structural racism; however, Berry does not address the broader systemic issues of racism at work, instead individualizing bullying behaviors as working toward maintaining logics of Black and white. Moreover, this narrative seemingly suggests that Black kids only bully other Black kids, which further works to maintain fixed racial categories.

While Wiseman (2002) does directly deal with racism, arguing, "Girls suffer because of racist standards of beauty" (p. 88), she too upholds the myth that bullying operates solely within racialized groups. For instance, when Wiseman moves on to discuss issues similar to those raised by Iman's story (i.e., "acting white"), she suggests this sort of bullying is an issue within all-black, "poorer schools" (p. 91). Wiseman concludes by suggesting that "if we don't challenge this kind of internalized racism, girls will keep attacking each other's sense of self" (p. 91). Again, while racism is mentioned, the racism is internalized, functioning to blame Black girls for bullying others based on racialized beauty standards, negating both structural racism and the idea that Black girls may also be bullied by Black boys, white girls, and white boys.

Simmons (2002) actually reframes racism as having a *positive* impact on girls' lives, suggesting "everyday threats of racism and oppression" lead Black girls to avoid making the sorts of close friendships that she argues lead to bullying among girls. That is, thanks to racism, Black girls do not bond with other girls in the way white girls do, so they are unlikely to suffer from clique based relational aggression. Beyond simply negating structural racism, this idea does the troubling work of situating racism as a good thing since it leads to Black girls not being victimized. One reason to negate bullying among Black girls is an insistence that Black girls are stronger, tougher, and have higher self-esteem than white girls. This process centers white middle-class girls as the most in need of saving when it comes to bullying. While the Reviving Ophelia discourse framed white girls as losing their voices upon entering adolescence, analyses of Black girls' communication point to a tendency of Black girls to use truth telling[3] (hooks, 1996; Simmons, 2002; Ward, 1996; Way, 1996). Black girls are represented as using open and forthright communication and approaching relationships from a less idyllic perspective than that of white girls (hooks, 1996; Ward, 1996). The Mean Girl discourse situates Black girls as using "direct conflict and truth telling" (Simmons, 2002, p. 11), and the presumption of Black girls' outspokenness is used to dismiss their need for protection.

The idea that Black girls are unlikely to get caught up in mean girl antics is brought to life in *Odd Girl Out*. The only Black girl in the film, Emily, refers to the mean girls as "white tornadoes," further securing the image of girl bullies as white. Emily is not impressed with Stacey and Nikki's popularity; on more than one occasion, she tells Nessa the popular girls "don't have anything that I want." The first time the viewer sees Emily, she is watching Nessa, Stacey, and Nikki's soccer practice. Later, in the cafeteria, Nikki calls Emily a "hobbit," but Emily ignores Nikki and instead looks directly at Nessa and says, "My club soccer team is recruiting new players. Truth? I think you'd be great." Emily's habit of beginning her sentences with "truth" is reflective of popular and academic discourses that maintain Black girls use truth-telling when communicating (hooks, 1996; Simmons, 2002; Ward, 1996; Wiseman, 2002). The Black girl who communicates in a forthright manner is seen as in direct contrast to white mean girls who are constructed as managing conflict in a covert and indirect manner. Emily is also *Odd Girl Out*'s moral center. Each time Nessa faces bullying, the camera pans to Emily's displeased face. When the girls are mean to Nessa in the cafeteria, Nessa throws out her food tray and runs away, and the camera zooms in on Emily who is shaking her head disapprovingly. Emily is supportive, friendly, and helpful, whereas the white mean girls are cruel without cause.

Mean Girl flattens out difference to suggest that issues like racism, sexism, and classism do not exist (or at least are not all that bad) and a fair and equal Girl World can be achieved if girls would just be nice to one another. For instance, in *Mean Girls*, when Cady is elected Prom Queen, she endorses social equality in her acceptance speech. Using her tiara as an analogy for popularity, specifically as a metaphor for The Plastics, Cady asks, "Why is everyone stressing over this thing? It's only plastic. We can all share it." She then breaks the tiara and passes out pieces to a diverse group of her peers (fellow nominees, a gay boy, a girl in a wheelchair, etc.). The narrative constructs popularity as a matter of hero worship, which relies on hierarchy (a hierarchy that seemingly has nothing to do with race, sexual orientation, gender performance, or ability). Cady refutes the idea that any one girl belongs at the top of that hierarchy, instead suggesting an impartial, just, and nondiscriminatory Girl World, ignoring difference and erasing structural discrimination. Whereas Girl Power was originally a feminist response to the eliteness of patriarchal culture, Mean Girl suggests *girls* reproduce elite hierarchy in troubling and dangerous ways. In turn, girls are encouraged to be "nice," retreating to dominant notions of femininity as passive and demure.

Are Girls Passive Victims, Empowered Agents, or Dangerous Aggressors?

As opposed to featuring new ideas about girls, Mean Girl is simply a continuation of the conversations U.S. culture has been having about girls for several decades. Girl Power and Reviving Ophelia converge in Mean Girl by situating girls in the worn-out "good/bad" binary; girls are (overly) powerful bullies or vulnerable victims. Mean Girl aims to produce nice (not mean), confident (but not too confident), middle-class white girls. The focus in the

Mean Girl discourse on the alleged damage girls are doing to one another sustains postfeminist ideas about women and competition while simultaneously contributing a more vicious and insidious enemy in the image of the mean girl. Reviving Ophelia suggests that the tendency of girls to become insecure is a result of being socialized in a sexist culture that does not allow girls to access or express their emotions. Mean Girl reframes this message; as opposed to patriarchy, other girls are shown as responsible for girls' low self-esteem.

Gonick (2006) suggests Girl Power and Reviving Ophelia both "direct attention from structural explanations for inequality toward explanations of personal circumstances and personality traits" (p. 2). Mean Girl operates similarly. Although "race-related bullying is significantly associated with negative emotional and physical health effects" (Rosenthal *et al.*, 2013), the discourse largely ignores race and racism, instead centering white girls. In a similar vein, Mean Girls ignores the dangers of patriarchal socialization and the "complexity of female competition in school" (Kelly & Pomerantz, 2009, p. 6), so the reasons why girls may legitimately experience anger are never considered. Girls are shown as instinctively brutal without cause, and girls' problems are framed as emanating exclusively from Girl World.

As the privileged and powerful begin to claim "victim," we see how clearly the Mean Girl discourse has taken hold and how little understanding we have of the realities of bullying. Anti-bullying programs offer individualized solutions to the problem of bullying, but are they worth their price tag given the other serious issues the education system currently faces (i.e., increasing class sizes, budget cuts, and standardized testing)? Although bullying has been declining for nearly a decade, "data suggests that's not because of anti-bullying programs" (Ferguson, 2013). In fact, anti-bullying programs "are not practically effective in reducing bullying or violent behaviors in the schools" (Ferguson, San Miguel, Kilburn & Sanchez, 2007) and "students attending schools with bullying prevention programs were more likely to have experienced peer victimization, compared to those attending schools without bullying prevention programs" (Jeong & Lee, 2013, p. 8). While the fight against bullying is to be commended, our misunderstandings of the structures that contribute to girls' anger and insecurity have created a cultural climate in which girls are situated in a one-dimensional manner as passive victims, empowered agents, or dangerous aggressors, ignoring the profound realities of sexism and racism in girls' lives.

Notes

1. Icons of postfeminism include Murphy Brown (Dow, 1996), Ally McBeal (Dubrofsky, 2002; Ouellette, 2002), Carrie Bradshaw (Arthurs, 2003; Gerhard, 2005), and Bridget Jones (McRobbie, 2004a).
2. In *Queen Bees and Wannabes*, Wiseman (2002) uses "Girl World" to talk about girls' day to day lives. As defined by Wiseman, "Girl World" is tribal, hierarchical, and composed of cliques (Hadley, 2003).
3. According to Ward (2007), "Truth-telling strategies emphasize constructive, critical affirmation of the individual and the collective" (p. 245).

References

Aapola, S., Gonick, M., & Harris, A. (2005). *Young femininity; Girlhood, power, and social change*. New York: Palgrave Macmillan.

Adelson, O. (Producer). (2005, April 4). *Odd girl out* [Television broadcast]. United States: Lifetime TV.

Anthony, M. A., & Lindert, R. (2010). *Little girls can be mean: Four steps to bully-proof girls in the early grades*. New York: St. Martin's Press.

Arthurs, J. (2003). *Sex and the City* and consumer culture: Remediating postfeminist drama. *Feminist Media Studies, 3*(1), 83–98.

Ashcraft, K. L., & Flores, L. A. (2003). 'Slaves with white collars': Persistent performances of masculinity in crisis. *Text and Performance Quarterly, 23*(1), 1–29.

Asthana, A. (2008, January 20). Crackdown on schoolgirl bullying epidemic. *The Observer*, p. 8.

Banet-Weiser, S. (2004). Girls rule!: Gender, feminism, and Nickelodeon. *Critical Studies in Media Communication, 21*(2), 119–139.

Banet-Weister, S. (2007). What's your flava? Race and postfeminism in media culture. In Y. Tasker & D. Negra (Eds.), *Interrogating postfeminism: Gender and the politics of popular culture* (pp. 201–226). Durham, NC: Duke University Press.

Baumgardner, J., & Richards, A. (2000). *Manifesta*. New York: Farrar, Strauss, and Giroux.

Berry, K. (2016). *Bullied: Tales of torment, identity, and youth*. New York: Routledge.

Bjorkqvist, K., Lagerspetz, K. M. J., & Kaukiainen, A. (1992). Do girls manipulate and boys fight? Developmental trends in regard to direct and indirect aggression. *Aggressive Behavior, 18,* 117–127.

Brown, L. M., & Gilligan, C. (1992). *Meeting at the crossroads: Women's psychology and girls' development*. New York: Ballantine Books.

Chesney-Lind, M., & Irwin, K. (2004). From badness to meanness: Popular constructions of contemporary girlhood. In A. Harris (Ed.), *All about the girl: Culture, power and identity* (pp. 45–56). New York: Routledge.

Chesney-Lind, M., Irwin, K. (2008). *Beyond bad girls: Gender, violence and hype*. New York: Routledge.

Crick, N. R., & Grotpeter, J. K. (1995). Relational aggression, gender, and social-psychological adjustment. *Child Development, 66*, 710–722.

Criswell, P. K. (2013). *Friendship troubles: Dealing with fights, being left out & the whole popularity thing.* American Girl Publishing.

Crothers, L. M., Field, J. E., & Kolbert, J. B. (2005). Navigating power, control and being nice: Aggression in adolescent girls' friendships. *Journal of Counseling and Development, 83*(3), 349–355.

Cultures of Dignity. (2016). About us—Owning Up online. Retrieved from http://owningup. online/case-studies-2/

Diedrich, L. (2005). Introduction: Genealogies of disability. *Cultural Studies, 19*(6), 649–666.

Dow, B. J. (1996). *Prime-time feminism: Television, media culture, and the women's movement since 1970.* Philadelphia, University of Pennsylvania Press.

Driscoll, C. (2002). *Girls: Feminine adolescence in popular culture, and the women's movement since 1970.* Philadelphia, University of Pennsylvania Press.

Dubrofsky, R. E. (2002). Ally McBeal as postfeminist icon: The aestheticizing and fetishizing of the independent working woman. *The Communication Review, 5*(4), 265–284.

Ferguson, C. J. (2013, October 10). Anti-bullying programs could be a waste of time. *Time.* Retrieved from http://ideas.time.com/2013/10/10/anti-bullying-programs-could-be-a-waste-of-time/

Ferguson, C. J., San Miguel, C., Kilburn, J. C., & Sanchez, P. (2007). The effectiveness of school-based anti-bullying programs: A meta-analytic review. *Criminal Justice Review, 32*(4), 401–414.

Foucault, M. (1972). *The archaeology of knowledge and discourse on language* (A. M. Sheridan Smith, Trans.) New York: Pantheon Books.

Foucault, M. (1978). *The history of sexuality: Volume 1: An introduction.* (R. Hurley, Trans.) New York: Vintage Books.

Foucault, M. (1984a). The birth of the asylum. In P. Rabinow (Ed.), *The Foucault reader* (pp. 141–168). New York: Pantheon Books.

Foucault, M. (1984b). Nietzsche, genealogy, history. In P. Rabinow (Ed.), *The Foucault reader* (pp. 76–100). New York: Pantheon Books.

Galen, B. R., & Underwood, M. K. (1997). A developmental investigation of social aggression among children. *Developmental Psychology, 33*(10), 589–600.

Gerhard, J. (2005). *Sex and the city:* Carrie Bradshaw's queer postfeminism. *Feminist Media Studies, 5*(1), 37–49.

Gill, R. (2012). Media, empowerment and the 'sexualization of culture' debates. *Sex Roles, 66*, 736–745.

Gonick, M. (2004). The "mean girl" crisis: Problematizing representations of girls' friendships. *Feminism & Psychology, 14*(3), 395–400.

Gonick, M. (2006). Between 'girl power' and 'reviving Ophelia': Constituting the neoliberal girl subject. *NWSA, 18*(2), 1–23.

Grindstaff, L., & West, E. (2010). "Hands on hips, smiles on lips!": Gender, race, and the performance of spirit in cheerleading. *Text and Performance Quarterly, 30*(2), 143–162.

Hadley, M. (2003). Relational, indirect, adaptive or just mean: Recent work on aggression in adolescent girls—Part 1. *Studies in Gender and Sexuality, 4*(4), 367–394.

Harris, A. (2004). *Future girl: Young women in the twenty-first century.* New York: Routledge.

Havrilesky, H. (2016, April 26). When the powerful cry 'bully.' *The New York Times Magazine.* Retrieved from https://www.nytimes.com/2016/05/01/magazine/when-the-powerful-cry-bully.html?_r=0

Helford, E. R. (2000). Postfeminism and the female action-advent hero: Positioning *Tank Girl.* In M. S. Barr (Ed.), *Future females, the next generation: New voices and velocities in feminist science fiction criticism* (pp. 291–308). Boulder, CO: Rowman & Littlefield Publishers.

Hill, A., & Helmore, E. (2002, March 3). Mean girls. *The Observer,* p. 19.

hooks, b. (1996). *Bone black: Memories of girlhood.* New York: Henry Holt and Company.

Jackson, S., & Lyons, A. (2013). Girls' 'new femininity' refusals and 'good girl' recuperations in soap talk. *Feminist Media Studies, 13*(2), 228–224.

Jardine, C. (2011, April 5). As Kate Middleton knows, girls make the best bullies. *The Telegraph.* Retrieved from http://www.telegraph.co.uk/news/uknews/kate-middleton/8427802/As-Kate-Middleton-knows-girls-make-the-best-bullies.html

Jeong, S., & Lee, B. H. (2013). A multilevel examination of peer victimization and bullying prevention in schools. *Journal of Criminology, 2013,* 1–10.

Kelly, D. M., & Pomerantz, S. (2009). Mean, wild, and alienated: Girls and the state of feminism in popular culture. *Girlhood Studies, 2*(1), 1–19.

Kilpatrich, H., & Joiner, W. (2012). *The drama years: Real girls talk about surviving middle school.* New York: Free Press.

Lamb, S. (2002). *The secret lives of girls: What good girls really do—Sex, play, aggression, and their guilt.* New York: The Free Press.

Leff, S. S., Waasdorp, Evian, T., & Crick, N. R. (2010). A review of existing relational aggression programs: Strengths, limitations, and future directions. *School Psychology Review, 39*(4), 508–535.

Mazzarella, S. R., & Pecora, N. O. (2008). Reflecting on girls' studies and the media: Current trends and future directions. *Journal of Children and Media, 2*(1), 75–76.

McNamara, B. (2016, December 21). Gabby Douglas opens up about being cyberbullied at the Olympics. *Teen Vogue.* Retrieved from http://www.teenvogue.com/story/gabby-douglas-opens-up-about-being-cyberbullied-at-the-olympics

McRobbie, A. (2004a). Notes on postfeminism and popular culture: Bridget Jones and the new gender regime. In A. Harris (Ed.), *All about the girl: Culture, power, and identity* (pp. 3–14). New York: Routledge.

McRobbie, A. (2004b). Post-feminism and popular culture. *Feminist Media Studies, 4*(3), 255–264.

McVeigh, T. (2002, November 10). Girls are now bigger bullies than boys. *The Observer,* p. 7.

Messick, J. (Producer), & Waters, M. (Director). (2004). *Mean girls* [Motion picture]. United States: Paramount Pictures.

National Education Foundation. (2000–2015). Resources for empowering girls and combating social aggression. Retrieved from http://www.nea.org/home/16792.htm

Negra, D. (2009). *What a girl wants?: Fantasizing the reclamation of self in postfeminism*. London: Routledge.

Olweus, D. (1991). Bully/victim problems among school children: Basic facts and effects of a school-based intervention program. In D. J. Pepler & K. H. Rubin (Eds.), *The development and treatment of childhood aggression* (pp. 411–448). Hillsdale, NJ: Erlbaum.

Orpinas, P., McNicholas, C., & Nahapetyan, L. (2014). Gender differences in trajectories of relational aggression perpetration and victimization from middle to high school. *Aggressive Behavior, 9999*, 1–12.

Ouellette, L. (2002). Victims no more. Postfeminism, television, and *Ally McBeal*. *The Communication Review, 5*, 315–335.

Pipher, M. (1994). *Reviving Ophelia: Saving the selves of adolescent girls*. New York: Riverhead Books.

Projansky, S. (2001). *Watching rape: Film and television in postfeminist culture*. New York: NYU Press.

Projansky, S. (2007). Mass magazine cover girls: Some reflections on postfeminist girls and postfeminism's daughters. In Y. Tasker & D. Negra (Eds.), *Interrogating postfeminism: Gender and the politics of popular culture* (pp. 40–72). Durham, NC: Duke University Press.

Remillard, A. M., & Lamb, S. (2005). Adolescent girls' coping with relational aggression. *Sex Roles, 53*(3/4), 221–229.

Ringrose, J. (2006). A new universal mean girl: Examining the discursive construction and social regulation of a new feminine pathology. *Feminism & Psychology, 16*(4), 405–424.

Rosenthal, L., Earnshaw, V. A., Carroll-Scott, A., Henderson, K. E., Peters, S. M., McCasline, C., & Ickovics, J. R. (2013). Weight- and race-based bullying: Health associations among urban adoelscents. *Journal of Health Psychology, 20*(4), 401–412.

Ryalls, E. D. (2012). Demonizing "mean girls" in the news: Was Phoebe Prince "bullied to death?" *Communication, Culture, & Critique, 5*, 463–481.

Siad, D. (2008, March 27). Girl fight. *The Toronto Star*, p. L01.

Simmons, R. (2002). *Odd girl out: The hidden culture of aggression in girls*. New York: Harcourt.

Springer, K. (2007). Divas, evil black bitches, and bitter black women: African American women in postfeminist and post-civil-rights popular culture. In Y. Tasker & D. Negra (Eds.), *Interrogating postfeminism: Gender and the politics of popular culture* (pp. 249–276). Durham, NC: Duke University Press.

Taft, J. (2004). Girl power politics: Pop-culture barriers and organizational resistance. In A. Harris (Ed.), *All about the girl: Culture, power, and identity* (pp. 69–78). New York: Routledge.

Talbot, M. (2002, February 24). Girls just wanna be mean. *The New York Times Magazine*, 24–34.

Tasker, Y., & Negra, D. (2007). Introduction: Feminist politics and postfeminist culture. In Y. Tasker & D. Negra (Eds.), *Interrogating postfeminism: Gender and the politics of popular culture* (pp. 1–25). Durham, NC: Duke University Press.

The Ophelia Project. (n.d.). Retrieved from http://www.opheliaproject.org/

Underwood, M. K. (2003). *Social aggression among girls*. New York: The Guilford Press.

Vavrus, M. D. (2010). Unhitching the "post" (of postfeminism). *Journal of Communication Inquiry, 34*(4), 222–227.

Walters, S. D. (1995). *Material girls: Making sense of feminist cultural theory.* Berkeley: University of California Press.

Ward, J. V. (1996). Raising resisters: The role of truth telling in the psychological development of African American girls. In B. J. R. Leadbeater & N. Way (Eds.), *Urban girls: Resisting stereotypes, creating identities* (pp. 85–99). New York: NYU Press.

Ward, J. V. (2007). Uncovering truths, recovering lives: Lessons of resistance in the socialization of black girls. In B. J. R. Leadbeater & N. Way (Eds.), *Urban girls revisited: Building strengths.* New York: NYU Press.

Ward, J. V., & Benjamin, B. C. (2004). Women, girls, and the unfinished work of connection: A critical review of American Girls' Studies. In A. Harris (Ed.), *All about the girl: Culture, power, and identity* (pp. 15–27). New York: Routledge.

Way, N. (1996). Between experiences of betrayal and desire: Close friendships among urban adolescents. In B. J. R. Leadbeater & N. Way (Eds.), *Urban girls: Resisting stereotypes, creating identities* (pp. 173–192). New York: NYU Press.

Wiseman, R. (2002). *Queen bees & wannabes.* New York: Three Rivers Press.

· 2 ·

BULLIES IN THE NEWS

The Tyler Clementi and Phoebe Prince Suicides[1]

On January 14, 2010, 15-year-old Phoebe Prince hanged herself in her family home with the scarf her sister gave her for Christmas. Prince did not leave a note, but, according to news reports, the relentless bullying by what the media labeled "mean girls" drove her to commit suicide. Less than a year after Prince killed herself, in September 2010, 19-year-old Rutgers University freshman Tyler Clementi committed suicide after his roommate, Dharun Ravi, used a Webcam to watch Clementi alone with a man in their dorm room. Unlike Prince, Clementi did leave a note of sorts, but it did not provide a reason for the suicide; his Facebook status read "Jumping off the gw bridge sorry." A "promising" student and a "brilliant violinist" (Sofair, 2011), Clementi killed himself, as the prevailing mainstream media narrative goes, after learning what he believed was a private moment was made public online.

Details of both cases were carried on news channels (for example, Fox and CNN), in national newspapers (e.g., *The New York Times*, *The Boston Globe*, and *USA Today*), magazines (i.e., *People* and *Newsweek*), and on morning television programs (for instance, *The Early Show*, *The Today Show*, and *The View*). Although, as I will show, the cases are different (i.e., habitual bullying vs. a one-time incident; cyberbullying vs. face-to-face bullying; high school students vs. college students), the media coverage drew a series of parallels, all of which articulate a cultural discourse in the United States about youth bullying. For example, the October 2010 story about Clementi's suicide in *People* magazine is titled "Tormented to Death?," while the cover of the April 2010 issue of *People* asks if Prince was "Bullied to Death?," framing both deaths as "bullycides" (suicide caused by bullying).

Critical media scholars note a tendency in popular mainstream media to ignore structural problems such as racism, sexism, and homophobia, and to focus instead on the stories of individuals (Dow, 2001; Grindstaff, 2002; Sloop, 2000, 2004), a process that frames structural issues as personal, relevant only for their impact on the individual, and solutions are individualized. This trend is replicated in the Prince coverage, which places blame squarely on the shoulders of so-called mean girls rather than within a larger context that is oppressive to young girls. Notably, news stories about Clementi's suicide consistently acknowledge systemic homophobia, potentially broadening the story from the individual (indeed, Clementi's story is often connected to suicides of other gay boys) to one of a homophobic culture. The incorporation of a cultural need to combat homophobia as part of popular mainstream discourse is seemingly progressive. However, I will show that the ways in which this discourse operates are problematic, as this potentially enlightened move is thwarted when the locus of blame for Clementi's death (like that of Prince) is placed on "bullies" who are constructed as murdering an innocent teen through bullying tactics. I argue that while Clementi's roommate, Ravi, may be a symptom of homophobia in our culture and the mean girls who reportedly bullied Phoebe may be reflective of structural sexism, the accused teens are not the source of these problems and the insistence in media to construct them as such obscures the systemic issues at work in teens' decisions to commit suicide.

Moral Panics

As discussed earlier, "moral panics" are the interplay of (over)reactions from the media, the public, politicians, and agents of social control to youthful deviance. Moral panics are "the momentarily intense, disproportionate, and dramatic manifestation of shock, anxiety, and hatred within society concerning the presumed morally deviant behavior of 'folk devils'" (Flinders & Wood, 2015, p. 644). The "folk devils" are stereotypically classified as deviants (Cohen, 2002), which leads to societal presumption that the behaviors are immoral (Flinders & Wood, 2015, p. 644). Generally aimed toward the actions of youth, moral panics suggest contemporary times have led to a moral decline in young people (Thompson, 1998). Thus, "moral panics act on behalf of the dominant social order by intervening in the space of public opinion through the use of highly emotive and rhetorical language which has the effect of requiring that 'something be done about it'" (McRobbie & Thornton, 1995, p. 562). In this way, moral panics are a process of moral regulation (Critcher, 2009), a process that calls for the threatening agents to be punished so that the panic can subside.

The moral panic about bullying, particularly when amplified by the ideas of cyberbullying and bullycide, is monolithic in its extreme overreaction. Bullying has become so prominent in the U.S. that many are now labeling it an "epidemic" (Yingst, 2010). Reactions by the media, politicians, law enforcement, and interest groups to youth bullying present teens accused of engaging in bullying behavior as wholly evil, unredeemable deviants and, thus, as in need of punishment. The Prince and Clementi cases are watershed accounts of bullying because of the large body of discourse they created and the serious criminal charges the alleged bullies faced. Using popular press coverage of Prince and Clementi as case studies, this analysis examines how a bullying epidemic is constructed in contemporary media and asks about the implications.

Analysis of the News Coverage

In order to discover a wide range of media texts to examine the two cases, I searched LexisNexis Academic database for "Phoebe Prince" and "Tyler Clementi" in all English news. In each case, I defined the time-period as one year after the day the teen died. Both cases received significant international media coverage, particularly Prince, as she was an Irish citizen; however, I was interested only in stories published in U.S. newspapers and magazines. The search for "Phoebe Prince," between January 14, 2010 and January 14, 2011, returned 338 stories published in the U.S., while searching for "Tyler Clementi" between September 22, 2010 and September 22, 2011 produced 315 U.S. articles. I was particularly attentive to stories that mentioned both Prince and Clementi. To find these articles, I searched LexisNexis Academic database for "Phoebe Prince and Tyler Clementi," between September 22, 2010 and September 22, 2014, which resulted in 25 articles in U.S. newspapers and magazines.

I analyzed magazines and newspapers with a national readership (e.g., magazines such as *Time* and newspapers like *The New York Times*) since they communicate messages about bullying to a large audience. Additionally, I looked at local Massachusetts and New Jersey newspapers. Because Prince and Clementi lived in these states respectively, there was significant attention paid to their cases locally. I excluded articles about beauty pageants, school plays, and rallies in which bullying was a key theme, but that mentioned Prince or Clementi only in passing. I did include letters to the editors because they are one important component of the cultural discourse about bullying, as they are a system of representation through which individuals understand the world (DeFoster, 2010; Mazzarella & Pecora, 2007a). Given these selection criteria, 193 articles from 67 newspapers and magazines were included in the final analysis.

Framing the Stories

The story about Phoebe Prince's suicide most often told in the media goes something like this: Four months prior to her death, in September 2009, Prince moved from Ireland to South Hadley, Massachusetts—described in *The Boston Globe* as "a nice, comfortable middle-class suburb" (Cullen, 2010b). After enrolling at South Hadley High School, Prince briefly dated the school's football quarterback, Sean Mulveyhill, earning the ire of several popular girls, including Mulveyhill's on-again, off-again girlfriend, Kayla Narey. Narey, Sharon Velazquez, Flannery Mullins, and Ashley Longe allegedly taunted Phoebe in school, through cell phone text messages, and on Facebook. On the day of her death, while Prince was walking home from school, a group of girls reportedly drove by yelling insults and threw an energy drink in her direction. This event has been constructed in the media as the last straw—the moment Prince decided to kill herself.

In the wake of Prince's suicide, in an unprecedented move, the district attorney charged five[2] South Hadley teenagers with felonies including criminal harassment and stalking. The teens were also charged with violation of civil rights with bodily injury, a statute that had previously been used to prosecute violence perpetrated by racist groups (Bazelon, 2014). The district attorney argued that Prince's civil rights were violated because the bullying interfered with her right to an education, and the bodily injury was Phoebe's death (Bazelon, 2014). At the time, this sharp response was the first of its kind: "Legal experts said they were not aware of other cases in which students faced serious criminal charges for harassing a fellow student" (Eckholm & Zezima, 2010a, p. 1). Media report that the girls bullied Prince through relational aggression, using tactics such as gossip and name-calling. Coverage of Prince's suicide does not include any reports of physical violence, yet these tactics of social aggression are presented as tools for murder.

Media coverage of Tyler Clementi's suicide generally tells this story: Following Clementi's request to have their dorm room to himself for three hours, Ravi reportedly used, fellow dorm mate, Molly Wei's computer to webcast Clementi's encounter with a man. Ravi tweeted, "Turned on my webcam. I saw him making out with a dude. Yay." Two days later, Ravi's 148 Twitter followers received another message: "Anyone with iChat, I dare you to video chat me between the hours of 9:30 and 12. Yes it's happening again." As the story goes, after learning that his encounter with a man had been streamed online, Clementi jumped off the George Washington Bridge. The Clementi case quickly became the focus of national discussions about cyberbullying and bullycide.

Ravi and Wei were charged with two counts each of invasion of privacy. Ravi was additionally charged with bias (based on Clementi's sexual orientation), as well as witness and evidence tampering because he deleted a post on Twitter alerting others to view the second encounter and replaced it with a false post. Thus, the Clementi case became the second case, following that of Prince, where students faced serious criminal charges for harassing a fellow student. Again, in the media coverage, there are no reports of physical violence. Unlike with the Prince case, the narrative relies on a single (as opposed to habitual) incident, and this one act of allegedly streaming Clementi's private moment online is presented as murderous.

Blaming Girls for Bullying

As noted above, in the popular press, blame for Prince's suicide is placed squarely on an alleged pack of mean girls. Prior to the Prince case, "mean girl" was a term used in popular culture but rarely in news stories, yet the media coverage of the Prince case relentlessly applies this label to the alleged bullies. The media's use of the term "mean girls" is important because it calls to mind the meaning associated with a particular referential context (Hall, Critcher, Jefferson, Clarke, & Roberts, 1978). The label "mean girl" depicts the "threat" in a form that is easily recognizable—the popular, cruel bully who will do anything to maintain her place atop the high school hierarchy.

The first time the term was used in this way was on January 24, 2010 (ten days after Prince committed suicide) when *The Boston Globe* ran an article by Kevin Cullen titled "The Untouchable Mean Girls." In the piece, Cullen uses the label "mean girls" eight times (including in the title) to refer to the girls who allegedly drove Prince to commit suicide. On February 4, 2010, Constantine (2010b) writing for a Springfield, Massachusetts newspaper, *The Republican*, also refers to "the 'mean girls' suspected of bullying the late Phoebe Prince" (p. A01). The trend of labeling the alleged bullies "mean girls" was not limited to newspaper coverage. For example, the April 26, 2010 issue of *People* magazine, on its cover, claimed to have new details about the accused "mean girls."

In the cultural discourse about girls' bullying, the tools of indirect aggression (i.e., gossip and not speaking to someone) are gendered, presented as used only by girls. For instance, in the media coverage of the Prince case there are no examples of boys using covert forms of aggression, only girls. In *The Boston Herald*, Eagan (2010) claims:

> Boys beat each other up. Girls spread vicious rumors. They call each other ugly names. They roll their eyes and laugh derisively and whisper as their victims squirm before them, helpless. Girls exclude. Their prey is banished from their cafeteria lunch table. She's not invited to the party. She's isolated, alone. (p. 006)

Eagan suggests that the use of indirect forms of aggression is specific to girls. Although Eagan's article is ostensibly about the "constant torment" Prince faced, she does not link the aforementioned description of girls' bullying to Prince's bullying. Instead, Eagan presents the fictionalized, hypothetical description of girls' bullying as the "truth" of Prince's torment and generalizes the narrative to be true of all girls. It is within this cultural context that the story of a young girl who committed suicide after the relentless bullying of, as described in *The Boston Globe*, "pretty and popular" mean girls is salient (Cullen, 2010b).

Media present the girls' verbal communication as just as damaging as physical aggression. This construction relies on a causal link between verbal aggression and suicide. The bullying tactics mentioned in *The New York Times* and *People* are verbal: taunting and physical threats (Eckholm & Zezima, 2010a), name-calling and verbal abuse (Eckholm & Zezima, 2010b), insults and hectoring (Meadows & Herbst, 2010). Although the bullying tactics Prince allegedly endured are reported to be verbal, there are links drawn that suggest

Narey, Velazquez, Mullins, and Longe killed Phoebe. For example, the tagline of a March 30, 2010 segment on CBS's *The Early Show* is "Teen Bullying Leads to Suicide," and Byrne (2010), in *The Patriot Ledger*, calls the girls "murderers" (p. 8). In turn, the girls' communication is vilified through hyperbolic, vague, pathos-ridden language such as "social blood-letting" (Gelzinis, 2010). In *The Boston Herald*, Gelzinis (2010) makes the link even more salient when he calls the tactics the girls reportedly used to bully Phoebe "weapons" that are "far more subtle, but just as deadly" as "teens gunning each other down" (p. 005).

The *Christian Science Monitor* calls the Prince case "this generation's Columbine moment for school bullying" (Khadaroo, 2010). There are multiple references to the Columbine massacre in the media coverage of the Prince case, but none discusses the differences in the shooters' physical violence and girls' indirect aggression. As a result, the two forms of aggression are represented in a particularly gendered manner, and indirect aggression, which uses verbal communication, is constructed as just as damaging as physical aggression. The seeming similarity between Columbine and South Hadley is salient in *The Boston Globe* where Cullen (2010a) explains that months before Phoebe's suicide, South Hadley High School invited Barbara Coloroso to talk to students, parents, teachers, and administrators about bullying. According to Cullen:

> Coloroso knows as much about the subject as anyone. She was brought into Columbine after two kids who were bullied decided to get even with guns. She was brought into the Red Lake reservation in Minnesota after a 16-year-old shot seven people dead at the high school where he was bullied.[3] And she was brought to South Hadley, ahead of the curve, ahead of a tragedy, five months before Phoebe Prince...hanged herself after being tormented by a group of girls who just wouldn't leave her alone.

Cullen describes the school shootings in a gender-neutral manner. As opposed to referencing that Klebold and Harris were boys, Cullen calls them "kids." Instead of referring to Weise as male, Cullen indicates a "16-year-old" committed the murders. In contrast, despite the fact that Sean Mulveyhill was also arrested for bullying Phoebe, Cullen is quite clear that the bullies in South Hadley were a "group of girls." The girls' gender is, thus, a necessary component in categorizing their actions as horrific.

In a manner similar to the representations of the Columbine shooters, the South Hadley mean girls are constructed as taking pleasure in aggression, which works to heighten the horror of their actions. The idea that the girls enjoyed bullying Phoebe contributes to their constructions as brutal without cause. For example, following the Columbine massacre, media reported the joy the shooters seemed to take from their rampage. In an interview on *The Today Show*, Katie Couric describes the boys as "laughing and carrying on" and a fellow Columbine student confirms "they were acting as if it was like a party" (Frymer, 2009). In a comparable manner, *The Boston Globe* reports the girls who reportedly bullied Phoebe:

> went on Facebook and mocked her in death. They told State Police detectives they did nothing wrong, had nothing to do with Phoebe killing herself. And then they went right back to school and started badmouthing Phoebe. They had a dance, a cotillion, at the Log Cabin in Holyoke two days after Phoebe's sister found her in the closet. (Cullen, 2010b)

Cullen's phraseology is interesting in that he claims the girls "had a dance… two days after Phoebe's sister found her." The girls did not host the cotillion; it was a school-sponsored event that Phoebe had planned to attend (Constantine, 2010a; Fanto, 2010; Smolowe, Herbst, Weisensee, Rakowsky, & Mascia, 2010), yet Cullen seems to suggest the girls threw a party to celebrate Phoebe's death. In this sense, Cullen ascribes the mean girls with a sense of power that he attributes to their privileged social status. Although the girls are vilified in some of the same ways as Klebold and Harris, they are not shown to be misfits and outcasts; instead, Cullen reports they are "pretty and popular," placing them in an influential position in the high school hierarchy.

Without acknowledgement of the interlocking systems of oppression that may contribute to girls' anger, jealousy emerges as the motive for the girls' bullying of Phoebe, feeding "the postfeminist media theme" (Dow, 1996, p. 148) of divisions among women. For example, *The New York Times* claims Prince's relationship with Mulveyhill caused his ex-girlfriend Narey to be so jealous that she and some of her friends started their campaign against Prince (Eckholm & Zezima, 2010d). The girls reportedly called Phoebe an "Irish whore" ("Why was Phoebe Prince bullied?," 2010) and "Irish slut" (Eckholm & Zezima, 2010b). The media attention to this case individualizes sexism as a bullying behavior, erasing boys and patriarchy from the narrative entirely.

Homophobic Bullying

While media coverage of the Prince case focuses on a small group of mean girls, thus individualizing the problem of bullying, stories about Clementi's suicide repeatedly reference structural homophobia. Many news stories connect Clementi's death to the suicides of other teenagers who reportedly also took their lives after being bullied because they were (or were perceived to be) gay (Khadaroo, 2010; McKinley, 2010; Turnbull, 2010). The demonization of the homophobic bullying these young boys faced and the empathetic cultural outpouring that followed their deaths is noteworthy. Importantly, however, the links drawn between homophobia and bullying are individualized since the story about Clementi's death remains one about evil homophobic bullies, as opposed to opening the discourse to include other negative (and potentially deadly) effects structural homophobia may have on LGBTQ youth. For instance, in a 2005 Harris poll, 90% of LGBTQ teens reported having been bullied in the past year (Tresniowki, 2010). LGBTQ students are 91% more likely to be bullied than their heterosexual peers (Seaman, 2016). Perhaps most troubling, one of every three children who commits suicide is LGBTQ (Yingst, 2010). Only 10% of teens self-identify as LGTBQ, so the fact that they account for 1/3 of all teen suicides is terribly distressing. Media largely reported these statistics on LGTBQ teen bullying and suicide in the coverage surrounding Clementi's death (Crisp, 2010; Dabkowski, 2010; McKinley, 2010; Turnbull, 2010). This is notable, as it is far more common in mediated representations of gay individuals to "refuse to recognize the existence of organized, systemic, or politically oppressive homophobia" and to never raise the political status of gays and lesbians (Dow, 2001, p. 133). However, in this case, the statistics about LGTBQ teen suicide are reshaped and connected to bullying, as opposed to the myriad other reasons an LGBTQ teen might commit suicide (i.e., rejection from family, sense of loss, religious persecution, etc.).

The insistence that homophobic bullying is *the* reason Clementi committed suicide is a persistent theme in the media coverage and the cultural discourse. For instance, in *The Christian Science Monitor*, Zimmerman (2010) notes that Secretary of Education Arne Duncan attributed Clementi's death to the "trauma" of homophobic bullying, pointing to the ways in which a moral panic involves the interplay of media, politicians, and the public. In turn, the bodies of Ravi and Wei (Clementi's alleged bullies) become the site where homophobia is placed, while other potential homophobic issues that may have played a role in Clementi's decision to commit suicide are ignored. Thus, homophobia is turned into a question of one person being mean to another as opposed to a systemic, normalized, mundane everyday form of oppression.

While seemingly demonizing Clementi's alleged bullies as homophobic, the media coverage remains gleefully homophobic in doggedly calling attention to Clementi's sexual orientation. Journalists consistently assert that what Ravi saw on the webcam was sexual in nature, contributing to the narrative that Clementi was so humiliated that he believed his only recourse was to kill himself. Although the webcam captured Clementi kissing another man, the incident is exaggerated when referred to as a "liaison" (Fanelli, 2010), a "rendezvous" (Alex & Naanes, 2011), or a "tryst" (Harris, 2011a, 2011b; Karoliszyn, 2011; Lemier, Feeney, & McShane, 2010), which would suggest the two men were lovers. In other cases, the idea that the men had sex is stated outright (DeFalco & Mulvihill, 2010; Lamb & Shilling, 2010; Michaelson, 2012). The headline for the May 7, 2011 story in *The Philadelphia Inquirer* refers to the case as the "sex webcam case," and claims that the webcam recorded "two male students engaging in sex" (Anastasia, 2011c, p. B01). Claims that Clementi was having sex are often followed by "with a man" or preceded by "gay," "homosexual," or "same sex," functioning to call attention to Tyler's same-sex desires in a way not typical when the subject is heterosexual. For instance, *The New York Post* writes that Clementi had a "gay encounter," and the headline labels it a "gay kiss" (Fenton, Calhoun, & Mangan, 2010).

The misinformation that Clementi was having sex is compounded by a narrative in which his sexual orientation was unknown to his friends and family, making Ravi's actions appear even more deplorable. Ravi's alleged homophobic bullying—online streaming of Clementi having a sexual encounter with a man—is presented in media coverage as "outing" Clementi (Bouthillette, 2011; Keyes, 2010; Khadaroo, 2010; Mangan, 2010; Mulvihill & Henry, 2010). For instance, a story in *The New York Post* states that Clementi's parents "were apparently unaware that their son was gay" (Fenton *et al.*, 2010, p. 4). Yet, other reports indicate that Clementi self-identified as gay to his family and others on campus ("Vengeful in Jersey," 2011). Indeed, on a December 10, 2011 interview on *The Today Show*, Clementi's mother explained that he had come out to his family prior to leaving for Rutgers and admitted she struggled with his sexuality. In an analysis of the television show *Ellen*, Dow (2001) argues "acceptance by family and friends" is framed as the most crucial issues a gay individual faces (p. 132). In this case, the difficulties of Clementi's relationship with his mother are ignored in favor of individualizing homophobia to a bullying behavior. In turn, the cause of Clementi's suicide is again reduced to the "creepy kids" who humiliated Clementi by spying on him (Fenton *et al.*, 2010).

Beyond negating the struggles LGBTQ youth may face with unaccepting family members, this narrative similarly ignores the distress many LGBTQ youth feel when faced with intolerant religious institutions. For instance, Clementi reportedly admitted that he was having doubts about God (Wiggin, 2011). Since many religious institutions position homosexuality as inappropriate and immoral (Adams, 2011; Bennett, 2003; Chavez, 2004), Clementi may also have been concerned about marginalization from his religion. We will likely never know the "true" story of what occurred between Clementi and Ravi. My point is that that there are many different stories that might have been told, but it is the story about how homophobic bullying caused Clementi's suicide that was taken up in the popular press, individualizing homophobia as a bullying behavior as opposed to asking critical questions about homophobia's structural impact on LGBTQ youth.

The Evil Bully vs. The Innocent Victim

The distinction between bully and victim is rarely clear-cut; more often, bullying is a learned behavior, suggesting the aggressor may have at one time been a victim (boyd & Palfrey, 2013). In fact, in a survey of 43,000 high school students completed in 2010, the Josephson Institute's Center for Youth Ethics found that 47% had been bullied, teased, or taunted at school but that 50% had been bullies themselves (Cloud, 2012). Yet in media, constructions of victim and bully are generally clearly delineated, setting up a dichotomy of the always evil bully and the endlessly innocent victim. Through this process, the evil bully and innocent victim operate simultaneously in a dialectic, functioning in tandem. The contemporary mediated bullying discourse simplifies the dynamics into good and evil, individualizing the problem, and not allowing for a more complex understanding of the issues, especially the structural issues.

The bullying discourse necessitates an innocent victim in order to demonize the evil bullies. In other words, the punitive treatment of bullies becomes compulsory when their victims are framed as virtuous. One of the ways media construct Prince as an entirely innocent victim is by framing the story of girl bullying as specific to the U.S. In turn, Prince is constructed as an outsider who is innocent to the ways of U.S. mean girls. The image of Prince as the ultimate victim—alone, scared, and without the tools or channels to combat the bullying—becomes salient through the construction of Prince's outsider status. In the majority of stories I analyzed, Prince's Irish heritage is discussed, if not attached to her name when first mentioned, as in "15-year-old Irish immigrant named Phoebe Prince" (Ollove, 2010). She is described as "a recent immigrant from Ireland" (Greenwald, 2010), "a newcomer from Ireland" (Cohen, 2010; Eckholm & Zezima, 2010d), "a transplant" (McNeil, 2010; Smolowe *et al.*, 2010), and "the despairing new immigrant from a small Irish village" (Nocera & Kennedy, 2010). Prince is shown to be a young girl who desperately wanted to participate in the normative U.S. school culture, but was marginalized because of her ethnic heritage and her naïveté regarding the mean girl way of life.

Since the actions of the mean girls are rarely outlined in any specific detail, the bullying tactics are not problematized; instead, the girls themselves are constructed as out-of-control and deviant. This trend contributes to a narrative about girls from good suburban families gone bad, amplifying the danger these girls pose to a quiet middle-class white community. It is common in times of moral panic to construct a group as engaging in immoral behavior that presumably has serious harmful consequences on society (Cohen, 2002; Goode & Ben-Yehuda, 1994). This process is reflected in *The Boston Globe* where a high school parent is quoted as saying, "Things like this aren't supposed to happen in South Hadley" (Cullen, 2010b). In *The Republican*, a Springfield, MA newspaper, the mean girls are represented as tarnishing the image of a "tight knit community" (Constantine, 2010c, p. 3). The discourse suggests that mean girls can shame an entire community—a white middle-class community that is unaccustomed to being in a negative position. Constantine (2010b) notes that on its website South Hadley describes itself as an "inviting and charming community," and the town's slogan is "A Great Place to Live" (p. A01). Using the voices of South Hadley residents, Constantine paints a picture of a town that is suffering because of the actions of a few deviant girls. For example, one long-time South Hadley resident claims, "It was always nice to say I was from South Hadley. That is no longer the case" (Constantine, 2010c, p. A01).

There is a coherent story that develops about the vulnerable outsider Prince and the evil insider mean girls. In newspapers, the mean girls are described as "a coterie of aspiring fascists…predatory…cruel, hedonistic, and self-absorbed" (Cohen, 2010, p. A13) and "criminal torturers" (Eagan, 2010, p. 006) who caused Prince to suffer "unending humiliation" (Ollove, 2010), "relentless, sadistic abuse" (Fitzgerald, 2010, p. 002), and "verbal torture" (Murphy, 2010, p. 9). Eagan (2010) in *The Boston Herald* calls them "criminal torturers" (p. 006). In *The Boston Herald*, Fitzgerald (2010) claims Prince's suffering is analogous to the "unspeakable horrors of internment at Dachau and Buchenwald" (p. 6). In turn, the girls are framed as like the Nazis who tortured and murdered millions of innocent people. The girls' construction as similar to the Nazis is heightened particularly through the myriad references to their bullying as "torture." Comparing Prince's experiences to those of individuals who were in concentration camps relies on representing not only the bullies as evil but also Prince as an innocent victim. That is, the girls can only be constructed as excessively evil if Prince is excessively innocent. The two constructions work in tandem; indeed, one is required by the other.

In newspapers, letters to editors, and political addresses, Clementi is similarly presented as an entirely innocent victim, while Wei and Ravi are seen as unredeemable evil bullies. Clementi is described as "innocent" (Akin, 2010), "polite, courteous" (Kindergan, Akin, Coutros, & Clunn, 2010), "bright" (Kalson, 2010), "shy" (Fenton *et al.*, 2010; Foderaro, 2010; Klein & Messing, 2011; Lemire *et al.*, 2010), "sensitive" (Tucker, 2010), and "tragic" (Gendar, Sandoval, & McShane, 2010). Many journalists reference Tyler as a "gifted" (Giordano, Simon, & Newall, 2010; Kindergan *et al.*, 2010), "talented" (Lemire *et al.*, 2010; Rosenberg, 2010), and "skilled" (Gendar *et al.*, 2010) musician. Daly (2010), in the *Daily News*, argues that being a violinist made Tyler "*more* sensitive" and "*more* vulnerable" (emphasis added). In constructing Clementi as the innocent victim, he is also made much more three-dimensional. In contrast, Ravi and Wei's descriptions as evil bullies are unidimensional. They are referred to as "cruel" (Fenton *et al.*, 2010; Sultan, 2010), "evil" (Norman, 2010), "vicious," "heartless" (Tucker, 2010), "tormentors" (Fenton *et al.*, 2010), and "cybercreeps" (Daly, 2010). Perhaps not surprisingly, given that Wei received fewer charges and testified against him, Ravi is made to appear most unredeemable. Reportedly, Wei described Ravi to investigators as "bombastic and egotistic" (Anastasia, 2011a) and "a braggart and a habitual liar" (Perez-Pena, 2011). He is further referred to as "self-absorbed" and "obnoxious" (Anastasia, 2011a). New Jersey Governor Chris Christie reportedly questioned how Wei and Ravi could "sleep at night" (Lemire *et al.*, 2010). Describing Ravi and Wei in this way simplifies the issue by suggesting they are hopelessly vicious and, in turn, the obvious solution is to remove them from society.

The evil bully/innocent victim dichotomy is a particularly useful tool in creating links that suggest what the alleged bullies did *caused* the suicides— the behaviors were murderous. In some cases, the use of a Webcam is made analogous to the weapons used by mass shooters. For instance, in the *St. Louis Dispatch*, Sultan (2010) claims that Ravi and Wei "did not bring an AK-47 to campus. But they were armed, nonetheless" (H6). While Moore (2010) calls Ravi and Wei's use of the Webcam "every bit as deadly as a bullet." In other cases, the Webcam incident is said to have caused "shy" and "sensitive" Clementi to have felt so "humiliated" that his only response was to kill himself (Fenton *et al.*, 2010; Kalson, 2010; Klein & Messing, 2011). Lastly, some journalists call what Ravi and Wei did "murderous" (Norman, 2010) or imply as much by comparing Tyler's suicide to the 1998 murder of Matthew Shepard (Dabkowski, 2010; Parker, 2010).[4] Again, as with the Prince case, the bullying behaviors of teenagers are represented as causing another's death, contributing to their presentations as wholly evil.

Court papers filed in preparation for both trials brought more information to light, much of which never made it into the media narratives and that complicates the portrayal of the always evil bully/wholly innocent victim relationship. For instance, according to Prince's mother, Prince began cutting herself in 2008, while still living in Ireland.[5] By February 2009, Prince was cutting again, and in May, she began taking Prozac (Bazelon, 2011). Then, in November, she was also prescribed Seroquel, a medication used to treat bipolar disorder. Not long thereafter, when Mulveyhill ended their relationship, Prince attempted to commit suicide by swallowing a bottle of Seroquel (Contrada, 2010). This information, which seems to suggest several potential reasons as to why Phoebe committed suicide, raises questions about the persecution of the alleged bullies. As opposed to exhibiting the presumption of innocence so integral to our legal system, the cultural discourse constructed the South Hadley mean girls as evil bullies who were guilty of murdering Prince.

In the Clementi case, transcripts of Internet chats provide a less clearcut innocent/evil binary, again pointing to the many different narratives that could have been told about this tragedy. In at least one exchange, Ravi indicated that Clementi's sexual orientation did not bother him: "I'm not really angry or sad idc (I don't care)" (Perez-Pena, 2011), while Clementi apparently wrote that Ravi "is 'sooo indian/first gen americanish' and 'his rents defs own a dunkin" (Akin, 2010, p. 17).[6] What may have been true is that, like many first year students at colleges and universities, the roommates had little in common, but this does not support a narrative in which Ravi bullied Clementi for being gay. In charging Ravi with bias-intimidation, the prosecution made a case that Clementi "reasonably believed" he was being harassed because he was gay, which was strengthened by constructing Clementi as a sympathetic innocent victim. Given that Clementi was unable to testify to his state of mind, the more wholly evil Ravi is made to appear, the more believable it is that his motive was homophobic in nature (as opposed to being immature, for instance). Despite, the complexities of these stories, the dominant narratives about evil bullies murdering innocent teens through bullying tactics became the "truth" about youth bullying.

The Weapon of Cyberbullying

The most commonly cited link between the Clementi and Prince cases is alleged to be cyberbullying. In popular culture, there is a tendency to represent cybertechnology (i.e., cell phone texting, social network sites, and so on) as a weapon in the hands of teens. Both the Clementi and Prince cases reflect public concern with youth and the Internet. As explained by Leslie (2010) in *The Atlanta Journal-Constitution*, "With the rise of Facebook, Twitter and other forms of social media still a relatively new mode of communication, cyber-bullying is unchartered territory for most parents and school officials" (p. 1A). A letter to the editor of *The Lebanon Daily News* in which Weaver (2010) suggests technology is a "most useful tool for citizens," but for students is a "weapon that's being used to harm society" reveals this concern. Note the way in which these comments are generational—technology is a great tool being misused *solely* by teens. An editorial in *The Washington Post* exacerbates the division between those who use technology for good versus those who use it for evil: "Technology has exponentially enabled and emboldened the mean or thoughtless among us" ("Cruelty at Rutgers," 2010). There is no way to currently know how prevalent cyberbullying is, yet as a culture we remain convinced that it is out of control and dangerous and that it *leads* to suicide. For instance, according to McHenry (2011), "Modern technology now plays a significant role in many teen suicides" (p. 232). When the myth that new forms of technology cause teen suicides takes hold, we risk incorporating more punitive responses to teen behaviors that are largely ineffective, ignoring gendered and homophobic oppression that exists outside of youth culture and beyond technology.

The alleged bullies are constructed as evil through the presentation of cyberbullying as just as dangerous (indeed, murderous) as physical violence and the tools of cyberbullying (cell phones and computers) as weapons. For example, a story in the *Daily News* about Clementi's death used the headline "Webcam suicide," suggesting the webcam was the murder weapon (Karoliszyn, 2011), and an editorial in the *Pittsburgh Post-Gazette* uses the headline

"Death by Internet." Similarly, in *The New York Times*, Schwartz (2010) argues Clementi "died from exposure in cyberspace." In *USA Today*, a text message is compared to "a tormentor's punch" ("Shame the cyber-bullies, 2010, p. 10A), and *The Christian Science Monitor* quotes Parry Aftab, the executive director of WiredSafety, an online safety group, as saying digital technology is "the weapon of choice often with older teens and young adults" (Khadaroo, 2010). In the *Daily News*, Lupica (2010) calls Ravi's use of a laptop "assault with a deadly weapon."

Suggesting that cybertechnology is a tool for murder functions to construct teens as malicious because they appear to be organized and scheming, like a network of terrorists. Indeed, a headline in the *Providence Journal* refers to cyberbullying as "terrorism of a personal kind" and suggests online bullying is "weaponry" that is more advanced than guns (Harrop, 2010). Harrop (2010) goes on to argue, "Communications technology has empowered terrorists (and) let young sadists injure others" (p. 7). Jim McGreevey, who resigned as Governor of New Jersey after announcing he was gay, claimed that Clementi was "being terrorized online" (Karoliszyn & Shapiro, 2010). In turn, technology is presented as a dangerous tool because it helps teens organize and coordinate their attacks. For example, in reference to the Prince case, Eckholm and Zezima (2010a) use the term "plotting" when discussing the cyberbullying Prince allegedly faced. This term works to create an image of a group of students working together to preplan warfare, making their actions seem more methodical and dangerous.

Moreover, there is little evidence to support the claims that Prince and Clementi were victims of cyberbullying. According to the prosecutor in the Prince case, the majority of the bullying took place on school grounds (Eckholm & Zezima, 2010c), yet early reports about her suicide nearly all blame cyberbullying for her death or reference cyberbullying as a key aspect of her case (Donelan, 2010; Eagan, 2010; McHenry, 2011; Van Sack, Wedge, & Weir, 2010). For example, Cullen (2010b) explains, "Cyberbullies using text messages and social networking websites were among those who hounded 15-year-old Phoebe Prince to the grave." Donelan (2010) asserts that Prince "committed suicide…after being inundated with cruel messages on her Facebook profile," yet according to Bazelon (2011), she did not have a Facebook account. Bhat (2010) maintains that Prince's suicide "highlights the tragic number of adolescents who have been cyber-bullied and see no recourse other than death" (p. 7). In each of these cases, cyberbullying is shown to have caused Prince to kill herself, so the criminalization of bullying and communication online is seen as acceptable, indeed necessary.

Similarly, cyberbullying is repeatedly said to be the reason Clementi killed himself. Hinduja and Patchin (2009) define cyberbullying as "willful and repeated harm inflicted through the use of computers, cell phones, and other electronic devices" (p. 5). This case does not meet the specifics of that definition since Ravi used a webcam to spy on Clementi once, so it was not a repeated act, but instead meets the criterion for invasion of privacy, a much less sexy accusation. Along with an insistence that Ravi is a cyberbully, media claim Ravi used the webcam to record a video of Tyler that he "posted," "streamed," or "broadcast" online (Barton, 2010; Daly, 2010; El-Ghobashy, 2010; Foderaro, 2010; Gardiner & Fox, 2010; Gendar *et al.*, 2010; Hu, 2010; Parker, 2010; Schweber, 2010; Siemaszko, 2010; Zimmerman, 2010). In *Time*, Cloud (2010) asserts that Ravi "secretly recorded a video of Clementi kissing a guy; the video went up on YouTube." Allegations that a video of Tyler was posted online to a site like YouTube suggest that it was viewed by an unknown number of people, and that Clementi would never be able to escape his shame—that the video would be online forever, but since the "encounter was shown live, authorities cannot retrieve the images" (Anastasia, 2011a, p. B01). Exacerbating the reality of what Ravi did with technology feeds into the contemporary moral panic about cyberbullying and the ways youth are using technology to harm one another.

Despite the fact that neither Clementi nor Prince was a victim of cyberbullying, in the media coverage the dangers of cyberbullying are amped up through hyperbole and hypothetical views about the potential outcomes if we continue to allow teens to run wild online. For instance, a letter to the editor published in *The Herald News* argues, "The harassment that infects nearly any school has been made especially pernicious by sophisticated home computers and Internet-equipped camera phones" ("Indictment is handed up in tragic case," 2011). Similarly, an editorial in *The Washington Post* claims:

> Technology has exponentially enabled and emboldened the mean or thoughtless. It allows those with less than noble intentions to hide behind screen names or lurk from afar, distancing themselves from their human targets and the possible consequences of their actions. And the trespasses are no longer contained to a circle of friends, a school or a town but are accessible to millions. ("Cruelty at Rutgers," 2010, p. A12)

Although these articles are presumably about the bullying Clementi and/or Prince faced, there is no link to the descriptions above to the specifics of their cases. Instead, these hypothetical, hyperbolic accounts are presented as the "truth" of the narrative of teen cyberbullying. When hypothetical stories, written by adults, about how youth use technology to bully become taken-for-granted, they may play a role in how authorities' respond to cyberbullying.

Media coverage of teen cyberbullying seems to suggest it is more dangerous and more common than face-to-face bullying, yet studies "show that face-to-face bullying is still more common—and youth consistently report that it has a greater negative impact—than what happens online" (boyd & Palfrey, 2013, p. 5). Although media have made cyberbullying more visible, cyberbullying "happens a third less than traditional bullying" (Bennett, 2010). Indeed, although LGBTQ youth experience more bullying online, they also regularly report finding peer support and access to health information online (GLSEN, 2012), highlighting the complexity of the issue of youth and emerging forms of media. While emerging forms of technology seemingly empower some youth, cultural conversations ignore the positive potential and instead use myths and problematic assumptions about teens and technology to make "bullies" responsible for suicides. The media coverage surrounding teen suicides contributes to the escalation of cultural concern about how teens use technology to bully.

Cultural Implications

In May 2011, the criminal cases against the South Hadley teens accused of bullying Phoebe Prince ended. The four girls admitted to certain facts about their role in bullying Prince that supported misdemeanor offenses. They each received probation and community service, and if they complete their probation successfully, they will have clean records.

In the Tyler Clementi case, Wei agreed to testify against Ravi and complete 300 hours of community service. If she keeps a clean record, the case against her will be dropped. Ravi was convicted of invasion of privacy and bias intimidation—a hate crime. He was eventually "sentenced to 30 days in prison, three years probation, mandatory counseling and a $10,000 fine, an amount that will go to victims of hate-based crimes" ("Proper punishment?," 2012). Ravi was released from prison after 20 days for good behavior (Zernike, 2015).

In March 2015, the New Jersey Supreme Court ruled that the bias-intimidation law used to prosecute Ravi was unconstitutional. The court found that the 2001 statute (the only one of its kind in the nation) was "unconstitutionally vague" (Zernike, 2015). In September 2016, six years after Clementi committed suicide, the court overturned Ravi's conviction while simultaneously condemning his conduct as "grotesque" (Harris, 2016). A month later, Ravi pleaded guilty to attempted invasion of privacy and was sentenced to time served and fines paid (Schweber & Foderaro, 2016).

The outcomes of these cases have far-reaching implications. First, both cases have been referenced in the passing of anti-bullying legislation, legislation that is often vague and subjective (as was the case with New Jersey's bias-intimidation law). As discussed earlier, in the bullying discourse, the bully is framed as wholly evil and unredeemable. The focus on the always evil bully is reflected in increasingly punitive anti-bullying legislation, highlighting the interplay of the media, politicians, and agents of social control in the moral panic about youth bullying. For example, on January 6, 2011, the New Jersey Legislature passed the Anti-Bullying Bill of Rights, considered the toughest measure in the country. According to the New Jersey Educational Association, the bill was passed in response to "media coverage of several student suicides," and Governor Christie cited the Clementi case when signing the bill into law (Anastasia, 2011b). Measures, such as this one, that focus on punishing and exiling bullies in order to protect the public do little to address the structural issues in our culture that contribute to the systemic sexism and homophobia that is wrongly placed on the individual bullies.

Troublingly, anti-bullying legislation, which media often celebrate, individualizes bullying, suggesting that we can easily identify and weed out those among us who are evil tormentors in order to protect the innocent victims, upholding a troubling bully/victim dichotomy. In this legislation, we see a reduction of systemic oppression to bullying, once again individualizing the issue. In turn, homophobia and sexism become a question of one person being mean to another as opposed to a normalized and mundane form of oppression that we need to be able to identify in order to properly deal with the issue of teen suicide.

The second important outcome is that the legal consequences coupled with the framing of the stories in the popular press of both cases contribute to a cultural belief that bullying *causes* suicide. On his December 5, 2011 show on CNN, Dr. Drew Pinsky claimed that Prince and Clementi were "tormented by their peers" and "driven to suicide." In laying the blame for suicide at the feet of bullies, the fact that suicide is the second leading cause of death among 15–24 year olds is ignored (Center for Disease Control, 2015). The cultural discourse about bullying relies on the idea that bullying can cause suicide, which works to frame teens as evil and malicious murderers. Suggesting that an individual can cause another to commit suicide discounts the myriad reasons an individual might choose to take her life.

Finally, the focus on the ways in which youth use technology to bully in these cases unnecessarily exacerbates cultural concern about youth and emerging forms of technology, driving schools and lawmakers to spend tremendous time, energy, and money to deal with the "problem" of cyberbullying. There is little evidence to suggest teens are bullying more than ever before (Bennett, 2010; Chesney-Lind & Irwin, 2004, 2008; Males & Chesney-Lind, 2010), and data show that cyberbullying happens less than traditional face-to-face bullying. In fact, the 2011 National School Climate Survey indicates "that a safer school climate directly relates to the availability of LGBT school-based resources and support, including Gay-Straight Alliances, inclusive curriculum, supportive school staff and comprehensive anti-bullying policies" (GLSEN, 2012), suggesting the focus on anti-bullying programs in school are not the quick solution many hope. The national conversation raised in response to these teens' deaths indicates a progressive desire to fight bullying, but the ways in which this discourse operates are problematic. While championing the escalation of punitive treatment of teens, the popular discourse reduces sexism and homophobia to a problem of individuals who bully and obfuscates a focus on challenging political institutions and an examination of structural issues.

Notes

1. This chapter is derived, in part, from an article I published in *Communication, Culture & Critique* on August 9, 2012, DOI: 10.1111/j.1753–9137.2012.01127.x
2. Along with Mulveyhill, Narey, Velazquez, Mullins, and Longe, eighteen-year-old Austin Renaud was arrested for statutory rape. The charge against him was eventually dropped.
3. On March 21, 2005, Jeff Weise shot and killed and seven people at Red Lake Senior High School before turning his gun on himself.
4. Matthew Shepard was a gay college student who was beaten to death in Laramie, Wyoming in 1998. Shepard's murder brought national and international attention to hate crime legislation at the state and federal levels.
5. Cutting is a form of self-harm in which an individual mutilates her skin, typically by burning or making scratches and cuts with a sharp object that are deep enough to break the skin and make it bleed.
6. Dunkin Donuts

References

Adams, T. E. (2011). *Narrating the closet: An autoethnography of same-sex attraction*. Walnut Creek, CA: Left Coast Press.

Akin, S. (2010, October 3). When lines of privacy get blurred. *Herald News*, p. A01.

Alex, P., & Naanes, M. (2011, April 21). Roommate faces 10 years. *The Record*, p. A01.

Anastasia, G. (2011a, September 12). Few clear answers in Rutgers webcam case. *The Philadelphia Inquirer*, p. B01.

Anastasia, G. (2011b, April 21). Former Rutgers student indicted for bias crimes in webcam-streaming of roommate's tryst. *The Philadelphia Inquirer*, p. A01.

Anastasia, G. (2011c. May 7). Woman in Rutgers sex webcam case cooperating with authorities. *The Philadelphia Inquirer*, p. B01.

Bazelon, E. (2011, April 8). What really happened to Phoebe Prince? *Slate Magazine*. Retrieved from http://www.slate.com/articles/life/bulle/features/2010/what_really_happened_to_phoebe_prince/the_untold_story_of_her_suicide_and_the_role_of_the_kids_who_have_been_criminally_charged_for_it.html

Bazelon, E. (2014). *Sticks and stones: Defeating the culture of bullying and rediscovering the power of character and empathy*. New York: Random House Trade Paperbacks.

Bennett, J. A. (2003). Love me gender: Normative homosexuality and 'ex-gay' performativity in reparative therapy narratives. *Text and Performance Quarterly, 23*(4), 331–352.

Bennett, J. (2010, October 11). From lockers to lockup. *Newsweek, 156*, 38.

boyd, d., & Palfrey, J. (2013). What you must know to help combat youth bullying, meanness, and cruelty. *Kinder & Braver World Project* (Vol. 2013–5). Cambridge, MA: The Berkman Center for Internet & Society.

Byrne, N. (2010, April 8). Bullying too weak to describe what kids did to Phoebe Prince. *The Patriot Ledger*, p. 8.

Center for Disease Control. (2015). *Suicide facts at a glance—2015*. Retrieved from file:///C:/Users/Emily/AppData/Local/Temp/suicide-datasheet-a.pdf

Chavez, K. (2004). Beyond complicity: Coherence, queer theory, and the rhetoric of the 'Gay Christian Movement.' *Text and Performance Quarterly, 24*(3/4), 255–275.

Chesney-Lind, M., & Irwin, K. (2004). From badness to meanness: Popular constructions of contemporary girlhood. In A. Harris (Ed.), *All about the girl: Culture, power and identity* (pp. 45–56). New York: Routledge.

Chesney-Lind, M., Irwin, K. (2008). *Beyond bad girls: Gender, violence and hype*. New York: Routledge.

Cloud, J. (2010, October 18). Bullied to death? *Time, 176*, 60–63.

Cloud, J. (2012, March 12). The myths of bullying. *Time*. Retrieved from http://content.time.com/time/magazine/article/0,9171,2108030,00.html

Cohen, S. (2002). *Folk devils and moral panics: The creation of mods and rockers* (3rd ed.). London: MacGibbon & Kee Ltd.

Cohen, R. (2010, April 6). Wanted: A few good parents, *The Washington Post*, p. A13.

Constantine, S. E. (2010a, January 16). 200 mourn death of South Hadley teen. *The Republican*, p. 3.

Constantine, S. E. (2010b, February 4). Online posts pose threat to innocent in bully case. *The Republican*, p. A01.

Constantine, S. E. (2010c, February 21). Bullies tarnish image of South Hadley, *The Republican*, p. A01.

Contrada, F. (2010, August 10). Defense says Phoebe Prince had history of troubles. *The Republican*, p. A01.

Crisp, J. M. (2010, October 13). Senseless loss of good people. *Sentinel Enterprise*.

Critcher, C. (2009). Widening the focus: Moral panics as moral regulation. *British Journal of Criminology, 49*, 17–34.

Cruelty at Rutgers. (2010, October 3). *The Washington Post*, p. A12.

Cullen, K. (2010a, January 21). Too little, too late against bully tactics. Retrieved from http://www.boston.com/news/local/massachusetts/articles/2010/01/31/too_little_too_late_against_bully_tactics/

Cullen, K. (2010b, January 24). The untouchable mean girls. *The Boston Globe*. Retrieved from http://archive.boston.com/news/local/massachusetts/articles/2010/01/24/the_untouchable_mean_girls/

Dabkowski, C. (2010, October 24). Bullies, gay teens and suicide. *Buffalo News*, p. F1.

Daly, M. (2010, September 30). Web allows bullies to make torment global. *Daily News*, p. 5.

Death by Internet. (2010, October 6). *Pittsburgh Post-Gazette*, p. A14.

DeFalco, B., & Mulvihill, G. (2010, September 30). N. J. student kills self after sex broadcast. *The Washington Post*, p. A03.

DeFoster, R. (2010). American gun culture, school shootings, and a 'frontier mentality:' An ideological analysis of British editorial pages in the decade after Columbine. *Communication, Culture, & Critique, 3*, 466–484.

Donelan, M. (2010, February 7). Cyber-bulling on increase, say experts. *Sentinel & Enterprise*.

Dow, B. J. (1996). *Prime-time feminism: Television, media culture, and the women's movement since 1970*. Philadelphia, University of Pennsylvania Press.

Dow, B. J. (2001). *Ellen*, television, and the politics of gay and lesbian visibility. *Critical Studies in Media Communication, 18*(2), 123–140.

Eagan, M. (2010, January 26). Teen's constant torment no child's play. *The Boston Herald*, p. 006.

Eckholm, E., & Zezima, K. (2010a, March 30). 9 Teenagers are charged after suicide of classmate. *The New York Times*, p. 14.

Eckholm, E., & Zezima, K. (2010b, April 9). Court documents detail a teenage girl's final days of fear and bullying. *The New York Times*, p. 12.

Eckholm, E., & Zezima, K. (2010c, March 31). Nine charged over bullied girl's suicide. *Sydney Morning Herald* (Australia), p. 13.

Eckholm, E., & Zezima, K. (2010d, April 2). Questions for school on bullying and a suicide. *The New York Times*, p. 1.

El-Ghobashy, T. (2010, September 30). Suicide follows secret webcast. *Wall Street Journal*, p. 27.

Fanelli, J. (2010, December 23). Parents file notice of suit in Rutgers gay suicide. *Daily News*, p. 10.

Fanto, C. (2010, February 7). Bullying tragedy was wakeup call, *The Bershire Eagle*. Retrieved from http://www.berkshireeagle.com/stories/bullying-tragedy-was-wakeup-call,120501?

Fenton, R., Calhoun, A., & Mangan, D. (2011, September 30). Cruelcam costs kid life. *The New York Post*, p. 4.

Fitzgerald, J. (2010, April 21). Phoebe, we're finally listening. *The Boston Herald*, p. 006.

Flinders, M., & Wood, M. (2015). From folk devils to folk heroes: Rethinking the theory of moral panics. *Deviant Behavior, 36*, 640–656.

Foderaro, L. (2010, September 30). Private moment made public, then a fatal jump. *The New York Times*, p. 1.

Frymer, B. (2009). The media spectacle of Columbine: Alienated youth as an object of fear. *American Behavioral Scientist, 52*(10), 1387–1404.

Gardiner, S., & Fox, A. (2010, October 2). Grief, outrage at Rutgers. *Wall Street Journal*, p. 19.

Gelzinis, P. (2010, March 31). Apathy, ignorance lethal combination. *The Boston Herald*, p. 005.

Gendar, A., Sandoval, E., & McShane, L. (2010, September 30). Secret sex webcast sparks suicide. *Daily News*, p. 4.

Giordano, R., Simon, D., & Newall, M. (2010, September 30). Rutgers freshman committed suicide over images on Internet of gay sex encounter. *The Philadelphia Inquirer*, p. B01.

GLSEN. (2012). *Gay, Lesbian & Straight Education Network: Research*. Retrieved from https:// www.glsen.org/research

Grindstaff, L. (2002). *The money shot: Trash, class, and the making of TV talk shows*. Chicago: The University of Chicago Press.

Hall, S., Critcher, C., Jefferson, T., Clarke, J., & Roberts, B. (1978). *Policing the crisis: Mugging, the state, and law and order*. New York: Holmes & Meier Publishers.

Harris, C. (2011a, May 24). Clementi roommate pleads not guilty. *The Record*, p. A01.

Harris, C. (2011b, May 24). Ex-Rutgers student faces charges ties to suicide. *The Herald News*, p. A01.

Harris, C. (2016, September 9). Conviction overturned for roommate in Tyler Clementi suicide, even as court blasts his "grotesque" behavior." *People*. Retrieved from http://people. com/crime/dharun-ravis-conviction-in-tyler-clementi-case-overturned/

Harrop, F. (2010, October 6). Bully with a secret lens: Terrorism of a personal kind. *Providence Journal*, p. 7.

Hinduja, S., & Patchin, J. W. (2009). *Bullying beyond the schoolyard: Preventing and responding to cyberbullying*. Thousand Oaks, CA: Corwin Press.

Hu, W. (2010, October 2). Legal debate swirls over charges in a student's suicide. *The New York Times*, p. 15.

Indictment is handed up in a tragic case. (2011, April 21). *Herald News*, p. A20.

Kalson, S. (2010, October 10). Bad intentions. *Pittsburgh Post-Gazette*, p. B3.

Karoliszyn, H. (2011, May 7). She'll talk, and get a walk, in Rutgers suicide. *Daily News*, p. 10.

Karoliszyn, H., & Shapiro, R. (2010, October 2). Call for compassion, *Daily News*, p. 7.

Keyes, B. (2010, October 19). Standing 'out' but not alone. *Portland Press Herald*, p. B1.

Khadaroo, S.T. (2010, October 1). Rutgers student death: Has digital age made students callous? *The Christian Science Monitor*. Retrieved from http://www.csmonitor.com/USA/Society/2010/1001/Rutgers-student-death-Has-Digital-Age-made-students-callous

Kindergan, A., Akin, S., Coutros, E., & Clunn, N. (2010, September 20). Gifted teen's suicide ties to webcast. *Herald New*, p. A01.

Lamb, W., & Shilling, E. (2010, October 1). Hate crimes penalties possible. *Herald News*, p. A01.

Lemire, J., Feeney, M. J., & McShane, L. (2010, October 1). He wanted roomie out. *Daily News*.

Leslie, K. (2010, October 22). School confronts online bullying. *The Atlanta Journal-Constitution*, p. 1A.

Lupica, M. (2010, October 4). Conducting symphony of sorrow at Rutgers. *Daily News*, p. 5.

Males, M., & Chesney-Lind, M. (2010). The myth of mean girls. *The New York Times*. Retrieved from http://www.nytimes.com/2010/04/02/opinion/02males.html

Mangan, D. (2010, October 2). Rutgers kid's kin speak out. *The New York Post*, p. 11.

Mazzarella, S. R., & Pecora, N. O. (2007a). Girls in crisis: Newspaper coverage of adolescent girls. *Journal of Communication Inquiry, 31*(1), 6–27.

McHenry, Amanda. (2011). Combating cyberbullying within the metes and bounds of existing supreme court precedent. *Case Western Reserve Law Review*, 231–262. Retrieved from http://www.thefreelibrary.com/Combating+cyberbullying+within+the+metes+and+bounds+of+existing...-a0287516658.

McKinley, J. (2010, October 4). Several recent suicides put light on pressures facing gay teenagers. *The New York Times*, p. 9.

McNeil, L. (2010, February 22). Suicide in South Hadley: Bullied to Death? *People, 73*, 62.

McRobbie, A., & Thornton, S. L. (1995). Rethinking 'moral panic' for multi-mediated social worlds. *The British Journal of Sociology, 46*(4), 559–574.

Meadows, B., & Herbst, D. (2010). Bullied to death? Justice for Phoebe. *People, 73*, 77.

Moore, John. (2010, October 19). Celebrities flooding Internet with anti-gay bullying posts, *Charleston Daily Mail*, p. 10B.

Mulvihill, G., & Henry, S. (2010, October 1). Rutgers student's suicide illustrates Internet dangers. *Lowell Sun*.

Murphy, W. J. (2010, February 13). And justice for some—Psychological abuse. *The Patriot Ledger*, p. 9.

Nocera, K., & Kennedy, H. (2010, March 31). 'Mean girl' ma puts blame on suicide victim. *Daily News*, p. 16.

Norman, T. (2010, October 5). Suicide is a sad reminder of homophobia. *Pittsburg Post-Gazette*, p. A2.

Ollove, M. (2010, April 28). Bullying and teen suicide: How do we adjust school climate? *The Christian Science Monitor*. Retrieved from http://www.csmonitor.com/USA/Society/2010/0428/Bullying-and-teen-suicide-How-do-we-adjust-school-climate

Parker, K. (2010, October 5). A private matter of public concern. *Chicago Daily Herald*, p. 12.

Perez-Pena, R. (2011, August 13). More complex picture emerges in Rutgers student's suicide. *The New York Times*, p. 17.

Proper punishment? (2012, June 13). *Christian Century*, p. 98.

Rosenberg, R. (2010, October 1). Suicide kid's cam pain. *The New York Times*, p. 16.

Ryalls, E. D. (2012). Demonizing "mean girls" in the news: Was Phoebe Prince "bullied to death?" *Communication, Culture, & Critique, 5*, 463–481.

Schwartz, J. (2010, October 3). Bullying, suicide, punishment. *The New York Times*, p. 1.

Schweber, N. (2010, December 23). Parents of students who committed suicide tell Rutgers University they may sue. *The New York Times*, p. 30.

Schweber, N., & Foderaro, L. (2016, October 27). Roommate in Tyler Clementi case pleads guilty to attempted invasion of privacy. *New York Times*. Retrieved from https://www. nytimes.com/2016/10/28/nyregion/dharun-ravi-tyler-clementi-case-guilty-plea.html?_r=0

Shame the cyber-bullies. (2010, October 7). *USA Today*, p. 10A.

Siemaszko, C. (2010, October 30). 2 tied to suicide quit Rutgers U. *Daily News*, p. 5.

Sloop, J. M. (2000). Disciplining the transgendered: Brandon Teena, public representation, and normativity. *Western Journal of Communication, 64*(2), 165–189.

Sloop, J. M. (2004). *Disciplining gender: Rhetorics of sex and identity in contemporary US culture.* Amherst: University of Massachusetts Press.

Smolowe, J., Herbst, D., Weisensee, E., Rakowsky, J., & Mascia, K. (2010, April 26). Inside her torment. *People, 73*, 66–70.

Sultan, A. (2010, October 10). Callous students can cause just as much damage online. *St. Louis Post-Dispatch*, p. H6.

Suniti Bhat, C. (2010, February 24). Protect your child from cyber-bullies. *Providence Journal-Bulletin*, p. 7.

Thompson, K. (1998). *Moral panics.* New York: Routledge.

Tresniowski, A. (2010, October 18). Tormented to death? *People.* Retrieved from http://people. com/archive/cover-story-tormented-to-death-vol-74-no-14/

Tucker, C. (2010, October 10). Outing internet cruelty. *The Atlanta Journal-Constitution*, p. 22A.

Tucker, R. (2012, March 25). Won't back down. *The New York Post*, p. 44.

Turnbull, L. (2010, October 17). Offering support, hope for gay teens who face bullying. *The Washington Post*, p. A12.

Van Sack, J., Wedge, D., & Weir, R. (2010, January 26). Pal: Suicide victim target of bullies. *The Boston Herald*, p. 006.

Vengeful in Jersey. (2011, April 22). *The New York Post*, p. 24.

Weitzman, E. (2012, March 30). When kids are the predators. *Daily News*, p. 49.

Wiggin, K. (2011, December 12). Tyler Clementi's parents give first interview about son's death. *CBS News*. Retrieved from http://www.cbsnews.com/8301-504083_162-57341548-504083/tyler-clementis-parents-give-first-tv-interview-about-sons-death/

Why was Phoebe Prince bullied? (2010, April 15). *People*. Retrieved from http://people.com/ celebrity/why-was-phoebe-prince-bullied/

Yingst, P. J. (2010, October 11). The painful moments are survivable. *Brattleboro Reformer*.

Zernike, K. (2015, March 17). Part of New Jersey's bias-intimidation law is ruled unconstitutional. *The New York Times*. Retrieved from https://www.nytimes.com/2015/03/18/nyregion/parts-of-new-jerseys-bias-intimidation-law-ruled-unconstitutional.html

Zimmerman, J. (2010, October 6). Homphobia hurts straight men, too. *The Christian Science Monitor*. Retrieved from http://www.csmonitor.com/Commentary/Opinion/2010/1006/Homophobia-hurts-straight-men-too

· 3 ·

"I CAN BE A BITCH WHEN I WANNA BE"

Queering "Mean Boys" Through Social Aggression

In December 2014, the academic journal *Aggressive Behavior*[1] published online an article that had the potential to alter cultural understandings of bullying. The article presented the outcome of the first U.S. longitudinal study of indirect aggression in which the researchers annually surveyed a group of Georgia teenagers between sixth and twelfth grade. Health promotion scholars, Orpinas, McNicholas, and Nahapetyan (2014) found that boys were consistently more likely to exhibit covert forms of aggression (for example, exclusion, duplicity, and starting rumors) than girls, while girls were more likely to be the victims of this type of aggression. Their findings stand in direct contrast to the taken-for-granted assumption that girls covertly bully other girls, while boys overtly bully only boys. Despite this seemingly shocking and counter-intuitive conclusion, the research barely made a blip, covered online in a series of publications (for instance, *The Huffington Post*, *Time*, and *BuzzFeed*) with little fanfare.

Prior to the release of these data, criminologists Chesney-Lind and Irwin (2008), in their book *Beyond Bad Girls*, pointed to the lack of academic and mediated attention paid to boys who bully indirectly, arguing, "We certainly have no popular culture image of the 'mean boy,' although we have plenty of images of mean girls. The mean boy story is simply not being told" (p. 115).

As I have discussed, contemporary constructions of mean girls rely on images of popular girls using covert forms of aggression to victimize other girls. In media representations of girl bullying, boys are generally absent from the narrative, unaware of what is occurring within the girls' friendship networks. This pattern situates indirect aggression as an authentically feminine form of aggression and changes the victim/aggressor dichotomy from boys victimizing girls to girls creating female victims. While this image of the mean girl has become common sense, the insistence that girls bully covertly while boys bully overtly has not always been so clearly delineated.

Before U.S. culture "discovered" mean girls, there were some filmic instances of popular *boys* using indirect forms of aggression to victimize girls. For example, in *She's All That* (Yacoub, 1999), released three years before the publication of Simmons and Wiseman's books, popular boy Zach bets his male friends that he can make "scary and inaccessible" Laney prom queen. While the boys, who are all in on the bet, manipulate Laney into believing they are genuinely her friends, they continue to gossip about and tease her (both covert forms of aggression). In contrast, the girls, completely unaware that anything is amiss, welcome Laney to their inner circle. Similarly, in *10 Things I Hate About You* (Jaret, 1999), the boys manipulate the film's narrative as well as the girls' actions. The representation of Joey, the most popular boy in school, is similar to that of the contemporary mean girl. He is self-involved, conceited, manipulative, and participates in gossip and exclusion.

In this chapter, I interrogate the cultural insistence that only girls use covert forms of aggression to bully, a claim that functions to demonize girls and ignore boys' use of indirect aggression. I argue that there are, in fact, contemporary images of "mean boys." In the film *Mean Girls* (Messick, 2004) and the television show *Gossip Girl* (Schwartz, 2007–2012), male characters who access social aggression are queered, troublingly aligning queerness with femininity. Gay men are commonly understood as being oppositely gendered, as being feminine as opposed to expressing the masculinity associated with heterosexual men (Battles & Hilton-Morrow, 2002; Sedgwick, 1990). This common sense notion is often seen in films and television programming where homosexuality is defined in opposition to masculinity, and gayness is that which is not masculine (Battles & Hilton-Morrow, 2002; Russo, 1985). These representations of gay men simply uphold the heteronormativity of mainstream society (Fejes, 2000) by situating gay men as like women.

This chapter adds to the literature on representations of gay men as feminine in media by suggesting that representing queer boys as using social aggression maintains the association of covert forms of aggression with femininity. In popular media sites, mean boys are gay or queer, cementing notions of indirect aggression as innately feminine. There are some notable differences between the queer mean boy and the gay mean boy. While representations of gay boys erase sexual desire and intimacy, the queer mean boy is (hetero)sexualized and much of his bullying behavior is framed as sexual in nature. The sexual violence perpetrated by the queer mean boy is reframed as individual bullying behaviors, as opposed to systemic misogyny, highlighting a troubling slippage between sexual violence and bullying. Additionally, the mean boy is not demonized to the extent that the mean girl is, despite using the same behaviors. This chapter is the first exploration of the similarities and differences in constructions of mean girls and mean boys.

The Search for Gender Equivalency in Aggression

As explained previously, in their books, Wiseman and Simmons based their claims about girl bullying on social scientific scholarship that seemingly discovered girls' aggression. Previous research on youth aggression and bullying, which focused on direct forms of aggression (physical and verbal), found that boys exhibited significantly higher levels of aggression than girls. Research in the late 1980s and early 1990s began the "search" for girls' "unique forms of aggression" (Crick & Grotpeter, 1995, p. 710), suggesting that if "pain" and "injury" are key features of aggression, then "these terms could also apply to damage to one's self-esteem or social standing" (Galen & Underwood, 1997, p. 589). For Crick and Grotpeter (1995), this meant looking for the ways in which girls attempt to harm other girls' relationships. They argued that forms of covert aggression are distinct from overt aggression and are "significantly related to gender" (p. 718).

Scholars applied a series of labels to this new conception of aggression, including "indirect," "relational," and "social" aggression, suggesting covert forms of aggression are more subtle (Galen & Underwood, 1997), are a form of social manipulation (Bjorkqvist, Lagerspetz, & Kaukiainen, 1992; Crothers, Field, & Kolbert, 2005; Galen & Underwood, 1997; Hadley, 2003, 2004; Remillard & Lamb, 2005; Underwood, 2003), and are aimed at destroying girls' relationships (Crothers *et al.*, 2005). While the terms are sometimes used interchangeably, Young, Boye, and Nelson (2006) suggest "indirect aggression focuses predominantly on social manipulation, specifically through circuitous means (i.e., the target is not directly confronted)" (p. 298). The bullying tactics associated with indirect aggression include gossip, social exclusion, verbal rejection, stealing friends, and not talking to someone (Crothers *et al.*, 2005; Galen & Underwood, 1997). "In contrast, relational aggression includes a broader range of socially manipulative behaviors and overt (direct) behaviors," (Young *et al.*, 2006, p. 298), including threatening to withdraw friendship. Social aggression includes both indirect and direct relationally aggressive behaviors and includes negative facial expressions or body movements (i.e., rolling eyes) (Galen & Underwood, 1997; Young *et al.*, 2006). The general conclusion of this research is that, when covert forms of aggression are taken into account, girls are just as (if not more) aggressive as boys (Bjorkqvist *et al.*, 1992; Crick & Grotpeter, 1995).

The research on girls' aggression was couched as a challenge to a perceived male bias in studies of aggression (Bjorkqvist *et al.*, 1992; Crick, Nelson, Morales, Cullen-Sen, Casas, & Hickman, 2001). Feminists previously highlighted the male bias in scientific "objectivity" in early psychological studies of human development, which generalized the experiences of men to describe the development of both men and women. "Gender neutral" scientific objectivity favored the masculine perspective of morality, founded on justice and duty, and, in turn, described the prominence of empathy and compassion in women's moral judgment as a deficiency in female development. In her groundbreaking book, *In a Different Voice,* Gilligan (1982) maintained that women follow an ethic of care in which they see themselves as participating in a world of connection. Chesney-Lind and Irwin (2004) maintain the research on girls' aggression is a "backlash to years of feminist research claiming that women are more nurturing, caring, and relationship oriented than men" (p. 49). Ringrose (2006) argues the sensationalized narrative of girls' bullying "incorporates and shifts Gilligan's claims about girls' nature, maintaining that it is girls' very caring and nurturing emotional relationships (through which their difference from boys is secured) that are used to wound other girls" (p. 412).

While this research was supposed to upend stereotypes of girls as not aggressive, the idea that girls are "manipulative, sneaky, mean spirited, and backstabbing…(is) hardly new" (Chesney-Lind & Irwin, 2008, p. 109). As Chesney-Lind and Irwin (2008) explain:

> The mean girl story is a new twist on a very old and damaging construction of women…Traditionally, women have been viewed as nice on the outside but venomous on the inside. That girls are mean to other girls is not a new popular or Hollywood theme in the slightest. (p. 21)

Although not a new image of girlhood, the mean girl and the damage she was reportedly doing to other girls took center stage in the early 2000s. In searching for evidence that girls aggress, this research simply "proved" long-held stereotypes of girls as brutal to one another.

Biological Determinism and Gendered Aggression

The scholarship on girls and indirect aggression had been around for over a decade when Wiseman and Simmons incorporated it into their books. Importantly, the research on covert forms of aggression does not show any consistent differences between genders (Young *et al.*, 2006), which seemingly contradicts the claims made by Simmons and Wiseman. In bringing this data to the mainstream, the books bastardized much of the research in order to present a more salient picture in which boys bully other boys through direct aggression and girls bully other girls through indirect aggression. For instance, Wiseman (2002) positions girls as "each other's worst enemies" (p. 3), yet, in his research on bullying, Olweus (1991) argued that girls "experience" more indirect forms of bullying, situating girls as more often the victims of social aggression, but not gendering the bully. Similarly, Simmons (2002) points to a "hidden culture of *girls'* aggression" (p. 3, my emphasis); however, in their study, Galen and Underwood (1997) found that fourth and seventh grade students engaged in indirect forms of aggression "equally often" (p. 596). Moreover, scholars suggest that boys might actually use social aggression as much (if not more) as girls in late adolescence. Wiseman and Simmons simplified the claims made in social scientific studies, a process that was then perpetuated by the news media when the books received significant mainstream attention and the authors were framed as experts on the issue of girl bullying.

The coverage of these studies in popular culture oversimplifies the science on indirect aggression, endorsing stereotypical thinking about girls and meanness (Chesney-Lind & Irwin, 2008). Because constructions of girl bullying are rooted in developmental psychology, they function to maintain essentialist modes of girlhood and put forth indirect aggression as part of girls' "nature" (Ringrose, 2006). Indeed, this is not uncommon. Representations of science in the mainstream press often distort and exaggerate scientific information (Hasinoff, 2009). For example, in an analysis of genetic discoveries in major daily newspapers in Canada, the United States, Great Britain, and Australia, Bubela and Caulfied (2004) found that "media do seem to overemphasize particular topics, such as behavioural genetics" (p. 1403). Scholars have previously shown "an ongoing dialogue between common sense and scientific knowledge" (Hasinoff, 2015, p. 50) in which biological determinism (the myth that gendered behaviors are predetermined by our genetic makeup) is reinforced.

In a postfeminist context, scholarship aimed toward proving what has always been taken as fact—that girls are inherently cruel and evil—focused attention on girl bullying, ignoring entirely the roles boys may play in bullying girls.[2] In turn, "direct aggression is held as a neutral, normative masculine standard of aggression against which the feminine is constructed as indirect, repressed and aberrant" (Ringrose, 2006, p. 411). Implicitly connecting social aggression to femininity situates indirect forms of aggression as biologically determined—as part of girls' and women's "nature."

Gossip Girl

The television show *Gossip Girl* "is narrated by an omniscient blogger, the titular Gossip Girl, who intersperses plot development with cutting remarks about the protagonists" (Martin, 2009, p. 21). The Gossip Girl blog functions similarly to contemporary gossip websites (such as TMZ.com). An individual sends a piece of gossip, a picture or video, or an unsubstantiated rumor to Gossip Girl who then sends a "blast" (usually a text message or email) to her followers. The hour-long drama follows upper- and middle-class teenagers who attend elite preparatory schools in the Upper East Side (UES) of Manhattan.[3] On *Gossip Girl*, Blair Waldorf is the Queen Bee of her preparatory school's most powerful clique, The Girls on the Steps. Jenny Humphrey's narrative revolves around her status as a "Wannabe" (a teen girl who desperately desires access to the elite social scene) and her ambitions to become a member of The Girls on the Steps and the world of the UES elite society outside of school. Jenny's brother, Dan Humphrey, is happily a social outsider who reluctantly becomes an insider when he begins dating "it-girl" (Blair's best friend and sometimes rival) Serena van der Woodsen. Although the show's Nielsen ratings were weak (averaging 2.5 million viewers), *Gossip Girl* was the most downloaded, DVRed, and streamed show among its teen fan base (Hampp, 2009), making it one of the most popular contemporary television shows aimed at adolescents.[4]

As I will show, *Gossip Girl* features two "mean boys." In the series premiere, Serena's brother, Eric van der Woodsen, is a patient at the Ostroff Treatment Center following a suicide attempt. Eric explains to Jenny that he attempted suicide because he felt "lonely," and his mother, Lily van der Woodsen, calls him "depressed" (Season 1, Poison Ivy). When Georgina, a friend of Serena's, visits the family for dinner, she "outs" Eric by mentioning his "boyfriend," the "hot piece" she saw him kissing in front of school. Lily's response is far from supportive, "This doesn't make any sense because that would mean that Eric is…and he's not. He's just not. Are you? Oh God" (Season 1, All about my Brother). In this moment, Eric's suicide attempt is implicitly tied to his homosexuality, aligning with stereotypes of gay men and boys as tragic victims (Gross, 1992; Russo, 1985).

UES "bad boy" Chuck Bass, although seemingly heterosexual (during the first season, he has sex with girls and women of all ages, including with multiple women at once), is queered in a series of ways. As Battles and Hilton-Morrow (2002) point out about the character of Will in their analysis of the television show *Will and Grace*, the queer male "is defined as being different from (more feminine than) his masculine" heterosexual buddies (p. 90). In contrast to his best friend, UES "golden boy" Nate Archibald, who runs cross-country and plays lacrosse and soccer, Chuck is framed as uninterested in sports and exercise. As well, Chuck's favorite color is purple, which has been associated with the LGBTQ community.[5] Although the viewer only sees Chuck engage in sexual contact with women, in the Season 3 episode, "All about Eve," Chuck suggests he has experience with men as well. When Blair manipulates Chuck into kissing a man, Chuck replies, "You really think I've never kissed a guy before?"

Mean Girls

As discussed previously, *Mean Girls* was written by Tina Fey, who based her screenplay on Wiseman's book. *Mean Girls* was the third most discussed girl film of the 2000s (Projansky, 2014). The film was a hit with viewers and critics, and "led to sustained public debate over girls" (Projansky, 2014, p. 9). Over a decade after its release, the film continues to garner discussion (for instance, in May 2016, Funko released a toy line featuring the film's characters, and a musical based on the film will premiere October 31, 2017). In *The New Yorker*, Brody (2014) calls the film "a classic," known for its catchphrases (e.g.,

"You go, Glenn Coco!" and "I'm the cool mom"), stellar performances by rising stars (i.e., Rachel McAdams and Amanda Seyfried), and its roots in actual observation (based on situations that arose in Wiseman's interviews with teen girls). Kelly and Pomerantz (2009) argue *Mean Girls* is at pains to reveal the "'mean girl problem' as a closed loop that does not implicate boys or men in any way" (p. 6), missing entirely the key role that the character Damien plays as part of the bullying that occurs among the girls.

After a "stressful and surreal" first day at Northshore High School, Cady meets best friends Damien and Janis, who show her the ropes of the social and political layout of the school. Within seconds of meeting Damien, the viewer learns he is gay. When Cady sits next to Damien in homeroom, he reaches over and pulls her hair onto his own, exclaiming to Janis, "You see this? This is the hair color I want." Janis then narrates Damien's sexuality, introducing him to Cady by saying, "This is Damien. He's almost too gay to function." Unlike the other boys in the film who seem entirely removed from Girl World, Damien appears fascinated by its intricacies. According to Damien, The Plastics, the school's most powerful clique, are "teen royalty. If Northshore was *US Weekly*,[6] The Plastics would always be on the cover." Regina George is the Queen Bee of The Plastics. Regina's minions, her "two little workers" are Karen Smith who, according to Janis, is "the dumbest girl you will ever meet," and Gretchen Weiners who "knows everything about everyone."

Femininity and the Mean Boy

As discussed previously, it is common for media representations of gay men to conflate femininity with homosexuality (Battles & Hilton-Morrow, 2002; Fejes, 2000; Sandercock, 2015). This trend continues in constructions of mean boys, bolstering common sense claims that indirect aggression is a normatively feminine way to aggress. The reliance on similar stereotypical tropes of femininity in constructing Damien in *Mean Girls* and Eric and Chuck in *Gossip Girl* is worth noting. For instance, all three are shown to care about appearance and fashion. As discussed previously, Damien wants to dye his hair the color of Cady's, while Serena tells Eric, "That hair color is all wrong for you" (Season 1, A Thin Line between Chuck and Nate), and Jenny comments on Eric's roots (Season 1, Blair Waldorf Must Pie!). None of the boys shies away from normatively feminine colors, such as pink and purple. For example, when The Plastics invite Cady to eat lunch with them, they tell her,

"On Wednesdays, we wear pink." Although neither Cady nor Janis owns a pink shirt, Damien is able to provide one for her to wear. As discussed earlier, Chuck's wardrobe features quite a bit of purple, as well as pastel colors, and his outfits include flourishes such as a popped collar, a bowtie, or an ascot. In the first season, he is also rarely seen without what he calls his "signature" scarf. Beyond being interested in their own appearances, the boys evaluate girls' and women's fashion. In the mall, Damien asks if he is "morally obligated to burn that ladies' outfit?;" when Serena first introduces Eric to Jenny, he claims to be her "stylist (and) personal shopper" (Season 1, Pilot); and Chuck recognizes women's designer clothing and "good taste" in high end jewelry (Season 1, The Handmaiden's Tale).

While all three boys are aligned with femininity, with the gay boys, Eric and Damien, the slippage between homosexuality and femininity is additionally accomplished by constructing the characters in a one-dimensional manner. Scholars have noted that, in media, people of color are often made one-dimensional (Dubrofsky, 2013; Ono, 2013). Through a lack of back-story and characterization (Dyer, 2000; Giroux, 1997; Ono 2013), characters of color are deprived of emotional resonance (Dubrofsky, 2013; Dyer, 2000). The representation of mean boys functions similarly in that their primary characterization is as gay. The boys' narratives are underdeveloped and used mainly to center stories about girl bullying.

One of the only aspects of Damien's identity of which the audience is aware is that he is gay. Unlike with many of the girls in the film, we never see Damien's home or his family, and we have no knowledge of what he does after school. Additionally, there is no discussion of what Damien's life as an openly gay boy in a public high school is like. During the school talent show, Damien sings Christina Aguilera's "Beautiful," contributing to his construction as feminine, since he sings a song by a female artist. However, this scene also briefly provides insight into the fact that life may not be so easy for Damien when the boys in the front row throw a sneaker at him. That Damien might also face bullying remains underdeveloped, though, and is never referenced again. While *Gossip Girl* does provide insight into Eric's family and home life,[7] unlike with the heterosexual characters on the show, his romantic relationships are never fleshed out and very little information is provided about his partners. For instance, in the Season 3 episode "Inglorious Bassterds," Eric meets Elliot. The two are in a relationship for 18 episodes (a lifetime on a show where "serious" relationships last less than half a season), but Elliot only appears in three (Season 3, The Unblairable Lightness of Being; Season 3, It's a Dad, Dad, Dad, Dad World; and Season 4, The Witches of Bushwick).

Additionally, Eric and Damien's primary function is to center storylines about social aggression and female bullying. Neither boy appears to have any male friends. While Eric spends most of his time with his sister, Serena, and, best friend, Jenny, Damien is only ever shown in scenes in which Cady or Janis is also present, and he is consistently situated within female spaces. For instance, he uses the girls' bathroom and attends an all-girl assembly. As well, Damien is the only boy featured in The Plastics "Burn Book," in which the girls write scathing captions beneath pictures of all the girls in the junior class. Damien and Eric's intimate knowledge of Girl World provides no insight into who they are, but instead works to center storylines about girl bullying. Like characters of color, the gay boys are prominent secondary characters that are relegated to the background (Dubrofsky & Ryalls, 2014; Giroux, 1997). The seemingly progressive move of including prominent gay characters is impeded by the fact that their primary purpose is to center stories about girls behaving badly.

Desexualizing Gay Boys

On *Gossip Girl*, the sexual escapades of the upper-class adolescents are a primary plot device, so much so that the Parents Television Council (PTC), which dubs itself "a non-partisan education organization advocating responsible entertainment," was outraged by the first season of the program (Parents Television Council, 1998–2010). Despite the potentially negative framing of the series by the PTC, the CW used the PTC's warnings as part of the marketing campaign for the second season premiere. In order to generate awareness for the show, the CW released a series of print ads and commercials featuring stills of the adolescent characters in various stages of undress, during or after sex, over which were placed the PTC's critiques (e.g., "mind-blowingly inappropriate"). *Gossip Girl* treats sex scenes erotically, and intercourse rarely leads to any repercussions (minus Blair's single episode, "A Thin Line between Chuck and Nate," pregnancy scare); however, Eric, the only primary character who self-identifies as gay, is desexualized. This finding is not necessarily surprising. As explained by Fejes (2000), contemporary "representations of gay males in media often separate same sex desire from the males who practice it…Mainstream media gay masculinity is a curiously de-sexed, de-eroticized phenomenon" (p. 116). The erasure of same sex desire in media does important cultural work in that it "fails to challenge the homophobic sanction against same sex desire" (Battles & Hilton-Morrow, 2002, p. 96). The image of the mean boy, thus, upholds heteronormative ideals of gender roles by presenting gay mean boys as feminine and de-sexualized.

The Season 1 episode "All about My Brother" provides access to how Eric is desexualized, as well as the ways in which his homosexuality is implicitly connected to his ability and desire to damage girls' social status. When Jenny begins dating Asher Hornsby, Eric suggests, "He's not the right guy for you." Jenny dismisses his concern, believing his true motive to be romantic feelings he harbors for her; however, when, Jenny's brother, Dan sees Asher kissing a boy, Eric's concern is validated. Importantly, this scene only suggests male-on-male kissing; the viewer, from Dan's perspective, sees the back of Asher's head, as he leans down to apparently kiss another boy (we see the other boy's khaki pants and brown dress shoes). In an attempt to get his sister to break up with Asher, Dan sends a tip to Gossip Girl, who blasts her followers: "This just in: Asher Hornsby spotted locking lips just before class, but not with his girlfriend. Looks like gentlemen don't always prefer blondes, little J. They prefer other gentleman." Blair, who is battling Jenny for Queen Bee of The Girls on the Steps, steals Asher's phone, hoping to discover information that will confirm Asher's sexual orientation and, in turn, ruin Jenny's social status. When she unearths a series of conversations between Asher and a boy that appear to be a "little more than friendship," she decides not to use them because Asher's "friend is someone I actually care about." At that moment, after being outed by Georgina during family dinner, Eric enters the party and tells Blair, "I got this. Gossip Girl was right. Asher was kissing someone this morning. Me," giving Blair permission to forward the texts and photographs she discovered on Asher's phone to the entire school. In this way, Eric's inside information about Jenny's boyfriend provides capital to align with Blair and dethrone Jenny, who is left alone because, according to her friends, "Dating a gay guy's an honest mistake, but lying to your girlfriends…is unforgivable." In this episode, Eric is desexualized; although Dan, Georgina, and Gossip Girl narrate the kiss, the image remains invisible.

In Season 2 of *Gossip Girl*, Eric introduces Jonathan Whitney to Serena and Blair as his "boyfriend" (Chuck in Real Life). If not for the references to Jonathan as Eric's boyfriend, there would be nothing to indicate the two are in a romantic relationship; they never kiss, hold hands, or showcase any physical affection. However, it is his relationship with Jonathan that serves as the foundation for Eric's foray into meanness, again implicitly connecting his gay identity to a normatively feminine form of aggression. In Season 3, Jenny becomes Queen of The Girls on the Steps. It is commonly understood among UES teens that no one is allowed to sit above the Queen on the steps of the "Met" (the Metropolitan Museum of Art), where the girls meet before and after school and during lunch. In "How to Succeed in Bassness," Eric and Jonathan move to the top of the steps because their typical spot is covered in pigeon excrement, so Jenny asks them to shift down a few levels. When they refuse, Jenny orders her minions to dump yogurt on Eric's head. Although willing to forgive Jenny for this attack, Eric becomes enraged when Jenny's minions strike again by throwing eggs at an unsuspecting Jonathan as he enters a Halloween party. This event, in which Jenny bullies Eric's boyfriend, is framed as the impetus for him to again use covert forms of aggression to ruin Jenny's social status. When Jenny makes her debut at cotillion, she believes the disadvantages she faces due to her middle-class upbringing (for example, her lack of skill in ballroom dancing) can be assuaged as long as she has the perfect escort—elite prep school jock Graham Collins. Although Eric's date, Kira (their mothers arranged for Eric to be Kira's escort), tells Eric she can call Graham (the two are friends), he dissuades her, claiming, "Jenny hates it when people get involved in her personal life" (Season 3, They Shoot Humphrey's Don't They). When Jenny apologizes to Eric for bullying Jonathan, he convinces her to take Jonathan to cotillion, telling Jonathan, "We have to stop her before she truly turns to the dark side," framing his manipulation and attempt to potentially damage Jenny's social status as benevolent.

Eric's manipulation continues when he sees a text on Jenny's phone from Graham offering to be her escort and, using Jenny's phone, replies, "Already got one. Thanks!" When Jenny learns of Eric's duplicitousness, she is furious, but Eric insists, "I knew that if you had the chance to go with Graham, you'd make the wrong choice…I was trying to save you," again framing his actions as benevolent. Jenny immediately dumps Jonathan and agrees to go to cotillion with Graham; however, on the night of cotillion, Jenny is humiliated when Kira is introduced with Graham, and she is left with no escort. When Blair asks Eric how he was able to convince Graham to go as Kira's escort, he explains that he told him, "What happens at Camp Suisse doesn't always stay at Camp Suisse." Blair replies, "I'm impressed with your *natural* talents," situating Eric's use of social aggression, a normatively feminine form of aggression, as part of his "nature." Moreover, this example solidifies a pattern on the show for Eric to discuss his past relationships with boys (who identify as heterosexual) when doing so can ruin Jenny's attempts to climb the social ladder. Eric's sexual orientation is at the heart of his bullying—he showcases "natural" ability to use social aggression, and his relationships with other boys provide the currency he needs to be a part of the machinations of Girl World.

Projansky (2014) argues *Mean Girls* articulates a queer sensibility; however, "while queer girls do emerge in provocative ways in *Mean Girls*, the film does not explicitly articulate queer sexuality" (p. 116). Like Eric, the viewer does not see Damien engage in same-sex desire; however, unlike Eric, Damien's same-sex desire is also not alluded to. He never identifies as gay (only Cady and Janis label him as such), and, in turn, he expresses no sexual desire. Indeed, the only person Damien kisses is Janis. Dancing together at the Spring Social, Damien and Janis kiss briefly, only to separate quickly, expressing disgust. As Damien walks away, fellow student Kevin G. approaches and articulates his attraction to Janis. By the film's end, the two are dating, while Damien remains romantically alone.

Battles & Hilton-Morrow (2002) argue, in media sites, gay characters often find their most successful relationships in heterosocial dyads. This is true of both Damien and Eric. Despite the failed attempt at romance, *Mean Girls* frames Janis as Damien's partner, not a boy with whom he might express homoerotic desire. Although *Gossip Girl*, at times, situates them as enemies, Jenny and Eric's relationship is similarly portrayed as the strongest of any the two have. While Eric dates a series of boys (e.g., Jonathan, Elliot, and Damien) and has relationships with others (for instance, Asher and Graham), when the series ends, he is apparently single. Similarly, Jenny has a series of romantic relationships with boys, many of them the same boys whom Eric dates (i.e., Damien, Asher, Graham), but she, too, ends up alone. In the series finale, "New York, I Love You XOXO," Jenny and Eric make their final appearance as guests at Dan and Serena's wedding. While nearly *all* the other characters are shown to be in satisfying relationships,[8] Jenny and Eric are again shown as a heterosocial dyad—seemingly only capable of maintaining a platonic friendship.

Framing Sexual Violence as Bullying

In contrast to Eric and Damien, Chuck is queered but not situated as gay and, as such, he is (hetero)sexualized and much of his bullying behavior is framed as sexual in nature. As a mean boy, Chuck's presentation points to the ways in which sexualized misogyny can often be implicit in forms of covert aggression. For instance, Chuck expresses sexist viewpoints regarding men's access to sex with women, telling Nate, who is dating Blair, that he should "seal the deal because you're also *entitled* to tap that ass" (Season 1, Premiere). Indeed, consent seems to play no role in Chuck's encounters with girls. Although *Gossip Girl* queers Chuck, he remains attractive to a bevy of women. As explained by Heasley (2005), queer heterosexual men may receive attention from girls who are attracted to a gay aesthetic. In this case, the progressive potential of queering, which ideally serves to disrupt heteronormative constructions, is lost. Instead, such a performance of masculinity simply muddies the waters on the way to a heterodetermined goal (Ryalls, 2013). Being attractive to women allows Chuck to aggress in particularly misogynistic ways. For instance, when Dan's best friend, Vanessa, attempts to blackmail Blair, she devises a scheme to have Chuck "seduce and humiliate" Vanessa (Season 2, Chuck in Real Life). Chuck blames Dan for stealing his best friend, Nate, so he agrees to Blair's plan as a form of retaliation. In order to seduce Vanessa, Chuck presents himself as someone who he is not—charitable, kind, and caring. Before Chuck is able to complete their devious plan, Blair reveals the "game" to Vanessa, telling her, "We were playing chess. (You) were just another piece he needed to knock down before getting to the Queen." In this instance, Chuck puts on an act in order to have sex with a girl he cares nothing about, so he can exact revenge on his ex-best friend's new friend. Despite lying to, manipulating, and potentially sexually assaulting Vanessa, Chuck still manages to come out on top when Vanessa tells Dan, "Chuck ended up being the more human of the two (Chuck and Blair). At least Chuck felt bad about it" (Season 2, Pret-a-Poor J).

While in the above instance Chuck tried to trick Vanessa in to having sex with him, in other cases, he attempts rape. Troublingly, in each case, his sexual violence is reframed as a bullying tactic. For example, in the series premiere, Chuck attacks two girls. After finding Serena drinking alone at a bar in the hotel his father owns, Chuck offers to get her a truffle grilled cheese sandwich. In the kitchen of the hotel, he dismisses the staff, rubs Serena's thigh, and begins kissing her throat. Serena yells, "No! Get off of me," but Chuck persists until Serena kicks him in the groin and runs off. Later in the same episode, at the first party of the school year, Chuck similarly attacks Jenny on a rooftop, but Serena and Dan thwart the attempted rape. When Serena pushes him, exclaiming, "Don't you ever touch her again," Chuck replies to

Serena, "Your life is over, slut" (Season 1, Premiere). In the first episode of *Gossip Girl*, Chuck attempts to rape both Serena and Jenny, and then resorts to gendered name calling when things do not go his way. Moreover, since his behavior is framed as bullying, he faces no legal retribution for his behavior as a sexual offender.

Despite his ongoing attempts to force or trick girls into having sex with him, Chuck then shames girls who do choose to have sex with him. For example, when Chuck hears that Blair might be pregnant and that she is unsure as to whether he or Nate is the father, he tips off Gossip Girl who blasts her followers: "Who's your daddy, B? Baby daddy that is. Two guys in one week? Talk about doing the nasty, or is that just nasty?" (A Thin Line between Chuck and Nate). Despite having sex with his best friend's long-term girlfriend, Chuck walks away unscathed, while Blair's friends isolate her, the entire school gossips about her, and she is called "a self-righteous bitch" and a "pregnant little hypocrite." Aside from slut-shaming, Chuck is quick to insult girls in other gender-specific ways. For instance, Jenny later exacts revenge on Chuck for attacking her. At a masked ball, he attempts to seduce Jenny, mistaking her for a "hot bitch from Chapin" (another UES private school). Jenny plays along, suggesting a game of Hide and Seek in which Chuck leaves a trail of items of clothing for her to follow. When Jenny finds Chuck in boxers and tank top on the rooftop, she takes his clothes and closes the door, locking him on the roof. Chuck yells, "Hey, what the hell? I'm stuck up here, bitch" (Season 1; The Handmaid's Tale). Chuck's only repeated retaliation is name-calling, a form of direct relational aggression.

While some of Chuck's actions are overt (i.e., name-calling and sexual assault), he seems unwilling or incapable of participating in any physical violence with boys. For example, when Dan finds Chuck on the rooftop with Jenny, he punches Chuck in the face. Chuck does nothing. When Serena pushes Chuck, his response is to call her a "slut," not to respond physically. In "The Wild Brunch," Chuck baits Dan by referencing the "unfinished business" he and Jenny have. Dan violently pushes Chuck into a statue that crashes to the floor, and Chuck again does not respond. In fact, it seems taken-for-granted that Chuck will not engage in physical violence. When he tells Nate that he plans to "hunt (Dan) down and kill him," Nate laughingly retorts, "Cause you kill people now? You gonna strangle him with your scarf?" (Season 1, The Wild Brunch). Chuck generally does not show any aggression to boys; instead, he aims most of his aggression at girls. Throughout his time in high school (and even after graduating), he is intricately involved in Girl World, seemingly naturally inclined to its stratagems and how to operate within its boundaries (discussed later). Because he is portrayed as physically non-threatening to boys and men and since his queerness aligns him with femininity, Chuck's sexual harassment and assault is troublingly reframed as part of the way that he bullies and not as illegal.

Mean Boy Manipulation

In her book, Simmons (2002) upholds myths of the differences between how boys and girls aggress, arguing, "Unlike boys who tend to bully acquaintances or strangers, girls frequently attack within tightly knit networks of friends" (p. 3). *Mean Girls* and *Gossip Girl* frame mean boys as manipulating girls in order to end friendships and to decrease girls' power. For instance, when Cady decides to join forces with Damien and Janis to overthrow Regina's dictatorship, they formulate a plan to "cut off her resources," including her "ignorant band of loyal followers" or "army of skanks." Although Janis indicates she cares nothing about the social politics of Northshore High School, Damien is "an active member of the student activities committee," so he takes an interest in who is elected Spring Fling Queen, as that person becomes head of the committee. When Damien explains why he is concerned with who wins Queen, Janis dismisses this interest as solely aligned with his sexual orientation and therefore his femininity when she says, "Wow, Damien. You've truly out-gayed yourself." In this way, Damien is situated as naturally inclined to the inner workings of Girl World. In order to "crack" Gretchen, Damien, dressed as Santa Claus, delivers "Candy Cane Grams" to Cady and Karen (grams that Cady bought) on which they have forged Regina's signature, leaving Gretchen to believe Regina is angry with her. Then, since Damien collects the votes for Spring Fling Queen, he is able to stuff the ballot box with fake nominations so that Gretchen is nominated along with Regina. These moments begin to create a rift between the girls, causing Gretchen to feel rejected and eventually leading her to spill all of Regina's secrets. Although Cady and Janis are also a part of the plan to ruin Regina, Damien manipulates and controls the plan through his actions and inner knowledge of Girl World.

Similarly, on *Gossip Girl*, in order to humiliate Jenny, Eric goes after her minions. In the Season 3 episode "The Debarted," Jenny arrives to school with the new "it bag," and her minions admire it lovingly: "Can I touch it?

Oh, it's beautiful. I've never seen one in the flesh." Jenny revels in the moment until Sawyer, another minion, joins the group with the same bag, exclaiming, "Twins!" Jenny insists that Sawyer take her bag back, but Sawyer refuses, "I'm sorry, Jenny, my mom brought this back for me from Paris." Jenny coldly replies, "Since you apparently love your new bag more than your old friends, I guess you can carry it—across the street. Enjoy being BFFs with a hunk of leather." As Sawyer walks away dejectedly, she finds Eric waiting and mumbles, "Ok, that was totally humiliating." Eric explains that, in order to ruin Jenny's social position, they have to turn all of her friends against her by making it appear as though she is "the meanest Queen ever." He then approaches the other minions to point out that bullying has gotten worse since Jenny became Queen. As in *Mean Girls*, the mean boy is shown to understand how to manipulate Girl World in order to weaken girls' friendships and damage girls' social status.

Chuck is also presented as implicitly involved in Girl World and as having a knack for social aggression. For instance, when Blair wants revenge on Serena, she turns to Chuck as opposed to any of her minions. She tells Chuck, "I want answers and no one likes to be on the ground floor of a scandal like Chuck Bass" (Season 1, Poison Ivy). Chuck agrees, "I can be a bitch when I wanna be." Chuck follows Serena and takes pictures of her entering the Ostroff Treatment Center (she is there to visit Eric). Blair then uses the pictures to humiliate Serena by (incorrectly) publicly announcing that she is coping with addiction. In Season 2, when Chuck wants to dismantle Blair's fiefdom, he manipulates Serena into fighting for the position of Queen. Chuck devises an elaborate plan that involves hiring a girl to pretend to be a new student, Amanda, who is interested in Dan (Serena's ex-boyfriend). Dan invites Amanda to lunch, but she stands him up. Chuck explains to Dan that once the Girls on the Steps "anoint Amanda into their fold, she'll be bound by their laws. Mainly, she won't be able to date ex-boyfriends, namely you," but Dan insists, "Serena wouldn't do that" (The Ex-Files). When Amanda goes on a date with Dan, Chuck continues his behind the scenes plotting, telling the Girls on the Steps that Amanda defied their rules and needs to be punished, even going so far as to suggest "a Nair-tini" (a prank that involves dumping a martini glass full of hair remover on another girl's head). Dan immediately misplaces blame for the mean trick on Serena, who, in response to Dan's reprimand, decides to take her place as Queen. As Gossip Girl narrates, "Spotted: a beautiful blonde Phoenix rising from the ashes of a major public humiliation. Welcome back,

Queen Serena." Through a series of power plays, Chuck is able to reinstate Serena as Queen, leaving Blair on the outskirts of the clique and damaging the girls' friendship. Chuck's innate abilities with social aggression are confirmed as feminine when Gossip Girl says, "Hell hath no fury like a Chuck Bass scorned," replacing the word "woman" in the idiom with "Chuck Bass", tacitly connecting him to femininity.

Cementing Cultural Assumptions

Since the publication of Wiseman and Simmons's books in 2002, relational aggression has culturally been understood as an authentically feminine form of aggression, despite social scientific data that suggests boys also engage in relational aggression. The insistence that only girls access social aggression demonizes girls who are seen as "naturally" mean and damningly ignores the fact that boys use indirect forms of aggression to bully girls. This process functions to tie meanness to femininity as a "natural" biological result of being a woman or (in the cases of the media sites analyzed here) queer. Girls and queer boys' access to covert forms of aggression is framed as instinctual, speaking to assumptions about gendered forms of aggression.

In this chapter, I explored three images of the mean boy in popular culture. Although Chesney-Lind and Irwin (2008) suggest no such image exists, I argue that, while the mean boy does exist, he functions to uphold heteronormative ideals of gender. The mean boys in *Mean Girls* and *Gossip Girl* are gay or queer, and, in turn, aligned with representations of homosexuality in media as feminine. This problematic association of queerness with femininity, as seen in constructions of mean boys, works to cement cultural understandings of social aggression as a normatively feminine way to aggress. The mean boy is constructed as feminine through a reliance on stereotypical tropes of femininity. Moreover, the gay mean boy is framed in a one-dimensional manner; the boys' narratives are underdeveloped and used mainly to center stories about girl bullying. The mean boy upholds normative gender roles by presenting gay boys as feminine and de-sexualized. Indeed, their homosexuality is never about romantic or sexual desire, but instead implicitly connected to their ability to damage girls' social status. Being gay or queer provides the mean boy with a "natural" instinct to use social aggression.

The construction of Chuck Bass as queer, as opposed to gay, operates differently in some noteworthy ways. Much of his bullying behavior is framed as sexual in nature, potentially illuminating how misogyny can often be implicit in forms of covert aggression. Because Chuck is shown to be physically non-threatening to boys and because his queerness aligns him with femininity, Chuck's sexual harassment and assault is situated as simply how he bullies. One of the issues with anti-bullying legislation is the effort to link bullying with sexual harassment. In states such as New Jersey and Oregon, anti-bullying legislation "specifically defined bullying to include harassment (sexual or non-sexual)" (Chesney-Lind & Irwin, 2008, p. 103). Even in academic literature, "sexual harassment" is considered "the most prevalent form of cyber-bullying among adolescents and adults" (Shariff & Gouin, 2006, p. 28). Considering sexual harassment and violence as bullying puts girls in serious danger when their claims to harassment and violence are brushed off as simply a part of school bullying culture. Chuck's representation is bound within this slippage. His sexual harassment and attempted rapes are minimized as part of his bullying behavior.

Notes

1. *Aggressive Behavior* is published on behalf of the International Society for Research on Aggression (International Society for Research on Aggression, 2016), which, according to the organization's website, is "a professional society of scholars and researchers engaged in the scientific study of aggression and violence."

2. In a previous article, I (2012) explored the case of Phoebe Prince and argued the media completely ignored the role Sean Mulveyhill may have played in bullying Phoebe, instead placing the onus on so-called "mean girls." This trend continued even when Phoebe's mother, in court, blamed Sean for her suicide, and Sean received a harsher penalty than the girls did.

3. In the season two finale, several of the main characters graduate from high school and attend Manhattan based colleges, such as New York University.

4. At the time of this writing, all six seasons are available on Netflix.

5. Purple is worn on "Spirit Day" to show support for young people who are bullied because of their sexual orientation. The purple hand is another symbol sometimes used by the LGBT community during parades and demonstrations.

6. *US Weekly* is a magazine that features celebrity photographs and gossip.

7. Much of the information the viewer receives about Eric's home life is tangential. His sister, Serena, is a lead character in the show, so the show provides insight into *her* life (family and home) of which Eric is a part.

8. Nate does not have a date for the wedding, but the viewer learns he is considering a run for mayor of New York and the polls already show him as potentially winning the race.

References

Battles, K., & Hilton-Morrow, W. (2002). Gay characters in conventional spaces: *Will and Grace* and the situation comedy genre. *Critical Studies in Media Communication, 19*(1), 87–105.

Bjorkqvist, K., Lagerspetz, K. M. J., & Kaukiainen, A. (1992). Do girls manipulate and boys fight? Developmental trends in regard to direct and indirect aggression. *Aggressive Behavior, 18*, 117–127.

Brody, R. (2014, April 30). Why 'Mean Girls' is a classic. *The New Yorker.* Retrieved from http://www.newyorker.com/culture/richard-brody/why-mean-girls-is-a-classic

Bubela, T. M., & Caulfield, T. A. (2004). Do the print media 'hype' genetic research? A comparison of newspaper stories and peer-reviewed research papers. *CMAJ, 170*(9), 1399–1407.

Chesney-Lind, M., & Irwin, K. (2004). From badness to meanness: Popular constructions of contemporary girlhood. In A. Harris (Ed.), *All about the girl: Culture, power and identity* (pp. 45–56). New York: Routledge.

Chesney-Lind, M., Irwin, K. (2008). *Beyond bad girls: Gender, violence and hype.* New York: Routledge.

Crick, N. R., & Grotpeter, J. K. (1995). Relational aggression, gender, and social-psychological adjustment. *Child Development, 66*, 710–722.

Crick. N. R., Nelson, D. A., Morales, J. R., Cullen-Sen, C., Casas, J. F., & Hickman, S. E. (2001). Relational victimization in childhood and adolescence: I hurt you through the grapevine. In J. Juvonen & S. Graham (Eds.), *Peer harassment in school: The plight of the vulnerable and victimized* (pp. 196–214). New York: The Guilford Press.

Crothers, L. M., Field, J. E., & Kolbert, J. B. (2005). Navigating power, control and being nice: Aggression in adolescent girls' friendships. *Journal of Counseling and Development, 83*(3), 349–355.

Dubrofsky, R. E. (2013). Jewishness, whiteness, and Blackness on *Glee*: Singing to the tune of postracism. *Communication, Culture, & Critique, 6*, 82–102.

Dubrofsky, R. E., & Ryalls, E. D. (2014). *The Hunger Games*: Performing not-performing to authenticate femininity and whiteness. *Critical Studies in Media Communication, 31*(5), 395–409.

Dyer, R. (2000). The matter of whiteness. In L. Back & J. Solomos (Eds.), *Theories of race and racism: A reader* (pp. 539–548). London: Routledge.

Fejes, F. (2000). Making a gay masculinity. *Critical Studies in Media Communication, 17*(1), 113–116.

Galen, B. R., & Underwood, M. K. (1997). A developmental investigation of social aggression among children. *Developmental Psychology, 33*(10), 589–600.

Gilligan, C. (1982). *In a different voice: Psychological theory and women's development.* Cambridge, MA: Harvard University Press.

Giroux, H. A. (1997). Racial politics and the pedagogy of whiteness. In M. Hill (Ed.), *Whiteness: A critical reader* (pp. 294–304). New York: New York University Press.

Gross, L. (1992). Out of the mainstream: Sexual minorities and the mass media. In E. Seiter, H. Borchers, G. Kreutzner, & E. M. Warth (Eds.), *Remote control: Television, audiences, and cultural power* (pp. 130–149). New York: Routledge.

Hadley, M. (2003). Relational, indirect, adaptive or just mean: Recent work on aggression in adolescent girls—Part 1. *Studies in Gender and Sexuality, 4*(4), 367–394.

Hadley, M. (2004). Relational, indirect, adaptive or just mean: Recent work on aggression in adolescent girls—Part 2. *Studies in Gender and Sexuality, 5*(3), 331–350.

Hampp, A. (2009, May 18). OMFG! A show with a few TV viewers is still a hit. *Advertising Age, 80,* 14.

Hasinoff, A. A. (2009). It's sociobiology, hon!: Genetic gender determinism in *Cosmopolitan* magazine. *Feminist Media Studies, 9*(3), 267–283.

Hasinoff, A. A. (2015). *Sexting panic: Rethinking criminalization, privacy, and consent.* Urbana, IL: University of Illinois Press.

Heasley, R. (2015). Crossing the borders of gendered sexuality: Queer masculinities of straight men. In C. Ingraham (Ed.), *Thinking straight: The power, the promise, and the paradox of heterosexuality* (pp. 109–129). New York: Routledge.

International Society for Research on Aggression. (2016). *Purpose and mission.* Retrieved from http://www.israsociety.com/about/purpose-and-mission/

Jaret, S. (Producer), & G. Junger (Director). (1999). *10 things I hate about you* [Motion Picture]. United States: Touchstone Pictures.

Kelly, D. M., & Pomerantz, S. (2009). Mean, wild, and alienated: Girls and the state of feminism in popular culture. *Girlhood Studies, 2*(1), 1–19.

Martin, J. (2009, October 19). The kids are all right. *America, 711,* 21–25.

Messick, J. (Producer), & Waters, M. (Director). (2004). *Mean girls* [Motion picture]. United States: Paramount Pictures.

Olweus, D. (1991). Bully/victim problems among school children: Basic facts and effects of a school-based intervention program. In D. J. Pepler & K. H. Rubin (Eds.), *The development and treatment of childhood aggression* (pp. 411–448). Hillsdale, NJ: Erlbaum.

Ono, K. A. (2013). *Mad Men's* postracial figuration of a racial past. In L. M. E. Goodlad, L. Kaganovsky, & R. A. Rushing (Eds.), *Madmen, mad world: Sex, politics, style and the 1960s* (pp. 300–319). Durham, NC: Duke University Press.

Orpinas, P., McNicholas, C., & Nahapetyan, L. (2014). Gender differences in trajectories of relational aggression perpetration and victimization from middle to high school. *Aggressive Behavior, 9999,* 1–12.

Parents Television Council. (1998–2010). Retrieved from http://www.parentstv.org/

Projansky, S. (2014). *Spectacular girls: Media fascination & celebrity culture.* New York: NYU Press.

Remillard, A. M., & Lamb, S. (2005). Adolescent girls' coping with relational aggression. *Sex Roles, 53*(3/4), 221–229.

Ringrose, J. (2006). A new universal mean girl: Examining the discursive construction and social regulation of a new feminine pathology. *Feminism & Psychology, 16*(4), 405–424.

Russo, V. (1985). *The celluloid closet: Homosexuality in the movies.* New York: Harper & Row.

Ryalls, E. D. (2012). Demonizing "mean girls" in the news: Was Phoebe Prince "bullied to death?" *Communication, Culture, & Critique, 5*, 463–481.

Ryalls, E. D. (2013). Emo angst, masochism, and masculinity in crisis. *Text and Performance Quarterly, 33*(2), 83–97.

Sandercock, T. (2015). Transing the small screen: Loving and hating transgender youth in *Glee* and *DeGrassi. Journal of Gender Studies, 24*(4), 436–452.

Schwartz, J. (2007–2012). *Gossip girl* [Television series]. Burbank, CA: Warner Brothers Television.

Sedgwick, E. (1990). *Epistemology of the closet.* London: Penguin.

Shariff, S., & Gouin, R. (2006). Cyber-dilemmas: Gendered hierarchies of power in a virtual school environment. *Atlantis, 31*(1), 27–37.

Simmons, R. (2002). *Odd girl out: The hidden culture of aggression in girls.* New York: Harcourt.

Underwood, M. K. (2003). *Social aggression among girls.* New York: The Guilford Press.

Wiseman, R. (2002). *Queen bees & wannabes.* New York: Three Rivers Press.

Yacoub, L. (Producer), & Iscove, R. (Director). (1999). *She's all that* [Motion Picture]. United States: The Weinstein Company.

Young, E. L., Boye, A. E., & Nelson, D. A. (2006). Relational aggression: Understanding, identifying, and responding in schools. *Psychology in the Schools, 43*(3), 297–312.

THE HIERARCHY OF VICTIMHOOD IN *BULLY*

The documentary *Bully* (Waitt, 2011), directed by Lee Hirsch and released by The Weinstein Company, follows three victims of bullying over the course of a school year: Alex Libby, the 12-year-old at the center of the film, is a white boy who lives in Iowa; Kelby Johnson is a white 16-year-old lesbian from Oklahoma; and Ja'Meya Jackson is a 14-year-old Black girl living in Mississippi. The documentary also features the stories of 17-year-old Tyler Long from Georgia and 11-year-old Ty Smalley from Oklahoma, both white, whom the film constructs as having killed themselves in response to school bullying.

The Motion Picture Association of America (MPAA) initially gave the film an R rating for language, raising the ire of many who believed the rating would make it difficult for the film to reach its intended audience of middle and high school students. Over the years, uber-producer Harvey Weinstein has become somewhat of an expert at turning a ratings controversy into a publicity campaign, which he did first in 1995 when *Kids* received an NC-17 rating and most recently when the transgender teen film, *Three Generations*, was slapped with an R rating. However, in the case of *Bully*, media represented Weinstein as "fighting the good fight" by backing the film's director (Gleiberman, 2012, p. 52). Hirsch argued that editing the offensive language in the film would diminish the painful reality of bullying. According to Hirsch, "The few instances of the use of the F-word are meaningful because it's how kids bully. The truth is you'd be hard-pressed to find someone who's 13 who had never heard that language before" (Sacks, 2012a, p. 7). Fellow documentarian Michael Moore agreed with Hirsch and suggested that the MPAA should make an exception since "anything that might help end the problem of bullying can't be seen as a negative" (Vilkomerson, 2012, p. 16). Eventually, Hirsch removed three expletives from the film in order to earn a PG-13 rating.

In the long run, the rating scandal may have served the film well, as it was paid significant cultural, political, and media attention directly before its release. The film received support from celebrities, politicians, and the public. For example, Meryl Streep hosted a screening of the film ("*Bully* boosters," 2012). Katy Butler, a 17-year-old girl, spearheaded a cross-country pilgrimage to draw attention to an online petition, which collected nearly a half-million signatures, asking the MPAA to overturn the rating (Sacks, 2012a; Tucker, 2012). The Reverend Jesse Jackson urged the MPAA to change the film's rating, arguing the "harsh reality" of the film "must not be edited especially considering how bullying has become a horrible form of violence" (McClintock, 2012). As well, Vincent Gray, the mayor of the District of Columbia, announced a citywide plan to deal with bullying, which culminated in a screening of the documentary, while Randi Weingarten, president of the American Federation of Teachers, explained, "Our job is to keep kids safe, and films like this help to do that, even if it's tough to watch" (Sacks, 2012b). In newspapers and magazines, journalists described *Bully* as "powerful" (Lumenick, 2012, p. 42), "sensitive and eye-opening" (Gleiberman, 2012, p. 52), "heartbreaking" (Sacks, 2012a, p. 7; Weitzman, 2012, p. 49), "intimate, straightforward, often wrenching" (Hornaday, 2012, p. T31), "moving and troubling" (Scott, 2012, p. 10).

In this chapter, I explore *Bully* as a lens into how the U.S. bullying discourse is raced and gendered. Walters (1995) contends, "As is true of so many 'explosive' media moments, we can learn more from the contentious public discourse that surrounded the film than from the film itself" (p. 6). *Bully* is symptomatic of a larger discourse on raced and gendered representations in the dominant U.S. bullying narrative. While the film is certainly emotionally wrenching, it is also deceptively simple, contributing to a cultural discourse that constructs a causal link between bullying and suicide ("bullycide") and presents bullies as one-dimensional evil tormentors. The fact that politicians, filmmakers, educators, and celebrities all point to *Bully* as a pedagogical tool for the United States to fight bullying situates the film as part of the debate over how to best deal with bullies. Thus, the film is a "symptomatic" text (Walters, 1995), which speaks to larger cultural anxieties and issues surrounding youth, aggression, race, gender, and sexuality.

Presenting the themes of bullying in an overly simplistic manner is particularly damaging since *Bully*'s use of documentary filmmaking tropes, such as shaky handheld cameras, undressed sets, and the use of evidentiary editing rather than the continuity editing of Hollywood fiction, structures the film as a representation of reality (Schoen, 2012). That is, *Bully* appears to depict "real" people behaving in "real" ways in the "real" world. Documentary films are politically forceful because they make experience available to a variety of audiences and institutions (Kahana, 2008). As explained by Irwin (2013), although audiences likely recognize the constructed nature of the experiences documented in the films, the genre's "persuasive accomplishment is achieving epistemic authority despite this duress" (p. 77). Through persuasive rhetorical efforts, documentaries can "effect change, not only within the sphere of the 'political' but also within that of the 'cultural'" (Rabinowitz, 1994, p. 8).

As Rabinowitz (1994) explains, "Political documentary has seen its mission to point out 'problems' within the social fabric of a nation with the aim of changing them" (p. 11). In this sense, *Bully* is no different. The documentary is symptomatic of a popular mainstream discourse that suggests a cultural desire to fight bullying (a worthwhile goal) but how this discourse operates is problematic. Although concern is theoretically placed with victims of bullying, there are victims who "matter more"—white, middle-class girls and boys. When victims are "othered"—they are not white or they are lesbians— the narrative receives less attention. The production of who is a victim in U.S. culture is important because these images are "emotional and effective representational modes for mobilizing sympathy, for producing outrage about social injustice and for political action" (Stabile, 2006, p. 2). Constructions of "appropriate" victimhood in the dominant U.S. bullying discourse have three important outcomes: first, whiteness is centered through an erasure of black victims; second, a space is created in which white masculinity is privileged; third, the appropriate response to being bullied is presented as turning the other cheek. In these ways, even when articulating concern over children and adolescents, *Bully* (and the discourse to which it contributes) fails to be progressive since it hierarchizes appropriate victims as male, white, and passive.

The Privilege of Whiteness

In all facets of society (law, literature, popular culture, religion), "whiteness is privileged, normalized, deified, and raceless" (Johnson, 1999, p. 1). The term "whiteness" refers to "mostly undefined attributes and assumptions (not confined to physical characteristics) constructed as normative in a particular context and providing a set of unacknowledged advantages" (Dubrofsky & Ryalls, 2014, p. 397). The invisibility of the assets and privileges inherent in whiteness contributes to commonsense notions that whiteness is the norm and that white culture and identity have no content, that white people are just people (Dyer, 1997). Although (or perhaps because) whiteness remains unarticulated, it plays a role in not only white identity, but also in the raced identities of others (Nakayama & Krizek, 1999). Whiteness maintains its privilege through both its lack of articulation and the process by which whiteness is defined in opposition to color, thereby making white the norm. Whiteness centers itself while defining anything nonwhite as "other" (Dyer, 1997). In this way, whiteness becomes the "default identity against which all is measured" (Dubrofsky & Hardy, 2008, p. 384). Thus, the experiences of whites are presented as the norm from which others are marked (Nakayama & Krizek, 1999). This trend is replicated in media sites, which tend to "recenter whiteness and decenter interests of people of color" (Ono, 2000, p. 168).

As discussed in Chapter 1, discourses of bullying rarely overtly mention race, highlighting the ways in which whiteness operates as the taken-for-granted norm. For instance, scholars have argued that the reason the Columbine massacre "generated higher public interest than any other (news) story of 1999 and was the third most closely followed story of the 1990s" (Muschert, 2007, p. 355) is the shooters were white. The shootings at the middle-class Denver high school were "the subject of a dramatic media spectacle," much of which revolved around the fact that Klebold and Harris were white and middle-class (Kellner, 2008, pp. 118–119). Columbine occurred alongside school shootings in Arkansas,[1] Kentucky,[2] Mississippi,[3] and Oregon,[4] all similarly committed by white boys (Katz & Jhally, 1999). By the late 1990s, stories of white middle-class teens seeking revenge against their classmates took primary focus in the cultural discourse about youth and bullying (Chesney-Lind & Irwin, 2004).

Similarly, girls' studies scholars note that the mean girl phenomenon (much like the discourse about the Columbine shooting) is overwhelmingly perceived as a white, middle-class problem (Aapola, Gonick, & Harris, 2005;

Chesney-Lind & Irwin, 2004, 2008; Gonick, 2004; Ringrose, 2006; Ryalls, 2012). Thus, the bullying discourse contributes to what Projansky and Ono (1999) call "strategic whiteness": recentering whiteness without calling explicit attention to this fact. Popular media participates in an "overall habit of marginalizing people of color" (Ono, 2000, p. 164). Whiteness in popular media "functions through its seamless taken-for-grantedness, the mundane ways in which it gains salience" (Dubrofsky & Ryalls, 2014, p. 400). Representations in media of bullying victims are nearly always of white boys and girls; *Bully* is thus an important media site as the film is one of the very rare instances to feature a Black female victim.

Melodrama and the Prioritization of the White Male Victim

Throughout history, whiteness "has been the taken-for-granted norm of American identity" (Butterworth, 2007, p. 231). Madison (2009) labels the patriotism that emerged during the 2008 Presidential Campaign as "crazy patriotism," a sort of patriotism that dehistoricizes U.S. identity into a white identity, "where whiteness becomes the (unspoken) default identity of 'American' and the 'American patriot'" (p. 322). The narratives of the three white boys in *Bully*—Alex, Ty, and Tyler—are shrouded in tropes of patriotism, which work to situate them (and white boys more generally) as most in need of saving, while othering the girls in the film. For example, when we first meet Alex, he describes his family as "all-American." The image of Alex and his white skinned, blue eyed, light haired family sitting together at the dinner table only serves to strengthen this description. Living in Iowa, the film situates Alex within the "heartland," a place that is constructed in media as innocent and the bedrock of family values (Sloop, 2004). Indeed, each of the boys is shown to come from an "all-American" nuclear family. In all three cases, the boys' parents are middle-class and married, they live in houses or farms (not apartments or trailers), and have dogs.

The boys' constructions as innocent victims are bolstered by the amount of screen time given to images of them as babies (we do not see similar images of the girls). For example, Alex's mom explains that he was born prematurely (at 26 weeks gestation). While we watch video of his tiny body in an incubator, his mother says, "They said he wouldn't live 24 hours." This scene situates Alex as immediately vulnerable and as at risk. We then see home video of Alex as a baby with chubby cheeks and a big smile, bouncing on his bottom while music plays in the background; next is a video of Alex as a towheaded toddler laughing wildly and waving at the camera. Similar video of Tyler opens the film; the first shot of *Bully* is a close up of Tyler, his head tilted horizontally, his face covering the entirety of the screen. The viewer's attention is drawn to his bright blue eyes and the smattering of freckles across his nose, as he begins to giggle while he makes faces and sticks out his tongue. The montage continues with an image of a baby in a diaper walking through green grass and splashing in puddles, and next to video of a father tickling his son, as they both roll around on the floor laughing uncontrollably. The film introduces Ty's story with a photograph that reveals him to also be fair skinned with blonde hair, freckles, and blue eyes. In the picture, Ty wears a St. Louis Cardinals jersey; as the camera pans his bedroom, we see a shelf lined with baseballs, and two Cardinals jerseys and several baseball bats hang from hooks along the bottom of the shelf. Baseball is "uniquely constitutive of American national identity…often viewed as a symbolic expression of what *is* American" (Butterworth, 2005, pp. 108–109, original emphasis). Baseball is, after all, the "national pastime." Wearing a t-shirt that says, "I love my wife," Ty's father explains, "My family's been here for over a hundred years. My farm is a Centennial Oklahoma home….Ty's name is in the foundation of the house we're living in. He helped me build it." In this way, Ty is situated as deserving of our attention; he is a "true" American, part of a nuclear family, which has long-standing roots in the community. This focus on the nuclear family in the boys' narratives is important as it lends itself to the melodramatic ways their stories are told.

One of the ways in which the white boys are situated as most in need of saving is through their construction as all-American. The second way this is accomplished is by presenting two of the boys as having killed themselves as the result of the bullying they endured. The boys' suicides are heartbreaking, but the film uses their deaths to increase the narrative emotional punch in a manner that is exploitive. Both narratives are melodramatic, and, through sensationalized appeals to emotion, stereotypical representations of bullycide are forefronted. For instance, although the film begins with seemingly joyous videos of Tyler, the joy is undercut by his father's narration as it begins to take a far more sinister turn: "He was never the most athletic…no one would be on his team because they said he was a 'fag'…If there is a heaven, I know Tyler's there." Tyler's father claims, "We had heard that he had his head shoved in to a wall locker. Some kids had told him to go hang his self, that he was worthless." This horrifying statement is followed by a five second silent lingering shot of Tyler's father with tears in his eyes. There is little doubt that Tyler's death was a tragedy, but note that Tyler's father supplies nothing but hearsay—"we had heard." According to Bazelon (2012), Murray County High School "has 42 video cameras installed throughout the school and grounds. They cover the hallway where Tyler's locker was. The police looked at the tape on the relevant days and saw no one pushing Tyler's head into a locker or doing anything else to him." The film does not substantiate any of the rumors that Tyler's father repeats (by speaking with other students or staff at Tyler's school, for example), yet they are taken as fact. Similarly, the segment on Ty opens with a news reporter stating, "A Perkins boy, just 11 years old, believed to be desperate enough to kill himself." Although the school superintendent claims, "There is no indication that bullying was a factor," the journalist continues, "but, despite what the superintendent says, friends say that Ty Fields was a victim of bullying." By relying on the journalist's narration, the film forefronts the conclusion drawn that bullying was a factor in Ty's death.

In representing Tyler and Ty's deaths as bullycide, *Bully* contributes to the contemporary U.S. moral panic regarding the effects of bullying. Typically, in the case of a moral panic, the media redefine the "threat" to society in their search for an original twist to a news story (Welch, Price, & Yankey, 2002). More specifically, "the media convey the newness of a breaking story in the form of an expression, word, or phrase" (Welch *et al.*, 2002, p. 5). "Bullycide" is one such phrase. According to the Centers for Disease Control (2015), suicide is the second leading cause of death among 15–34 year olds (among 10–14 year olds, it is the third leading cause). Moreover, according to the National Center for Educational Statistics (2011), one in three students between the ages of 12 and 18 experiences bullying. There is nothing new about these troubling statistics; however, combining ideas about suicide and bullying in the term "bullycide" provide media a "new" story to tell.

Bully's representation of Tyler and Ty's suicides are similarly simplistic in the insistence that the bullying they faced is *the* reason they committed suicide. Tyler's father explains, "As he grew older, he kind of reverted and was a loner. He couldn't stand big crowds. He couldn't stand the noise of it all." This seemingly small point may actually reveal a deeper issue—one that certainly questions the ostensibly straightforward connection between bullying and suicide. As explained by Bazelon (2012), in sixth grade, Tyler was diagnosed with Attention Deficit Hyperactive Disorder, bipolar disorder, and Asperger's (autism with a normal to high IQ). Adolescents with Asperger's

Syndrome have severe trouble in social situations, causing them to become withdrawn and socially isolated, often leading to depression or anxiety (Web-MD, 2012). Given the pain of isolation, it is perhaps not surprising that research shows a link between Asperger's Syndrome and suicide (Bazelon, 2014; Soraya, 2010). *Bully* never addresses any of these issues; instead, the viewer is left to believe that *the* cause of Tyler's suicide is bullying. Similarly, the only of Ty's friends interviewed in the film is Trey, who claims that, "This kid who used to pick on (Ty) all the time came up and started being mean…when I saw him last, he was really sad and crying," seemingly confirming the link between bullying (being mean) and Ty's suicide. Ty's father claims, "We're just simple folks. We're nobodies. I guarantee that if some politician's kid did this because he was getting picked on in a public school, there'd be changes made tomorrow." Again, there is no specificity about what was happening to Ty or any indication of why he killed himself; instead, that this is an example of bullycide is taken as fact.

Weinberg (2004) notes a trend in documentary filmmaking to slide into melodrama by minimizing reporting and emphasizing character and emotion. This trend is replicated in *Bully* when, for instance, Tyler's mother takes the camera on a tour of the family's house to describe in detail where and how Tyler killed himself. She explains that on the day of Tyler's death, when his father opened Tyler's bedroom door, "He yelled for me, and that woke Troy (Tyler's younger brother) up, so Troy saw everything. All we see when we come in here still is the picture of Tyler hanging there." Moreover, the final shot of the five minute and ten second sequence that opens *Bully* is of Tyler's parents in the cemetery; they stand at Tyler's gravesite and place tulips on a fresh mound of dirt. Ty's narrative is similarly wrenching. In this case, the cameras are allowed in to the funeral, which includes an open casket. We watch as Ty's friend Trey collapses over the casket, audibly weeping, until an adult wraps her arms around him and guides him away. Ty's mother is nearly catatonic walking into the church, leaning against her husband's shoulder, as he whispers, "We're going to tuck him in one more time and put him to bed," emphasizing Ty's portrayal as a baby, a young innocent boy. The cameras follow as the pallbearers carry Ty's coffin to his gravesite, focusing in on young Trey who is half the height of the adult men. During the funeral, Ty's parents (both in Cardinals jerseys) grasp each other, tears streaming down their faces. The final shot of this emotional scene is of Ty's casket being slowly lowered into the ground.

The melodramatic bullycide narratives bookend *Bully*—Tyler's story begins the film, and Ty's father's story about beginning a Facebook group, "Stand for the Silent," provides the final scenes. We see images of nationwide vigils, people holding pictures of victims of bullycide and wearing t-shirts that read, "Stand for the Silent." Tyler's father attends one of the vigils, and the final scene of the film is of the back of his shirt, which reads "Tyler, your voice will be heard." In the midst of the narratives of Tyler and Ty, receiving far more screen time than that of any of the other kids, is Alex's story.

In some ways, Alex's bullying is most troubling, as, unlike with the other victims in the film, we actually see him punched, stabbed (with a sharpened pencil), and choked. On his first day of school, Alex tentatively approaches the bus stop, his nervous breathing is audible. The two boys already at the bus stop watch a video on a cell phone; when Alex approaches to also watch, one tells him, "Don't even try. I'll break your Adam's apple, which will kill you." Once on the bus, Alex asks the boy sitting next to him to be his "buddy." The boy replies, "I'm not your buddy. I will fucking end you, shove a broomstick up your ass. You're gonna die in so much fucking pain. I'm gonna cut your face off. I'll bring a knife tomorrow. Know what I'm sayin'?" Alex, chuckling, replies, "Yeah, I know what you're saying." These images are quite harrowing. Weinberg (2004) notes narration is "an anathema to most documentary filmmakers today"; however, in some cases, "filmmakers use narration 'in disguise' as printed paragraphs on screen" (p. 58). Midway through *Bully*, a paragraph printed in white appears on a black screen reading: "Due to escalating danger to Alex, the filmmakers show footage of him being bullied to his parents and school officials," thus breaking the third wall in a way that suggests the danger to Alex is so severe, the filmmakers must step in to "save" him. The highly emotional ways in which Alex, Tyler, and Ty's stories are told works to prioritize these boys as *most* in need of saving. I do not mean to suggest that the boys featured in *Bully* are not victims, but instead to show the ways in which their narratives are prioritized over those of the female bully victims, a troubling sleight-of-hand that marginalizes young women.

Lesbian Erasure

Kelby, a 16-year-old from Oklahoma, is doubly marginalized—first, by her town for being a lesbian and then again by the film, which pushes aside her narrative in favor of those of the white boys. *Bully* is notable for its inclusion of a lesbian bullying victim, an identity group that has largely been ignored by the U.S. cultural discourse surrounding bullying, which is particularly noteworthy given how much attention has been paid to boys who are bullied for being or appearing to be gay. Problematically, *Bully*'s focus on the white boys as "all-American" situates Kelby as "other" than all-American. As explained by Hahner (2008), patriotism for girls has often been associated with domesticity and the performance of American womanhood. Because Kelby is a lesbian, she is immediately situated as non-normatively feminine. According to Projansky (2014), queer girls are largely invisible in media culture. Ciasullo (2001) suggests when lesbians do appear, they "are normalized— heterosexualized or 'straightened out'—via the femme body" (p. 578). In a seemingly progressive move, in choosing to feature a lesbian victim, the film did not select a girl who embodied hegemonic femininity. Kelby's presentation is decidedly normatively masculine—she wears her hair very short, at times covered with a knit cap, her face is not adorned with makeup, and her wardrobe is made up largely of loose fitting jeans, flannel shirts, and hooded sweatshirts.

Although "butch" lesbians are virtually invisible in media sites, "when they do appear, they are often pathologized" (Ciasullo, 2001, p. 578). As opposed to pathologizing Kelby, the film appears driven to present her as an entirely average teenager, and, in doing so, the harsh realities of her bullying are erased. Driver (2007) argues that the inclusion of queer youth in media "is increasingly privileged as evidence of liberal tolerance" (p. 8). This "tolerance trap," as explained by Walters (2014), works to show gay and lesbian individuals as nonthreatening others. For Walters, contemporary culture has reached "a phase of banal inclusion, normalization, assimilation, and everyday unremarkable queerness in which tolerance is finally achieved" (p. 8). Walters's suggestion is brought to life through Kelby's narrative. Although Kelby is shown to be a victim of bullying, her storyline is one in which her bullying is situated as really not all that bad, so she is included in the narrative about bullying but in a way that suggests her story is fairly innocuous and not nearly as upsetting or dangerous as those of the boys. For example, in stark comparison to Alex, we see no images of Kelby's bullying. Instead, the film relies on Kelby as the narrator of her experiences, and her narration is often vague, lacking the specificity of the images of Alex being punched, for instance. In one story, Kelby explains that when she walked in the street to approach a group of "older guys, driving in their mom's minivan," they "sped up, and I flew into the windshield." As opposed to presenting this moment with gravity, as is the case with the boys, Kelby and her friends are shown laughing about the assault, while Kelby jokes, "I couldn't have gotten hit by something cool, like a Jeep." Moreover, as opposed to framing her bullying as specifically homophobic, Kelby suggests the bullying is due to "the culture" of Oklahoma, where "anytime someone comes around that's the least bit different, they make sure to put 'em down." This apolitical perspective seemingly dismisses homophobia as a structural, systemic issue, instead flattening out difference.

Perhaps even more notable is that Kelby's story is told through a series of tropes that situate her as happy. As the film's introduction to Alex ends, he explains, "People think I'm not normal. Most kids don't want to be around me. I feel like I belong somewhere else." Following this statement, the film switches to Kelby, who contrastingly appears to be a happy U.S. teenager and who seems to fit in with her peers well. Kelby's introductory scene begins with an image of her in the back of a truck with another girl—they are laughing and smiling, having a good time. There are several images of Kelby with her girlfriend that "indicate some intimacy, but they do not indicate *sexuality*" (Ciasullo, 2001, p. 586, original emphasis). For instance, the girls innocently hold hands while walking, hug, and Kelby puts her arm around her girlfriend's shoulder while kissing her on top of her head. Showing Kelby as accessing intimacy with other girls is important in that it works to situate her as having friends (unlike Alex). In a later scene, Kelby, her girlfriend, and their friends run and dance in the rain. At one point, Kelby's girlfriend jumps on her back and the camera lingers on them as they walk across the green grass with a rainbow visible in the background.[5] The music that frames this scene is decidedly upbeat. Kelby explains that her friends are what make her "get up and walk to school every morning."

In contrast, in the next scene, Alex's mother has to explain to him that the bullies who punch and choke him are not his friends: "Friends are supposed to make you feel good. That's the point of having them." In response, Alex asks, "If you say these kids aren't my friends, then what friends do I have?" As opposed to aligning Kelby's narrative of bullying with those of the white boys, the film stresses her "ability to prevail against consistent homophobia, highlighting the liberal narrative of individual triumph against systemic oppression" (Skerski, 2007, p. 369). Whereas Alex is unable to tell the difference between a friend and a tormentor, and Tyler and Ty are seen as so tortured their only option was suicide, Kelby is reframed as a victim of oppression who is able to overcome her circumstances and remain upbeat in her desire to make a "change" in the world. Importantly, although their level of victimhood is clearly hierarchized, with the white boys situated as more important than the white girl, all of the white victims in the film are shown to be innocent. As I explore next, the same presumption of innocence is not ascribed to Black victims of bullying.

Appropriate Victims

In an analysis of local TV news coverage of Freaknik,[6] Meyers (2004) argues Black women who are victims of sexual assault are stereotyped and dismissed, while the perpetrators of their assaults are absolved of responsibility. I extend her analysis through a focus on Black 14-year-old Ja'Meya, a victim of bullying who is similarly blamed for her victimage while the bullies are absolved. In *Bully*, Ja'Meya's storyline is pushed aside in order to center those of the white boys, highlighting how media sites "structure the status of people of color as secondary and how minor characters work through a larger power structure that foregrounds whiteness" (Ono, 2000, p. 180). This is particularly damaging because, as explained by Dubrofsky (2011), media sites that rely on the rhetoric of realism (featuring the activities of "real" people doing "real" things) naturalize the constructions of race they promote. The fact that *Bully* includes a Black victim of bullying is of note, as the bullying narrative has largely erased Black victims (as discussed in Chapter 1). This is perhaps not surprising, as Stabile (2006) argues the "contrast between the quality and quantity of coverage of white victims of all genders and ages and that accorded to (B)lack victims is stunning in its consistency and continuity" (p. 1). Thus, the construction of Ja'Meya as not performing victim correctly and the larger bullying discourse to which her narrative contributes are situated within the historical erasure of black victimage.

Like the narratives of the boys who committed suicide, a parent tells Ja'Meya's story, but as opposed to structuring Ja'Meya as all-American, she is immediately represented as working class through a long shot of the trailer that she and her mother live in. While her mother takes the camera on a tour through Ja'Meya's bedroom, she explains, "She said when she finished school, she wanted to go to the Navy because she didn't want me to work so hard, and she wanted to help me out." In this instance, far from the "all-American" nuclear families of the white boys in the film, Ja'Meya is situated as being raised by a single mother. Although, like the stories of Ty and Tyler, Ja'Meya's mother narrates this opening scene for the viewer, a trip to the cemetery or another tragic story of suicide does not follow. Instead, the next image is of the closed door of the Yazoo County Juvenile Justice Center, and we learn that Ja'Meya was incarcerated for taking a gun on her school bus. In this instance, Ja'Meya is situated within long standing tropes of Black girls and women as having a "predilection for violence and confrontation" (Dubrofsky & Hardy, 2008, p. 377). Images of anger or violence situate Black woman as "unpatriotic" (Madison, 2009, p. 322) and, hence, un-American.

Through the narration of the white male police sheriff, the viewer learns Ja'Meya was charged with 45 felonies (including 22 counts of kidnapping and 22 counts of attempted aggravated assault, presumably one for each student on the bus). Sitting at a table with the American flag hanging on the wall behind him, the sheriff watches video of Ja'Meya on the bus, shaking his head and pursing his lips in disapproval. The security footage shows Ja'Meya standing toward the front of the bus, waving the gun in her upraised hand. Dubrofsky and Magnet (2015) argue surveillance practices and technologies are used to normalize and maintain whiteness. In this case, the camera on the bus functions to surveil Ja'Meya and is used as evidence against her, contributing to "the surveillance and criminalization of women of color (the fastest growing demographic to be included in the prison industrial complex)" (Dubrofsky & Magnet, 2015, p. 2). Toward the end of the video, the sheriff provides his judgment on the case:

> For me, there's nothing. There's no amount of bullying, there's no amount of teasing, of picking on, of whatever, there's nothing unless someone was actually whipping on this girl, unless someone was hitting this young lady in the head and being physically brutal to her, there's nothing that justifies this girl bringing a gun on that bus. Nothing.

Importantly, we do not see similar footage of the bullying that Ja'Meya claims to have suffered (kids calling her "stupid" and "dumb," throwing things, and laughing at her). According to Ja'Meya, the bullying she encountered occurred on her bus, so it seems likely that there would also be footage available of her torment, yet we only see the grainy black and white image of her brandishing a gun. Through the use of surveillance, Ja'Meya's body is marked as unworthy of being protected; she does not perform victimage correctly. Ja'Meya's representation is situated within mediated images that normalize the ways that "people of color and people of the working and poverty classes are effectively criminalized by virtue of their class or race/ethnicity" (Shugart, 2006, p. 84).

As explained by Meyers (2004), "The convergence of gender, race, and class oppressions minimizes the seriousness of the violence" (p. 96). Unlike Alex, who passively sits by during his suffering on the bus and later tells his parents that his tormentors are actually his friends, Ja'Meya is positioned within stereotypical representations of Black women's supposed predilection for excessive aggression (Andrejevic & Colby, 2006; Dubrofsky & Hardy, 2008; Hill-Collins, 2004). Chesney-Lind and Irwin (2008) suggest that constructions of Black girls as violent work to justify the incarceration of large numbers of Black girls since they are shown to be just as violent and scary as Black men and boys. Ja'Meya's bullying is never shown, so she is denied a construction as victim; instead, the film presents her as retaliating through potentially overt and violent aggression, only making her problems worse. This sort of victim blaming is particularly troubling because representing a Black girl as possibly violent and as having the potential to commit a school shooting works to ignore the fact that boys are overwhelmingly the perpetrators of gun violence in schools (Chesney-Lind & Irwin, 2008).

The choice to feature a Black girl victim of bullying is important in that Black girls have been nearly erased from the bully narrative; however, the video of Ja'Meya wielding a weapon only serves to contribute to an increasing normalization (if not celebration) in the U.S. of Black girl violence. Her violent response to the bullying she faced is housed within her raced construction; as the only person of color in the film, her difference is secured through her presentation as reacting the "wrong" way to bullying, while the other victims in the film performed victim correctly by either turning the other cheek or turning the violence upon themselves. Ja'Meya becomes confrontational, as opposed to remaining a passive victim, and, in turn, she is presented as less in need of cultural protection. Because the film does not show or blame the bullies, the fault seemingly lies solely with Ja'Meya. Her violent conduct links her "to the bad behavior and moral lapses associated with Black women and poverty" (Meyers, 2004, p. 112), in line with popular cultural stereotypes of low-income Black individuals as criminally inclined, holding them responsible for their problems (Shugart, 2006).

While Ja'Meya's bullies are notably absent, the film works to paint young people who bully as one-dimensional evil tormentors. Following the emotional narrative that opens *Bully*, we see a boy sitting alone on a school bus. As the bus fills with students, the Belgian women's choir Scala & Kolacny Brothers sings "I'm a teenage dirtbag, baby."[7] The pairing of the image of the school bus with these lyrics (which sound as though young children are singing them) clearly cements the message—kids who bully are "dirtbags." Indeed, in *Entertainment Weekly*, Gleiberman (2012) refers to the bullies in the film as "junior sadists" (p. 53), and in the *Daily News*, Weitzman (2012) calls them "predators." Whereas we hear emotional and sympathetic narratives from all the victims' parents and some friends in the film, the bullies are superficially portrayed as criminals. This clear cut binary seems to apply to only the white victims in *Bully*. Ja'Meya, on the other hand, remains mired within a blame the victim narrative, and, in turn, her bullies are nearly erased from the film.

In the *Daily News*, Weitzman (2012) claims Ja'Meya "is incarcerated after she was pushed too far by mean girls" (p. 49). This statement signifies how powerfully the mean girl narrative has taken hold in our culture. *Bully* rarely genders Ja'Meya's bullies; instead, she and her mother typically refer to them as "kids." Indeed, the one specific story Ja'Meya tells is of a "guy" who "started talking about what he was going to do to me, talking about he'll fight girls." Despite this clear reference to the male bully, Weitzman recreates a mean girl narrative, strengthening cultural presumptions that *only* girls bully girls. The supposition of a female bully when the victim is a girl is a pattern in representations of youth bullying. For instance, the media coverage of the death of Phoebe Prince (discussed in Chapter 2) similarly ignored the role Sean Mulveyhill may have played in Phoebe's bullying in order to place the burden of her death on the alleged girl bullies. Court documents suggested that Sean was, in fact, the Queen Bee, a role so enmeshed with femininity it was difficult to conceive of a narrative in which a popular male football player would take on the characteristics of a mean girl (Ryalls, 2012). In both of these cases, the male bully remains invisible, instead relying on the culturally dominant mean girl narrative.

Justice for All-American White Boys

Media sites bound with realism, such as documentary, are saturated with a legitimacy not attributed to fiction. As such, when considering responses to bullying, individuals, politicians, and law makers are likely to reach for narratives presented in the news and documentaries as evidence of just how "bad" the problem is. The use of melodrama only complicates this process, as "melodrama solicits from its audience judgments based upon unequivocal codes of good and evil" (Sypher, 1980, p. 179). Justice is at the heart of melodrama, but justice for whom? In the case of *Bully*, the answer is clear—white middle-class boys are most in need of our protection. While the relative invisibility of the lesbian in popular culture has been a concern for lesbian feminist critics for years (Ciasullo, 2001, p. 582), *Bully* does little to forefront concerns about lesbian victims of bullying, instead contributing to a pattern in media sites to represent gay and lesbian individuals in ways that "support the 'natural' order" (Gross, 2001, p. 14).

Ja'Meya's construction is mired in tropes of black women and girls as violent, which works to recenter whiteness as the primary concern of the bullying discourse. In this way, *Bully*, like other forms of mainstream media, identifies which victims are deserving of societal attention and intervention (Jiwani, 2015). Media sites supply cultural information about how to identify a victim, which then justifies punishment. "Individuals, institutions, policy-makers, police, and politicians, that is, take news about crime as their rationale for action and legitimation for various practices and behaviors that might otherwise seem ill-advised" (Stabile, 2006, p. 2). For instance, as discussed in the introduction to this book, zero tolerance policies implemented in many schools as one way to fight against bullying have been shown to disproportionately punish Black girls. In the 2011–2012 academic year, Black girls in middle school were suspended six times as often as white girls (Krings, 2017). Narratives that refuse to acknowledge the victimization of black girls only function to reproduce the most harmful ideologies of race and gender (Stabile, 2006).

Notes

1. On March 24, 1998, Mitchell Johnson, 13, and Andrew Golden, 11, shot and killed four students and a teacher; 10 other students were injured ("A school shooting in Jonesboro, Arkansas kills five," 2017).
2. On December 1, 1997, 14-year-old Michael Carneal opened fire on a prayer group that met every morning in the lobby of Heath High School, killing three students and wounding five more (Holland, 2012).
3. On October 1, 1997, 16-year-old Luke Woodham murdered his mother and then entered Pearl High School where he shot nine classmates, killing two (Mitchell, 2016).
4. On May 21, 1998, 15-year old Kip Kinkel killed two students at Thurston High School and wounded 24 others (Griffin, 2014).
5. The rainbow was popularized as an official symbol of the gay community in 1978 when San Francisco artist Gilbert Baker designed the first modern gay pride flag. "When San Francisco gay activists marched to protest the 1978 assassination of city supervisor Harvey Milk, they marched with Baker's flags" (Wickman, 2013).
6. Freaknik was "an annual 'spring break' ritual that drew African American college students from throughout the country to Atlanta, Georgia in the 1990s" (Meyers, 2004, p. 95).
7. "Teenage Dirtbag" was a 2000 hit for the alternative rock group Wheatus.

References

A school shooting in Jonesboro, Arkansas, kills five. (2017). *History.com*. Retrieved from http://www.history.com/this-day-in-history/a-school-shooting-in-jonesboro-arkansas-kills-five

Aapola, S., Gonick, M., & Harris, A. (2005). *Young femininity; Girlhood, power, and social change*. New York: Palgrave Macmillan.

Andrejevic, M., & Colby, D. (2006). Racism and reality TV: the case of MTV's *Road Rules*. In D. S. Escoffery (Ed.), *How real is reality TV?: Essays on representation and truth* (pp. 195–211). Jefferson, NC: McFarland & Co.

Bazelon, E. (2012, March 29). The problem with *Bully*. *Slate Magazine*. Retrieved from http://www.slate.com/articles/news_and_politics/bulle/2012/03/bully_documentary_lee_hirsch_s_film_dangerously_oversimplifies_the_connection_between_bullying_and_suicide_.html

Bazelon, E. (2014). *Sticks and stones: Defeating the culture of bullying and rediscovering the power of character and empathy*. New York: Random House Trade Paperbacks.

Bully boosters. (2012, March 15). *The New York Times*, p. 18.

Butterworth, M. L. (2005). Ritual in the 'church of baseball:' Suppressing the discourse of democracy after 9/11. *Communication and Critical/Cultural Studies, 2*(2), 107–129.

Butterworth, M. L. (2007). Race in 'the race:' Mark McGwire, Sammy Sosa, and heroic constructions of whiteness. *Critical Studies in Media Communication, 24*(3), 228–244.

Center for Disease Control. (2015). *Suicide facts at a glance—2015*. Retrieved from file:///C:/Users/Emily/AppData/Local/Temp/suicide-datasheet-a.pdf

Chesney-Lind, M., & Irwin, K. (2004). From badness to meanness: Popular constructions of contemporary girlhood. In A. Harris (Ed.), *All about the girl: Culture, power and identity* (pp. 45–56). New York: Routledge.

Chesney-Lind, M., Irwin, K. (2008). *Beyond bad girls: Gender, violence and hype*. New York: Routledge.

Ciasullo, A. M. (2001). Making her (in)visible: Cultural representations of lesbianism and the lesbian body in the 1990s. *Feminist Studies, 3*, 577–608.

Driver, S. (2007). *Queer girls and popular culture: Reading, resisting, and creating media*. New York: Peter Lang.

Dubrofsky, R. E. (2011). *The surveillance of women on reality television: Watching The Bachelor and Bachelorette*. Lanham, MD: Lexington Books.

Dubrofsky, R. E., & Hardy, A. (2008). Performing race in *Flavor of Love* and *The Bachelor*. *Critical Studies in Media Communication, 25*(4), 373–392.

Dubrofsky, R. E., & Magnet, S. A. (2015). Introduction: Feminist surveillance studies: Critical interventions. In R. E. Dubrofsky and S. A. Magnet (Eds.), *Feminist surveillance studies* (pp. 1–17). Durham, NC: Duke University Press.

Dubrofsky, R. E., & Ryalls, E. D. (2014). *The Hunger Games*: Performing not-performing to authenticate femininity and whiteness. *Critical Studies in Media Communication, 31*(5), 395–409.

Dyer, R. (1997). *White*. New York: Routledge.

Gleiberman, O. (2012, April 6). *Bully* and the broken MPAA. *Entertainment Weekly, 1201*, 52–54.

Gonick, M. (2004). The 'mean girl' crisis: Problematizing representations of girls' friendships. *Feminism & Psychology, 14*(3), 395–400.

Griffin, A. (2014). Oregon school shooting: For former Springfield principal, Reynolds tragedy felt very personal. *The Oregonian*. Retrieved from http://www.oregonlive.com/gresham/index.ssf/2014/08/oregon_school_shooting_for_for.html

Gross, L. (2001). *Up from invisibility: Lesbians, gay men, and the media in America*. New York: Columbia University Press.

Hahner, L. (2008). Practical patriotism: Camp fire girls, girl scouts, and Americanization. *Communication and Critical/Cultural Studies, 5*(2), 113–134.

Hill-Collins, P. (2004). *Black sexual politics: African Americans, gender, and the new racism*. New York: Routledge.

Holland, S. S. (2012). Memories of a school shooting: Paducah, Kentucky, 1997. *The Atlantic*. Retrieved from https://www.theatlantic.com/national/archive/2012/12/memories-of-a-school-shooting-paducah-kentucky-1997/266358/

Hornaday, A. (2012, April 13). Kids being kids? Let's all grow up. *The Washington Post*, p. T31.

Irwin, M. J. (2013). "Their experience is the immigrant experience:" Ellis Island, documentary film, and rhetorically reversible whiteness. *Quarterly Journal of Speech, 99*(1), 74–97.

Jiwani, Y. (2015). Violating in/visibilities: Honor killings and interlocking surveillance(s). In R. E. Dubrofsky & S. A. Magnet (Eds.), *Feminist Surveillance Studies* (pp. 79–92). Durham, NC: Duke University Press.

Johnson, P. C. (1999). Reflections on critical white(ness) studies. In T. K. Nakayama & J. N. Martin (Eds.), *Whiteness: The communication of social identity* (pp. 1–9). Thousand Oaks: CA: Sage.

Kahana, J. (2008). *Intelligence work: The politics of American documentary*. New York: Columbia University Press.

Katz, J., & Jhally, S. (1999, May 2). Missing the mark. *The Boston Globe*, p. E1.

Kellner, D. (2008). *Guys and guns amok: Domestic terrorism and school shootings from the Oklahoma city bombing to the Virginia Tech massacre*. Boulder, CO: Paradigm.

Krings, M. (2017). 'Zero tolerance' policies disproportionately punish black girls. *PhysOrg*. Retrieved from https://phys.org/news/2017-02-tolerance-policies-unfairly-black-girls.html

Lumenick. L. (2012, March 30). *Bully* deserves more than a blind eye. *The New York Post*, p. 42.

Madison, D. S. (2009). Crazy patriotism and angry (post)black women. *Communication and Critical/Cultural Studies, 6*(3), 321–326.

McClintock, P. (2012, February 29). Rev. Jesse Jackson urges ratings board to reverse *Bully*'s R rating. *The Hollywood Reporter*. Retrieved from http://www.hollywoodreporter.com/news/bully-rating-rev-jesse-jackson-harvey-weinstein-296021

Meyers, M. (2004). African American women and violence: Gender, race, and class in the news. *Critical Studies in Media Communication, 21*(2), 95–118.

Mitchell, J. (2016). Pearl High School shooter Luke Woodham wants parole. *Clarion Ledger*. Retrieved from http://www.clarionledger.com/story/news/2016/05/25/luke-woodham-wants-parole/32625191/

Muschert, G. W. (2007). The Columbine victims and the myth of the juvenile superpredator. *Youth Violence and Juvenile Justice, 5*(4), 351–366.

Nakayama, T. K., & Krizek, R. L. (1999). Whiteness as a strategic rhetoric. In T. K. Nakayama & J. M. Martin (Eds.), *Whiteness: The communication of social identity* (pp. 87–106). Thousand Oaks: Sage Publications.

National Center for Educational Statistics. (2011, August). Student reports of bullying and cyberbullying. Retrieved from file:///C:/Users/Emily/AppData/Local/Temp/2011336.pdf

Ono, K. A. (2000). To be a vampire on *Buffy the Vampire Slayer*: Race and ("other") socially marginalizing positions on horror TV. In E. R. Helford (Ed.), *Fantasy girls: Gender in the new universe of science fiction and fantasy television* (pp. 163–186). New York: Littlefield Publishers.

Projansky, S., & Ono, K. (1999). Strategic whiteness as cinematic racial politics. In T. K. Nakayama & J. M. Martin (Eds.), *Whiteness: The communication of social identity* (pp. 149–174). Thousand Oaks, CA: Sage.

Projansky, S. (2014). *Spectacular girls: Media fascination & celebrity culture*. New York: NYU Press.

Rabinowitz, P. (1994). *They must be represented: The politics of documentary*. New York: Verso.

Ringrose, J. (2006). A new universal mean girl: Examining the discursive construction and social regulation of a new feminine pathology. *Feminism & Psychology, 16*(4), 405–424.

Ryalls, E. D. (2012). Demonizing "mean girls" in the news: Was Phoebe Prince "bullied to death?" *Communication, Culture, & Critique, 5*, 463–481.

Sacks, E. (2012a, March 25). *Bully* pulpit. *Daily News*, p. 7.

Sacks, E. (2012b, March 28). *Bully* theaters are reel blind. *Daily News*, p. 45.

Schoen, S. W. (2012). *The Rhetoric of Evidence in Recent Documentary Film and Video* (Doctoral dissertation). Retrieved from http://scholarcommons.usf.edu/etd/4399/

Scott, A. O. (2012, March 30). Behind every harassed child? A whole lot of clueless adults. *The New York Times*, p. 10.

Shugart, H. A. (2006). Ruling class: Disciplining class, race, and ethnicity in television reality court shows. *Howard Journal of Communication, 17*, 79–100.

Skerski, J. (2007). From prime-time to daytime: The domestication of Ellen DeGeneres. *Communication and Critical/Cultural Studies, 4*(4), 363–381.

Sloop, J. M. (2004). *Disciplining gender: Rhetorics of sex and identity in contemporary US culture*. Amherst: University of Massachusetts Press.

Soraya, L. (2010, November 17). The pain of isolation: Asperger's and suicide. *Psychology Today*. Retrieved from https://www.psychologytoday.com/blog/aspergers-diary/201011/the-pain-isolation-asperger-s-and-suicide

Stabile, C. A. (2006). *White victims, black villains: Gender, race, and crime news in US culture*. New York: Routledge.

Sypher, W. (1980). Romeo and Juliet are dead: Melodrama of the clinical. In D. Gerould (Ed.), *Melodrama* (pp. 179–186). New York: New York Literary Forum.

Tucker, R. (2012, March 25). Won't back down. *The New York Post*, p. 44.

Vilkomerson, S. (2012, February 9). Hollywood battle brews over *Bully*. *Entertainment Weekly, 1197*, 16.

Waitt, C. (Producer), & Hirsch, L. (Director). (2011). *Bully* [Motion picture]. United States: The Weinstein Company.

Walters, S. D. (1995). *Material girls: Making sense of feminist cultural theory*. Berkeley: University of California Press.

Walters, S. D. (2014). *The tolerance trap: How God, genes, and good intentions are sabotaging gay equality*. New York University Press.

WebMD. (2012). *Asperger's syndrome—symptoms*. Retrieved from http://www.webmd.com/brain/autism/tc/aspergers-syndrome-symptoms

Weinberg, H. (2004). The television documentary today. *Television Quarterly, 34*(2), 56–60.

Weitzman, E. (2012, March 30). When kids are the predators. *Daily News*, p. 49.

Welch, M., Price, E. A., & Yankey, N. (2002). Moral panic over youth violence: Wilding and the manufacture of menace in the media. *Youth & Society, 3*(4), 3–30.

Wickman, F. (2013, June 26). A rainbow marriage. *Slate*. Retrieved from http://www.slate.com/articles/life/explainer/2012/06/rainbows_and_gay_pride_how_the_rainbow_became_a_symbol_of_the_glbt_movement_.html

$$\cdot\ 5\ \cdot$$

"BEWARE OF YOUNG GIRLS"

Millennial Mean Girls in *Scream Queens*

"I know you think it's some kind of magical sisterhood, but it's actually *Game of Thrones* once you pull back the veneer." (Wes Gardner, Pilot, *Scream Queens*)

The FOX television show *Scream Queens* (Murphy, 2015–2017) is an hour-long amalgam of horror and black comedy. This chapter's title is a reference to the name of episode six of the show's first season. "Beware of Young Girls" encapsulates the show's ethos in which millennial mean girls are shown to be especially troubling because of their obsession with new communication technologies, an obsession that is constructed as causing the girls to lack compassion for others. *Scream Queens* is referential to past representations of girl bullying; however, the show presents millennial mean girls as even more pathological, antisocial, and narcissistic. As evidenced by the above quote from Wes Gardner, the father of a first year university student who hopes to join a sorority, contemporary mean girls showcase shocking displays of brutality in line with HBO's phenomenally violent *Game of Thrones* (2011–). The book series (the first book in the series is *A Game of Thrones*) upon which the television show is based is written by George R. R. Martin who claims "that though his books are fantasy fiction, one of his intentions has been to convey an accurately medieval sense of how the powerful prey upon the powerless"

(Orr, 2015). In this vein, the mean girls on *Scream Queens* are shown to use cruelty and violence when targeting their victims—girls who are less popular, queer, or differently abled.

Recently, a spate of books explored the seemingly negative effects of technology on youth morality (e.g., Keen's [2008] *The cult of the amateur: How blogs, mySpace, YouTube and the rest of today's user-generated media are destroying our economy, our culture, and our values*; Siegel's [2009] *Against the machine: Being human in the age of the electronic mob*; and Jackson's [2009] *Distracted: The erosion of attention and the coming dark age*). Perhaps no book title more clearly illustrates this anxiety than Bauerlein's (2009) *The dumbest generation: How the digital age stupefies young Americans and jeopardizes our future (*Or, don't trust anyone under 30)*. Bauerlein's book "charts a consistent and perilous momentum downward" in the "intellectual condition of young Americans," which he blames on technology (p. 7).

Jenkins (1999) and Mazzarella (2003) have suggested historical and contemporary panics about youth and technology frequently highlight adult fear of the ways in which youth use new technologies. Critical scholars have increasingly interrogated the taken-for-granted assumption that technology negatively affects youth, suggesting that adult responses to youth and technology are often unproductive. For instance, this book argues that the contemporary moral panic about how teens use technology to bully (i.e., cyberbullying) frames technology as a dangerous bullying tool and has led to responses to cyberbullying that potentially infringe on students' free speech rights (for instance, school officials monitoring students' social media). In an analysis of the rhetoric surrounding the suicide of Amanda Todd, which framed the teen as taking her life because she was being blackmailed for flashing her breasts on a live webcam, Penney (2016) contends the protectionist overtones surrounding youth and technology make teens "more exploitable through denying them agency" (p. 712). Hasinoff (2015) maintains the anxieties that surround teen girl sexting (the portmanteau of sex and texting) are based in adult fear of technology. Hasinoff argues cultural concern about technology, youth, and sexuality has led to "responses to sexting that are largely ineffective, such as strict sexting abstinence policies and the criminalization of consensual sexting" (p. 1).

The cultural anxiety about the effect of technology on young people's morality is brought to life in *Scream Queens*. Phillips (2005) suggests that the genre of horror functions as a site of representation of society's "collective fears and concerns" (p. 5). According to Phillips (2005), horror films, which are vitally interested in the politics of the culture within which they exist, draw upon and project our collective anxieties. Additionally, a wide range of scholarship has explored how the horror genre articulates cultural concern specifically about our understandings of race at a given time (Guerrero, 1993; Means Coleman, 2011; Young, 1996). This chapter asks what anxieties about youth, race, technology, and morality are revealed in *Scream Queens'* postracial (the myth that racism and race are not relevant in contemporary times) millennial context. I argue the show contributes to the bullying discourse by situating millennial mean girls as racist, selfish, and dangerous, highlighting cultural concern regarding millennials' supposed excessive connection with new communication technologies.

Scream Queens

Scream Queens, produced by Ryan Murphy,[1] debuted on FOX in September 2015. Although the show's ratings were not as high as *Glee* (another Murphy/FOX collaboration), according to the FOX (2016) website, *Scream Queens* was the highest rated new comedy among adults 18–34 and the number one downloaded series on Video on Demand. The show won the Critic's Choice TV Award for "Most Exciting New Series" and the People's Choice Award for "Favorite New TV Comedy;" *Scream Queens* also received nominations from the Hollywood Foreign Press (the Golden Globes), the Gay and Lesbian Entertainment Critics, and FANGORIA (the Chainsaw Awards). In 2017, *Scream Queens* concluded its second (and final) season. As Murphy has done with other shows (i.e., *American Horror Story, American Crime Story*), the second season features many new cast members and has moved to a new location (a hospital). Given the change in themes, this analysis focuses on the show's first season.

Scream Queens' storylines center on the Kappa Kappa Tau (Kappa) sorority at the fictional Wallace University and the "Red Devil" who stalks, brutalizes, and tortures the sorority's members. Kappa consists of a group of mean girls. Their Queen Bee (and president of the sorority) is white, upperclass Chanel Oberlin. Chanel cannot be bothered to learn her white minions' names, so she labels them simply Chanel #2, Chanel #3, and Chanel #5. Chanel explains, "There was a Chanel #4, but she got Meningitis. She was like, 'I'm sick; I have to go home.' I was like, 'No, stay,' but she went home anyway and then she died, so another thing I was right about" (Pilot). Cathy

Munsch is the white Dean of Students at Wallace University; she hates sororities and has made it her mission to close Kappa. To punish Kappa for "rampant reports of alcoholism, prescription drug abuse, racism, as well as allegations of bestiality," Dean Munsch forces the sorority to accept anyone who wishes to pledge (Pilot). The Dean's command drives away Kappa's typical pledges (i.e., white, upper-class, normatively attractive), leaving what Chanel refers to as "the dregs of society" (Pilot). Kappa's pledges include Grace, a white legacy[2] who hopes to join the sorority to feel closer to the mother she never knew; Grace's roommate, Zayday, Kappa's only Black pledge; Hester who is white and wears a neck brace; Sam, nicknamed by Chanel "Predatory Lez," is Asian American; and Jennifer, a white "candle vlogger," who rates candles on YouTube. The Kappas most often socialize with the Dicky Dollar Scholars, a "golf frat." When the murders begin and it is apparent that the Red Devil is targeting Kappa, Dean Munsch hires Denise Hemphill, a Black security guard to protect the sorority.

 Scream Queens begins at a Kappa party in 1994 when a pledge dies giving birth in a bathtub. After realizing the girl has had a baby, her sorority sisters are far from empathetic, callously telling her she is "officially the worst Kappa pledge of all time" and leaving her to bleed to death as they dance, drink, and enjoy the party. By connecting this decades-old image of mean girls to current day mean girls, *Scream Queens* calls attention to the fact that the mean girl is hardly a "new" image of girlhood. Along these lines, the show consistently references the 1988 mean girl cult comedy *Heathers*. For instance, (as in the show) in the film, the members of the most popular clique at school all have the same name, Heather. In the *Scream Queens* episode "Chainsaw," the Doris Day recording of "Que Sera Sera" plays over a scene of Hester surreptitiously trying on Chanel's designer clothes. *Heathers* opens with the same song. In *Heathers*, the girls are often shown playing croquet; there is a croquet set in the basement of the Kappa house. The implication is that if the Heathers graduated from high school and attended the same college, they would have been Kappas. There is potential for a poignant critique of the so-called "newness" of the mean girl; however, as I will show, instead *Scream Queens* reveals that millennial mean girls are "new" in that they are worse—more racist, more heartless, and more violent than their predecessors.

Millennials as "Digital Natives"

In 2000, William Howe and Neill Strauss published *Millennials Rising*, which popularized the term "millennials." The millennial generation (also known as Generation Y) is broadly defined as U.S. teens and young adults born between the 1980s and early 2000s (ages 18–35) (Taylor, 2016). One of the key characteristics of millennials is their designation as "digital natives"—"'native speakers' of the digital language of computers, video games, and the Internet" (Prensky, 2001, p. 1). Because they were born in to the digital world, millennials are said to comprehend and appreciate it as well or better than previous generations (Katz, 1996). The millennial generation is popularly understood as having technological intimacy (Serazio, 2015, p. 600), as being "active participants in, rather than passive recipients of" media (Stein, 2015, p. 3). U.S. culture takes for granted that millennials are both hyperconnected to and empowered by technology (Serazio, 2015).

The idea that millennials are digital natives in a context where adults are still immigrants has led to cultural anxiety regarding how young people use technology. Fears about millennials and technology are manifold, including "the alleged damage caused by violent or pornographic images, the addictive nature of some new technology, and the supposed loss of civilization and culture" (Katz, 1996). Media reflect this anxiety with images of "millennials who are morally challenged (and) trapped in their own digital excess" (Stein, 2015, p. 13). Stein (2015) argues that television shows featuring young people "negotiate anxieties about millennials, including anxieties about how millennials' excessive digital know-how may take them out of adult control" (p. 77). Katz (1996) echoes this cultural concern, arguing, "The idea that children are moving beyond our absolute control may be the bitterest pill for many to swallow in the digital era." A key concern regarding the millennial generation and its relationship with technology is "that young adults are obsessed and addicted to technology and media, and that these addictions cause them to become antisocial and narcissistic" (Stein, 2015, p. 30) and incapable of showing empathy (Poertner, 2016). *Scream Queens* is illustrative of these concerns. Next, I highlight how the show situates millennial mean girls as hyperconnected and, as a result, as lacking empathy for and awareness of the world around them.

Millennial Mean Girls and Technology

Millennials are commonly framed as a "narcissistic 'me' generation" (Tapscott, 2009, p. 5). *Scream Queens* brings this anxiety to life by showing mean girls who are obsessed with technological forms of communication, and who, as a result, lack empathy and are incapable of forming intimate relationships. In some cases, the girls are presented as so fixated on technology, they are unable to break free, even when to do so may save their lives. For instance, in the series' pilot, Chanel #2 live tweets her murder. Following the freak killing of the sorority's housemother Miss Bean,[3] Chanel #2 is terrified and determined to leave campus. As she packs, she receives a text, "Brave enough to open the door?" Despite her terror, she opens the door and finds the Red Devil standing on the other side. The two continue their text conversation, while looking at one another and flirting (she smirks, tosses her hair, bats her eyelashes), until the Red Devil types, "I'm going to kill you now." Even as the violent attack begins, Chanel #2 continues to communicate via text message, begging the Red Devil to "please stop!!!!!!!!!!" As he stabs her, she crawls toward her laptop, which is open to her Twitter account and begins to tweet: "The Red Devil is killing me! I let him into my room, and he's stabbing me to death. Please help me! Someone please help me! Please!" With her final dying breath, Chanel #2 sends the tweet. Despite being in a sorority house full of young women, Chanel #2 never screams or cries for help, and, although she is holding her phone, she never dials 911. Instead, until she dies, she engages only with new communication technologies (text messaging and tweeting). Similarly, candle vlogger Jennifer dies while speaking into her webcam, producing a vlog entry. Jennifer is furious when she hears her door open, exclaiming, "Guys, I'm recording," seemingly choosing communication via technology over face-to-face human connection. As she continues recording, the Red Devil approaches and drives an ice pick in to her skull. Jennifer does not turn around when the door opens to see who enters. Moreover, her laptop is set atop a vanity with a mirror. Jennifer would realize she is in grave danger if she only pulled her eyes away from her webcam for a moment to see the Red Devil reflected in the mirror, but she is seemingly unable, prioritizing her relationship with her webcam and vlog, even when to do so means her imminent death.

Scream Queens often takes aim at millennial girls' narcissism, as expressed via social media, by mocking "real life" millennial mean girls. For instance, in "Haunted House," the show ridicules Taylor Swift. Swift has been accused of being the Queen Bee of her clique or "squad." In September 2015, fellow pop-star and rumored Swift nemesis Katy Perry tweeted, "Watch out for the Regina George in sheep's clothing," comparing Swift to the infamous Queen Bee from *Mean Girls* (Willis, 2015). Swift's clique, which consists of beautiful, young, and rich models and actresses, has been critiqued for perpetuating elitism (Ellis-Petersen, 2015), and Camille Paglia (2015) suggests Swift only uses the celebrities as performance props to further her own career. Indeed, when Swift was taken to task for a lack of diversity among her friends, she quickly invited Zendaya and Serayah McNeill (two actresses of color) to the group, suggesting Swift's relationships are based on visibility as opposed to genuine friendship.

In December 2014, Swift surprised fans by gathering information from their social media profiles and using those details to buy them holiday gifts. In some cases, Swift personally delivered the presents, as documented in a video entitled "Swiftmas" posted to YouTube. On *Scream Queens*, Chanel dubs Halloween "Chanel-O-Ween" and follows Swift's suit by surprising some of her "752 Instagram fans" with parcels on their doorsteps ("gifts" include a rubber severed hand and glittering razor apples). In a montage video similar in format to Swift's, with Frida Sundemo's "You" playing in the background (the chorus taunts, "It's all about you"), Chanel explains, "Chanel-O-Ween is the one time of year where I can give these precious donkeys something to look forward to. They put down their hot pockets and bask in the warm glow of what it feels like to love me." While Chanel narrates the video, we see a "fan," wearing a Chanel T-Shirt, reading aloud the card that Chanel has sent: "I can't wait to see you in person, but before that I'd like you to post this all over social media to exploit it for my own gain." Another fan directly faces the camera and calls Chanel "the most important person in the world." Chanel's "generosity" (and, in turn, Swift's) is framed as solely a way for her to gain more attention and, as opposed to making others feel good, to feed her narcissism. The episode "Pumpkin Patch" animates this theme again. When Zayday decides to run for Kappa president against Chanel, she hosts a Haunted House fundraiser to eradicate Sickle Cell Anemia, so people will know she takes the position seriously and is not running just to be popular. In response, Chanel decides to throw a Halloween party to fight "black hairy tongue disease." Dean Munsch enrages Chanel when she enforces a Halloween curfew. Chanel sends an email to the entire student body claiming she will "honor the Halloween curfew, (but) I will not let anyone miss out on coming out in costume to support a great cause and make me look really good." A pattern develops in which it becomes clear that Chanel never does anything without an underlying motive—to "make me look really good."

A second instance of lampooning a "real life" mean girl occurs in "Dork-us." In April 2013, the president of the University of Maryland's Delta Gamma chapter, Rebecca Martinson, sent an email to her sorority sisters deriding them as "boring," "awkward," and "retarded" (Weaver, 2013). The email received significant attention and was the butt of many late-night television hosts' jokes. Martinson later deleted her Twitter account after the blog Jezebel posted screen shots of her racist, ageist, sexist, and homophobic tweets (Townsend, 2013). In the wake of the much-publicized rant, Martinson resigned from the sorority. On *Scream Queens*, Chanel sends a similar missive, which she addresses to "all useless Kappa sluts," referring to their "tiny manatee brains" and calling the girls "whores" and "trollops." In connecting Chanel's most narcissistic, selfish mean girl moments to "real life" mean girls, the show implicitly suggests that, while we are meant to laugh at Chanel, her meanness is grounded in reality—millennial girls truly are this awful.

Following the violent murder of Kappa pledge Tiffany, which is played for laughs, Dean Munsch articulates the connection of millennials' use of technology with their self-centeredness. Chanel dubs Tiffany "Deaf Taylor Swift" because Tiffany claims to "know the lyrics to every one of (Taylor Swift's) songs. And I don't let the fact that I'm deaf stop me from singing them at the top of my lungs." Tiffany wears a hearing aid, but she often asks the girls to "speak up" so she can hear them better. As part of the hazing process, the Kappa pledges participate in the "Sexy Gopher Whore Head Challenge," during which they are left over night, buried from the neck down below ground.[4] When the girls hear the sound of a lawn mower, they begin to scream. Tiffany asks them to "speak up" and then mistakenly believes they are singing a Taylor Swift song, so she joins in singing loudly until the Red Devil drives the lawn mower over her head, decapitating her. After Tiffany is murdered, Dean Munsch explains that social media has stripped power from college Deans who are no longer able to keep crime on campus quiet. Here, Dean Munsch expresses a common anxiety about millennials and technology—the loss of adult power over youth (explained earlier). As she walks through the crime scene, in the background we see students waving at news cameras and mouthing, "Hi, mom." Through voiceover, Dean Munsch explains:

> In the age of Twitter, students were Instagramming pictures of the crime scene and posting narcissistic Facebook posts about where they were when it happened before the police even arrived. I've got news for you, you self-involved junior, just because you know a guy who's in class with the dead girl's roommate does not mean it could have been you. (Hell Week)

The inability of contemporary university administrators to conceal crime may be seen as positive, given, for example, the recent realization that campuses have been covering up rampant sexual assault for decades. Moreover, many have heralded the use of social media platforms, like Twitter, to call attention to abuses of power (for instance, the ongoing murders of unarmed Black men by police officers). On *Scream Queens*, the critical role technology has played in fighting oppression is pushed aside to instead frame millennials as self-involved, self-centered, and narcissistic as a direct consequence of their relationship with technology.

Lacking Emotional Connectivity

Scream Queens represents millennial mean girls as choosing technology over intimate human bonds, highlighting a deficiency in their ability to feel empathy and compassion. The idea that all the girls lack emotional connections with others is seen most clearly in the episode "Seven Minutes in Hell." During a slumber party, the girls become alarmed when they realize the Red Devil has trapped them in the Kappa house. The Dicky Dollar Scholars, on their way to the house for a panty raid,[5] are able to break in through Chanel's bedroom window. As the boys climb a ladder to enter the window on the second floor, the Red Devil decapitates one of their brothers with a chainsaw. Once inside, no one calls the police or expresses concern; instead, they play Truth or Dare (a game that requires each participant to either answer any question truthfully or perform a dare). During the game, Chanel #3, who previously self-identified as heterosexual, admits to having feelings for ("Predatory Lez") Sam. When Sam chooses "truth," Grace tells her to reveal Chanel #3's biggest secret, and Sam divulges that Chanel #3's father is Charles Manson. Furious, Chanel #3 "dares" Sam to go down to the sorority house's "creepy" basement, where she is suffocated by the Red Devil in the same bathtub in which the Kappa pledge gave birth in 1994. Then, when the game changes to Seven Minutes in Heaven,[6] Chanel #5's boyfriend, Rodger, is shot repeatedly in the head and face with a nail gun when the Red Devil interrupts their make-out session. Despite the fact that both girls lose their romantic partners in the same night, they later nonchalantly discuss the murders while painting their toenails. Chanel #3 admits to feeling slightly guilty about "condemning (Sam) to die by telling her to go down to the basement alone," while Chanel #5 only expresses regret that she will never find another guy who likes her.

Finally, following the murder of three students, Chanel and Zayday decide to enter the tunnels below the house to find an escape route. When the Red Devil attacks Zayday, Chanel hits him over the head with a light fixture, saving Zayday's life. Over the course of a few hours, the Red Devil brutally slaughters three students and attempts to murder two more. Zayday, having only barely escaped the clutches of the Red Devil, exclaims, "No slumber party is over without a kick ass dance party," and the girls begin to dance, seemingly entirely unfazed by the deaths of their friends and lovers and the lack of personal safety.

This lack of emotional response to the girls' terrifying circumstances is seen repeatedly. Immediately after having a human head served to them on a platter for Thanksgiving dinner, the girls decide to hit the Black Friday sales. Then, when the Red Devil straps a bomb to a pizza delivery person and the girls unknowingly let him into the house, he explodes in their living room. The crime scene is brutal, with blood and body parts splattered everywhere. In this case, Chanel #5 actually shows a visceral reaction, crying, shaking, and calling the man's death "messed up," but she is shamed for her response. Chanel #3, annoyed, tells her, "Yes, a totally innocent man, who seemed super nice and probably did nothing wrong at all, just got blown up in our living room. Bummer. Now, let's honor his memory by moving on." Chanel concurs, "Get it together #5. Stop wallowing and start concentrating on what's really important here—restoring our reputation" (Dorkus). Even in this moment of violence, terror, and death, Chanel's only concern is with herself.

The girls' lack of emotional resonance is also connected to physical violence; they are incapable of forming any intimate ties or to feel compassion for others, so they easily slide from covert (being mean) to overt (attempting murder) aggression. Although seemingly focused on indirect forms of aggression, the Mean Girl discourse troubles the borders between meanness and violence (Ringrose, 2006). Ringrose (2006) argues the film *Mean Girls* highlights the presumed slippage between meanness and violence when, in the film, girls begin violently physically fighting one another after the Burn Book (a book that includes pictures of each girl in the junior class with a mean comment such as "has sex with hotdogs") is made public. *Scream Queens* is also indicative of this slippage. For instance, Chanel quickly moves from manipulation to overt threats of violence when she tells her sorority sisters, "I will make sure you end up lying right next to Miss Bean" if they tell anyone that she killed the sorority housemother (Pilot). Moreover, implicit to Chanel's ability to manipulate the girls is a series of rules, at least one of which involves physical violence. When Chanel #5 enters Chanel's room without knocking, Chanel calmly tells her, "You didn't knock. You know what that means, rules are rules" (Pilot). Chanel #5 slaps herself across the face—twice.

Chanel is not the only millennial mean girl to use physical violence; nearly all of the girls slip into overt physical violence at some point during the season. For example, it is not uncommon for the girls to push one another down the sorority house stairs. When giving the eulogy for Chanel #2, Chanel explains, "Whenever I found myself walking down a staircase in heels, you can bet #2 was right there behind me with a helpful little nudge" (Beware of Young Girls). In "Ghost Stories," Hester pretends to be pregnant with the baby of Chanel's on-off boyfriend, Chad Radwell. The girls are able to determine she is lying when she washes sushi and unpasteurized cheese down with a glass of champagne (items doctors advise pregnant women may hurt the health of the unborn child). Hester admits she is not pregnant, so Chanel pushes her down the stairs, and the other Chanels (who believe she is dead) hide the body in the sorority house's walk-in freezer. The girls are also quick to attempt to murder whomever they determine, on a whim, is the Red Devil. When an Ouija board spells out that Chanel is the murderer, they first buy a bowling ball to "bash her skull in" and then decide to kill her with rat poison (Beware of Young Girls). Then, in "Black Friday," the girls change their focus to Dean Munsch and attempt to kill her with poisoned apple cider. These narratives highlight what Ringrose (2006) calls culture's fears that, if left unchecked, the aggression of the mean girl "might be unleashed, run riot" (p. 417). Again, *Scream Queens* situates millennial mean girls as meaner and more violent than previous mean girls, specifically through an implicit connection between a complete lack of emotional connectedness and physical aggression.

Millennial Postracism on *Scream Queens*

As explained earlier, U.S. culture tends to express a view of technology as determining all human behavior in all situations, either negatively or positively (boyd, 2014). The introduction of new communication technologies tends to correspond with optimism and anxiety about their potential to affect society (Hasinoff, 2015). While many adults express anxiety about technology's negative effects on millennials, those with a more optimistic view consistently see this generation as more diverse and more attuned to and concerned with issues of marginalization. For instance, in an article in *TIME* entitled "The Kids are All Left," Taylor (2016) describes millennials as "racially diverse (and) socially liberal" (p. 36). Tapscott (2009) points to millennials' relationship with technology as a reason for their openness, stating, "As the first global generation ever, (they) are more tolerant of diversity than their predecessors. They care strongly about justice and the problems faced by their society and are typically engaged in some kind of civic activity" (p. 6). The millennial generation is situated as postracial—as having moved beyond racism and striving for equality. Postracism acknowledges the gains made by people of color, suggesting the Civil Rights Movement accomplished its goals and negating any need for ongoing anti-racist work. As explained by Joseph (2009), postracist discourse insists that "not only does racism no longer exist, but race itself no longer matters" (p. 239). The suggestion is that "we are living out our lives on a level playing field" (Vavrus, 2010, p. 222) when it comes to race. Contemporary culture takes for granted that millennials are postracist and color-blind. For instance, many media outlets reported that in the 2016 presidential election millennials overwhelmingly voted for Hillary Clinton instead of Donald Trump because of Trump's racist viewpoints on Black Lives Matter and his desire to "make America great again" (to rewind to a time when racism was an active, overt, and acceptable ideology) (Gara, 2016; Mosendz, 2016; Richmond, Zinshteyn, & Gross, 2016).[7]

A postracial ethos permeates *Scream Queens*: race is configured as irrelevant, while at the same time whiteness is centered (Dubrofsky & Ryalls, 2014). The episode "Haunted House" illuminates this process. The juxtaposition of Kappa pledge Zayday and the sorority house's security guard Denise, who attempted to rush Kappa in 1998, presents race as immaterial. In a flashback, during a Kappa rush event, a white member of Kappa tells Denise the historically Black sorority is down the street, explaining, "I don't think you'd like it here at Kappa house." This is the extent of the racism—a white sorority girl encourages Denise to join a Black sorority. She does not use a racial epithet, there is no physical violence, and when the show returns to present time, there is no discussion of the ongoing struggle to integrate traditionally white sororities. In essence, Denise not joining Kappa is situated as a choice she made when the sisters made a covertly racist suggestion. When Denise accuses Zayday of being the Red Devil killer, Zayday argues that Denise's suspicion of her can be traced to the fact that Denise sees in Zayday "everything you could have been...and you see me about to take it one step further by becoming the first ever Black president of Kappa house." In this way, racism is situated as in the past, a historical reality that was not really all that bad and is not relevant to the present day, since Zayday was able to successfully rush Kappa and may even be elected president.

While racism and race are seen as immaterial, whiteness is centered through Zayday's historical presidential run, which is precipitated and fortified by her white sorority sisters. Grace is the first person to suggest that Zayday run for president of Kappa, telling her, "If you're serious about becoming president [of the United States] someday, becoming president of Kappa is not a bad place to start" (Pilot). When the election results in a tie, Zayday and Chanel share the presidency, making Zayday the first Black Kappa president; however, privately Chanel reveals to the other Chanels that she voted for Zayday because she hoped not to win. Basing her ideas on information she garnered from watching documentaries about the mafia, she explains to her minions:

> You never ever want to be the boss in times of extreme crisis. As soon as you become the boss, you get a target on your back… Being president of Kappa house when there is a killer hunting down the sisters of Kappa house means you're the target. (Seven Minutes in Hell)

Zayday's race (and, in turn, racism) is made to seem irrelevant, as she seemingly accesses the same privileges as her white sorority sisters; at the same time, she gains these privileges through the actions of these same sorority sisters, centering whiteness.

Zayday's presidential run is consistently aligned with that of Barack Obama, the first Black president of the United States, securing the postracial context. Earl Gray, the only Black member of the Dicky Dollar Scholars, encourages Zayday to run for president, arguing, "The Greek system will be obsolete in a generation if things don't change. I believe you and I represent that change" (Haunted House). This mantra of "change" implicitly ties Zayday's campaign to that of Obama, who ran on a promise of "change you can believe in." Indeed, Chanel believes that Zayday will win the election because "we live in the age of Obama," bringing to life Esposito's (2009) claim that the election of Obama marks for some a postracial turn in "which race no longer matters" (p. 521). On *Scream Queens*, the postracial turn is accomplished by situating racism as a problem of the past (through flashbacks to the 1990s) and presenting race as irrelevant in contemporary culture, a process that relies on notions of millennials as having moved beyond race and racism, negating the realities of structural oppression and discrimination.

Racism and the Queen Bee

While millennials are often configured as a postracial generation, media implicitly connect the power of the Queen Bee to white privilege, suggesting mean girls are not postracial and situating them as responsible for perpetuating racism within a generation that has moved beyond it. For instance, in a *New York Times* article, Talbot (2002) explains that social marginalization and racism in schools have been linked to powerful groups of mean girls. Rebecca Martinson, Queen Bee of University of Maryland's Delta Gamma chapter (discussed above), deleted her Twitter account after her racist tweets were discovered. As discussed in Chapter 1, to combat girl bullying, Wiseman developed The Owning Up program, which encourages popular girls "to understand their privilege and to stop the cycle of exclusion that keeps many students on the social margins" (Chesney-Lind & Irwin, 2004, p. 50). The suggestion that mean girls are responsible for racism troublingly ignores the fact that racism is structurally evident in our culture and instead proposes that if mean girls would just be "nice," then we could achieve a society where everyone is equal. These claims are bound within a postracial ethos. Ono (2010) maintains that "postracism is a fantasy that racism no longer exists" (p. 227). I contend the myth of the mean girl is a fantasy that *if* racism exists it does so only among girls and that ending racism is as simple as encouraging mean girls to step down from their privilege and to be "nice."

In Chanel's opening monologue in the pilot episode of *Scream Queens*, she declares herself "Queen Bee of Kappa Kappa Tau." Further, the show constructs her as the Queen Bee in a series of ways. Wiseman (2002) argues the Queen Bee uses money, fear, and control to manipulate her peers to do her bidding. Chanel describes herself as "super gross rich" (Seven Minutes in Hell), and she uses her class privilege to manipulate those around her. In fact, when Grace calls Chanel a "terrible person," she shrugs, "I'm rich and I'm pretty, so it doesn't matter" (Pilot). When Chanel accidentally kills Miss Bean, her class privilege is the tool she reaches for to bribe the girls to stay quiet about the murder by promising to take them on her "dad's jet to Cancun for a Spring Break trip" (Pilot). Chanel's mother considers her "top of (her) class for destroying people's confidence" (Mommie Dearest). For example, she buys "deliberately cheap, totally forgettable Christmas gifts for friends, (because) the obvious cheapness of the gift makes them question our friendship and makes them way easier to manipulate as they try desperately to get back on my good side" (Black Friday). Despite her obviously cruelty, Queen Bee

Chanel is able to use money and manipulation to maintain her position of power in the sorority and to control the sisters of Kappa. Moreover, *Scream Queens* associates racism with Chanel through the outrageous things she says.

Dubrofsky (2013) theorizes the ways in which "humorous racism," rooted in a postracial ethos, functions on *Glee*, arguing overt racism invites "viewers to laugh at the characters for being so oblivious to their own obnoxious traits, rather than consider the characters racist: overt racism allows for the inference that racism is not a reality, and as such, funny and harmless" (p. 88). By associating racism with Queen Bee Chanel, *Scream Queens* invites viewers to laugh at the outrageous things she says, while situating her racism as innocuous. In turn, the onus for racism is placed on her, negating structural and systemic racism, in line with popular understandings of mean girls. Chanel's racism is situated as so overt that it is ridiculous and, as a result, humorous. For instance, Chanel is shown to rely on stereotypes when she claims to keep her "Asian…on retainer to come take tests with me, anything math or science" (Haunted House). When Dean Munsch insists that Kappa accept anyone who desires to pledge, Chanel warns that "ethnics" who will bring "weird spices from their home countries" will join the sorority (Pilot).

Postracism is also inherently nostalgic, "desirous of the past" (Ono, 2013, p. 300). As explained by Ono (2010), postracism "disavows history, overlaying it with an upbeat discourse about how things were never really that bad, are not so bad now, and are only getting better" (p. 228). Chanel's racism is similarly rooted in a disavowal of the realities of historical racism. For instance, in honor of Thanksgiving, she wears a brown suede fringe dress, with blue topaz jewelry and a feather headband, explaining she is dressed as Sacagawea who "taught the Pilgrims how to make cranberry sauce and sang 'Blue Corn Moon' or something" (Ghost Stories). Chanel confuses Sacagawea with Pocahontas, who is depicted in the 1995 animated Disney film of the same name. The film and Chanel's understanding of Native American history are largely nostalgic—perpetuating historical myths about the friendly relationships between the Native Americans and the Pilgrims (ignoring the brutal reality of genocide). Moreover, when Chanel's minions point out her mistake, she exclaims, "Are you serious? I just spent two hours dressing up as the girl who didn't realize she was third wheel on Lewis and Clark's gay camping extravaganza," dismissing the important role Sacagawea played in the success of the expedition to the Pacific Ocean. Further, Chanel rejects the horrors of the institution of slavery when referring to the sorority housemother as "white mammy" because "she's essentially a house slave" (Pilot). As explained by Ono (2010), "Postracism suggests historical racism and colonialism have been remedied or eliminated or perhaps were never that bad to begin with" (p. 228). Chanel's overt racism "allows for the inference that racism is not a reality, and as such, funny and harmless" (Dubrofsky, 2013, p. 88). Through humor, Chanel negates the troubling realities of historical racism and colonialism, allowing the viewer to see these issues as not really all that bad.

Chanel's racism remains uncommented on, dismissed, until she sends a crude and insulting missive to her sorority sisters (Dorkus). When the email goes public, Chanel faces intense public scrutiny. Unable to handle the shame, Chanel decides to kill herself with an asp (a venomous snake that Cleopatra[8] used to commit suicide). When Zayday finds her, Chanel says, "Get out please. I'm trying to kill myself." Zayday responds, "I understand that what you're going through is really intense, and I know that you and I haven't always seen eye to eye…I have a real problem with your casual racism, which is something we need to work on, but girl I promise I got your back." The dismissal of Chanel's racism as "casual" by the only Black member of Kappa negates its power, giving the viewer permission to laugh at the outrageous things Chanel says. If Chanel does not offend Zayday, then the white viewer is let off the hook. Moreover, Zayday's statement is presented as "unequivocal, authentic truth" because a person of color is uttering it (Joseph, 2009, p. 249); her statement "bears the authority of one speaking from knowledge of her own gender and race" (Meyers, 2004, p. 109). Zayday then leans back against the bed's headboard and has Chanel place her head in her lap, continuing, "Maybe this is like one of those teaching moments, like my grandmamma says. Maybe this is the moment where you learn that words… can hurt people, so you just can't always say the first thing that pops into your head." In this moment, Zayday symbolically functions as a mother-figure to Chanel who is positioned as a child, an update to the "mammy" figure of black women in popular culture, noted by McFarland (2015) in her analysis of the 2011 film *The Help*. Additionally, this scene activates a trend in the horror genre to show Black self-sacrifice and devotion to whites (Means Coleman, 2011). In the 1980s, Black characters in horror films were inevitably dead by the film's end and often were the first to die. This trope was so commonplace that Means Coleman (2011) refers to it as "We always die first." Importantly, however, Black devotion has generally been represented through the death of the Black character, yet, on *Scream Queens*, Zayday (and Denise) survives the Red Devil. As such, the show turns a racist generic convention on its head, further cementing its postracial ethos.

No Technology = Nice Girls

In featuring mean girls who are cruel, manipulative, and aggressive, *Scream Queens* is in line with contemporary mediated representations of girl bullying; at the same time, *Scream Queens* differs from many bullying discourses by referencing previous portrayals of girls behaving badly. As I have discussed, the image of the mean girl is hardly new, and *Scream Queens* seems positioned to bring this reality to life. However, in alluding to previous mean girls (i.e., sorority girls from the 1990s, Cleopatra, and *Heathers*), the show works to present millennial girls as *more* mean and *more* violent. Nostalgia is similarly rooted in the show's postracial ethos, which situates historical racism as not all that bad while centering whiteness. Through the portrayal of Chanel, *Scream Queens* confirms racism as at the heart of the Queen Bee's privilege, while allowing the viewer to laugh at her overt and ridiculous racism. In so doing, the show blames mean girls for perpetuating racial inequality, despite being part of a generation that has seemingly progressed beyond race and racism.

It is perhaps not surprising that *Scream Queens*, a television show on a major network, does not acknowledge institutionalized racism; however, the show's call to the audience to laugh at Chanel's overt racism as opposed to deride it is troubling. While one might argue it is progressive that the two primary Black characters are "allowed" to live, Chanel's overt racism and Zayday's soft acceptance of it within a postracial context only make room for the deaths of "Deaf Taylor Swift" and "Predatory Lez." The deaf woman and an Asian American lesbian provide the culturally visible marginalized identities to take the place in horror that Black character deaths once filled.

In the finale of *Scream Queens*, the Chanels are wrongly convicted of the murders and the judge, who deems them "insane," sentences them to an asylum. Importantly, the judge also calls the girls "rude, entitled, (and) narcissistic." As Worrall (2004) explains, behaviors by girls that previously may have been ignored are increasingly being dealt with by the criminal justice system, which redefines girls' bad behavior as criminal and their immoral behavior as "near criminal." Sending the girls to an asylum for being "rude, entitled, and narcissistic" is troublingly reminiscent of a time when women were sent away by their fathers, husbands, and doctors for being "hysterical," the symptoms of which included nervousness, sexual desire, or a general tendency to cause trouble (Ehrenreich & English, 2011). As opposed to being angered by their sentence, the Chanels "love" the asylum and hope to never leave. As Chanel explains, there "is no social media pressure to be the hottest or the meanest"

(The Final Girls). In this final statement, the show positions millennial girls' meanness as an aspect of their connection to social media and, as such, the patriarchal response to imprison girls who cause trouble is shown to be the right one since they are forced to separate from technology and are, in turn, happier and nicer.

Notes

1. Murphy is the producer for a wide range of television shows, including *Popular* (1999–2001), *Nip/Tuck* (2003–2010), *Glee* (2009–2015), and *American Horror Story* (2011–).
2. A student whose family member is a member of the sorority she desires to join.
3. Distressed that Dean Munsch is forcing Kappa to accept anyone who wishes to pledge the sorority, Chanel devises a plan to "scare the pledges off" by pretending to burn Miss Bean's face off. Chanel intends to shove Miss Bean's face into the fryer, which will be turned off, so the oil will be cold. However, unbeknownst to Chanel or Miss Bean, the Red Devil has turned on the fryer, and Miss Bean dies when Chanel pushes her into the hot oil.
4. This scene is in line with the show's impulse to reference historical images of mean girls. In the film *Heathers*, clique member Veronica is buried up to her neck in the lawn while the Heathers play croquet, hitting her with their balls.
5. Dating back to a time period when men were not allowed to enter female dorms, a panty raid is a prank that involves male students crashing a slumber party and stealing their underwear as "proof" of their illicit entrance to the female dorm.
6. Seven Minutes in Heaven is a game during which two young people enter a dark enclosed space (typically a closet) to do whatever they please (i.e., talk, make out, have sex) for seven minutes.
7. This coverage also highlights another cultural anxiety about millennials—their low voter turnout.
8. This reference to Cleopatra (known for her ability to manipulate even the most powerful of men) functions, again, as a historical nod to past Queen Bees.

References

Bauerlein, M. (2008). *The dumbest generation: How the digital age stupifies young Americans and jeopardizes our future (*Or, don't trust anyone under 30)*. New York: Penguin Books.

boyd, d. (2014). *it's complicated: the social lives of networked teens*. New Haven, CT: Yale University Press.

Chesney-Lind, M., & Irwin, K. (2004). From badness to meanness: Popular constructions of contemporary girlhood. In A. Harris (Ed.), *All about the girl: Culture, power and identity* (pp. 45–56). New York: Routledge.

Dubrofsky, R. E. (2013). Jewishness, whiteness, and Blackness on *Glee*: Singing to the tune of postracism. *Communication, Culture, & Critique, 6*, 82–102.

Dubrofsky, R. E., & Ryalls, E. D. (2014). *The Hunger Games*: Performing not-performing to authenticate femininity and whiteness. *Critical Studies in Media Communication, 31*(5), 395–409.

Ehnreich, B. & English, D. (2011). *Complaints & disorders: The sexual politics of sickness* (2nd ed.). New York: The Feminist Press.

Ellis-Petersen, H. (2015). Taylor Swift an 'obnoxious Nazi Barbie," writes Camille Paglia. Retrieved from https://www.theguardian.com/music/2015/dec/11/taylor-swift-an-obnoxious-nazi-barbie-writes-camille-paglia

Esposito, J. (2009). What does race have to do with *Ugly Betty*? An analysis of privilege and postracial (?) representations on a television sitcom. *Television & New Media, 10*(6), 521–535.

FOX. (2016). *Scream queens* renewed for a second season. Retrieved April 23, 2016, from http://www.fox.com/article/%E2%80%9Cscream-queens%E2%80%9D-renewed-for-a-second-season.

Gara, A. (2016, November 16). Donald Trump's economic reality rides on the millennial generation he lost at the polls. *Forbes*. Retrieved from https://www.forbes.com/sites/antoinegara/2016/11/16/donald-trumps-economic-reality-rides-on-the-millennial-generation-he-lost-at-the-polls/#15ccdd467757

Guerrero, E. (1993). *Framing blackness: The African American image in film*. Philadelphia, PA: Temple University Press.

Hasinoff, A. A. (2015). *Sexting panic: Rethinking criminalization, privacy, and consent*. Urbana, IL: University of Illinois Press.

Howe, W. & Strauss, N. (2000). *Millennials rising: The next great generation*. New York: Vintage Books.

Jackson, M. (2009). *Distracted: The erosion of attention and the coming dark age*. New York: Prometheus Books.

Jenkins, H. (1999). Professor Jenkins goes to Washington. Retrieved from file:///C:/Users/Emily/AppData/Local/Temp/Professor_Jenkins_Goes_to_Washington.pdfhttp://henryjenkins.org/2008/11/professor_jenkins_goes_to_holl.html

Joseph, R. L. (2009). "Tyra Banks is fat": Reading (post-)racism and (post-)feminism in the new millennium. *Critical Studies in Media Communication, 26*(3), 237–254.

Katz, J. (1996, July 1). The rights of kids in the digital age. *Wired*. Retrieved from https://www.wired.com/1996/07/kids-2/

Keen, A. (2008). *The cult of the amateur: How blogs, mySpace, YouTube and the rest of today's user-generated media are destroying our economy, our culture, and our values*. New York: Doubleday.

Mazzarella, S. (2003). Constructing youth: Media, youth, and the politics of representation. In S. N. Valdivia (Ed.), *A companion to media studies* (pp. 227–246). Malden, MA: Blackwell Publishing.

McFarland, M. D. (2015). Anti-racist white hero, the sequel: Intersections of race(ism), gender, and social justice. *Critical Studies in Media Communication, 32*(2), 81–95.

Means Coleman, R. R. (2011). *Horror noire: Blacks in American horror films from the 1980s to present*. New York: Routledge.

Meyers, M. (2004). African American women and violence: Gender, race, and class in the news. *Critical Studies in Media Communication, 21*(2), 95–118.

Mosendz, P. (2016, November 9). What this election taught us about millennial voters. *Bloomberg.* Retrieved from http://www.bloomberg.com/news/articles/2016-11-09/what-this-election-taught-us-about-millennial-voters

Murphy, R. (Producer). (2015). *Scream queens* [Television series]. Los Angeles, CA: FOX Broadcasting Company.

Ono, K. A. (2010). Postracism: A theory of 'post'—as political strategy. *Journal of Communication Inquiry, 34*(3), 227–233.

Ono, K. A. (2013). *Mad Men's* postracial figuration of a racial past. In L. M. E. Goodlad, L. Kaganovsky, & R. A. Rushing (Eds.), *Madmen, mad world: Sex, politics, style and the 1960s* (pp. 300–319). Durham, NC: Duke University Press.

Orr, C. (2015, June 17). Why does *Game of Thrones* feature so much violence? *The Atlantic.* Retrieved from https://www.theatlantic.com/entertainment/archive/2015/06/game-of-thrones-sexual-violence/396191/

Paglia, C. (2015, December 10). Camille Paglia takes on Taylor Swift, Hollywood's #girlsquad culture. *Hollywood Reporter.* Retrieved from https://www.theatlantic.com/entertainment/archive/2015/06/game-of-thrones-sexual-violence/396191/

Penney, R. (2016). The rhetoric of mistake in adult narratives of youth sexuality: The case of Amanda Todd. *Feminist Media Studies, 16*(4), 710–725.

Phillips, K. R. (2005). *Projected fears: Horror films and American culture.* Westport, CT: Praeger.

Poertner, C. (2016, January 28). What 'new school' bullying looks like, and what we can do about it. *The Huffington Post.* Retrieved from http://www.huffingtonpost.com/carla-poertner/what-new-school-bullying-_b_9090420.html

Prensky, M. (2001). Digital natives, digital immigrants part 1. *On the Horizon, 95*(5), 1–6.

Richmond, E., Zinshteyn, M., & Gross, N. (2016, November 11). Discussing the youth vote. *The Atlantic.* Retrieved from https://www.theatlantic.com/education/archive/2016/11/dissecting-the-youth-vote/507416/

Ringrose, J. (2006). A new universal mean girl: Examining the discursive construction and social regulation of a new feminine pathology. *Feminism & Psychology, 16*(4), 405–424.

Serazio, M. (2015). Selling (digital) millennials: The social construction and technological bias of a consumer generation. *Television & New Media, 16*(7), 599–615.

Siegel, L. (2009). *Against the machine: Being human in the age of the electronic mob.* New York: Random House.

Stein, L. E. (2015). *Millennial fandom: Television audiences in the transmedia age.* Iowa City: University of Iowa Press.

Talbot, M. (2002, February 24). Girls just wanna be mean. *The New York Times Magazine,* 24–34.

Tapscott, D. (2009). *Growing up digital: How the net is changing your world.* New York: McGraw Hill.

Taylor, P. (2016, February). The kids are all left. *TIME, 187,* 34–41.

Townsend, C. (2013, April 25). "This email should never have been sent": Sorority girl who sent furious rant to fellow sisters resigns from Delta Gamma. *Daily Mail.* Retrieved from http://www.dailymail.co.uk/femail/article-2314752/Sorority-girl-Rebecca-Martinson-sent-furious-email-rant-fellow-sisters-resigns-Delta-Gamma.html

Vavrus, M. D. (2010). Unhitching the "post" (of postfeminism). *Journal of Communication Inquiry*, 34(4), 222–227.

Wagmeister, E. (2017, January 11). "Scream Queens" season 3? Fox execs give an update. *Variety*. Retrieved from http://variety.com/2017/tv/news/scream-queens-season-3-renewed-or-cancelled-1201957633/

Weaver, C. (2013, April 18). The most deranged sorority girl email you will ever read. *Gawker*. Retrieved from http://gawker.com/5994974/the-most-deranged-sorority-girl-email-you-will-ever-read

Willis, J. (2015, January 30). Katy Perry confirms 'mean girl' tweet was aimed at Taylor Swift. *ET*. Retrieved from http://www.etonline.com/music/158932_katy_perry_says_mean_girls_tweet_was_about_taylor_swift/

Wiseman, R. (2002). *Queen bees & wannabes*. New York: Three Rivers Press.

Worrall, A. (2004). Twisted sisters, ladettes, and the new penology: The social construction of "violent girls." In C. Alder & A. Worrall (Eds.), *Girls' violence: Myths and realities* (pp. 41–60). New York: State University of New York Press.

Young, E. (1996). Here comes the bride: Wedding gender and race in *Bride of Frankenstein*. In B. K. Grant (Ed.), *The dread of difference: Gender and the horror film* (pp. 309337). Austin: University of Texas Press.

· 6 ·

PREPPING THE QUEEN BEE

Mean Girls and Bad Wannabes on *Gossip Girl*[1]

"You need to be cruel to be queen. Anne Boleyn thought only with her heart and got her head chopped off, so her daughter Elizabeth made a vow never to marry a man. She married a country. Forget the boys. Keep your eye on the prize, Jenny Humphrey. You can't make people love you, but you can make them fear you." (Blair Waldorf, Season 2, The Goodbye Girl)

When *Gossip Girl* (Schwartz, 2007–2012) premiered on The CW in 2007, it was touted in *The New Yorker* as an inside look at the "tantalizing spectacle" of the "most privileged part of Manhattan" (Franklin, 2007, p. 171). As discussed in Chapter 3, the show follows upper- and middle-class students at elite preparatory schools in the Upper East Side (UES) of Manhattan,[2] with a narrative focus on the white middle-class Humphreys. The show frames father, Rufus, and son, Dan, as morally upright citizens who must take care of younger sister, Jenny. On *Gossip Girl*, white Blair Waldorf is the Queen Bee of Constance Billard's most powerful clique, The Girls on the Steps. Blair is the gatekeeper of the upper-class, maintaining her place in the social hierarchy of her school and the UES by manipulating and rejecting others. In turn, as the Wannabe, Jenny's narrative revolves around her ambitions to become a member of The Girls on the Steps at her preparatory school and the world of the UES elite society outside of school. These aspirations are motivated by access to greater social power, as well as to material benefits and social privileges not available to her as an outsider of these groups. *Gossip Girl* frames Jenny's attempts to become a part of The Girls on the Steps as analogous to social climbing.

On *Gossip Girl*, a pattern develops that suggests middle-class girls' attempts to improve their social standing will alter them from authentically "good" to dangerously "bad." Chesney-Lind and Irwin (2008) explain, for nearly a century, "bad" girls have been framed as seeking equality with men in terms of violence and sex, but, at the start of the twenty first century, "popular culture suddenly discovered 'mean' girls" (p. 1). As opposed to showing these two images of girlhood as disparate, *Gossip Girl* suggests that middle-class girls are doomed to failure when attempting to be mean (a quality the show situates as authentic only to upper-class femininity), so they inevitably become bad. Given that bad girls are more often conceived of as working-class girls of color, the show's tendency to show white middle class girls as bad functions, as Ringrose (2006) argues about the Mean Girl discourse, as a warning about failed white middle-class femininity, highlighting the slippage between meanness (covert aggression) and badness (violence). *Gossip Girl* is illustrative of this slippage, showing middle-class girls who attempt to rise in the social hierarchy (of eliteness, popularity, or class) as moving from "good" to "mean" and finally to "bad."

This analysis of *Gossip Girl* provides access to the important work the show does in representing girlhood, class, and social climbing. While the show confirms many of the generalizations of the Mean Girl discourse I have thus far highlighted, its narrative concentration on class makes it interesting and important on its own. It can be difficult to examine classed representations in popular culture because, as hooks (2000) and Mantsios (2000a, 2000b) argue, the United States remains dedicated to notions of a classless society. In fact, very little attention is paid to class in popular culture and, in turn, public discourse (Foster, 2005; Mantsios, 2000b). On the other hand, *Gossip Girl* takes as its central narrative class-based relations, specifically those between the middle- and upper-classes. As a result, a case study of the program allows for a detailed and nuanced examination of the role of class in the Queen Bee/ Wannabe relationship.

In much of the social scientific literature about the mean girl, middle-class girls are situated as bullies and poor girls as their victims, leading girls' studies scholars to note that the discourse is reflective of a cultural concern with the moral character of middle-class girls (Aapola, Gonick, & Harris, 2005;

Chesney-Lind & Irwin, 2008; Gonick, 2004; Ringrose, 2006). This investigation focuses on an aspect of the Mean Girl discourse not yet studied since *Gossip Girl* shows upper-class girls to be bullies and middle-class girls their victims. I argue that shifting the class construction of the Queen Bee from middle-class to upper-class alters how the same set of behaviors (bullying, meanness, aggression) is viewed, while simultaneously maintaining cultural concern with the moral character of white middle-class girls. I base this investigation on the first three seasons of *Gossip Girl* (2007–2010) because my primary interest is with the show's presentation of the Queen Bee and Wannabe, girlhood images that have been conceived of as specific to junior and high school (Simmons, 2002; Wiseman, 2002), so storylines that revolve around characters in high school are most relevant. By season four, all the primary characters on the show have graduated from high school (or left the UES).

The Queen Bee and the Wannabe

The Mean Girl discourse frames the Queen Bee as the leader of the clique, an (overly) empowered agent who can persuade her peers to do anything she wants, can argue anyone down (including teachers and parents), and has an eye-for-an-eye worldview (Wiseman, 2002). According to Simmons (2002), popularity is a "cutthroat contest into which girls pour boundless energy and anxiety…Popularity changes girls, causes a great many of them to lie and cheat and steal" (p. 156). *Gossip Girl* reflects Simmons's claim by showing the middle-class Wannabe as so desperate to be popular that she is quick to lie, cheat, and steal. Because the Wannabe desires to be a part of the Queen Bee's clique, she will do anything to please her. For example, in Jenny's attempts to win Blair's favor, she mimics her style, runs her errands (i.e., picks up her dry cleaning), and keeps her secrets. Blair lives in a penthouse on the UES with her mother, a successful fashion designer. Despite living in New York City all her life, Blair has never ridden the subway, preferring instead a private car or limousine. When her boyfriend attempts to teach her the ropes of public transportation, she exclaims, "There's no way I'm going down there. It's full of mole men and middle-class professionals. That's why God created drivers. Rats go underground, not Waldorfs" (Season 2, Southern Gentlemen Prefer Blondes). Blair wields her elite class status and its attendant privileges as weapons. She brandishes a sort of political power by using boundary maintenance, which works to protect her elite position by allowing her to choose whom to include and exclude from her elite clique. Boundary maintenance is, according to Kendall (2010), also the primary goal of upper-class individuals, cementing the show's association of the eliteness of popularity with elite upper-class society.

In contrast, middle-class Wannabe Jenny is always at pains to keep up with her upper-class peers' lifestyles, predominantly due to a lack of economic resources. She sews her clothes because she cannot afford designer labels, and, at times, she sells personal belongings in order to go on vacation or to dinner with her classmates. Blair takes pride in her ancestral bloodline and good breeding, while sarcastically encouraging Jenny to "pretend you're well bred" (Season 3, Ex-husbands and Wives). In doing so, Blair points to the ways in which Jenny's forays into upper-class society are always inauthentic; she is pretending, putting on an act. Additionally, there are a series of metaphors that work to distinguish Jenny as not belonging to the upper-class. For example, (the show's narrator) Gossip Girl calls her "poor little orphan Jenny" in need of a "Daddy Warbucks" (Season 2, Bonfire of the Vanity), and, when Jenny is invited to the Masquerade Ball, her father refers to her as "Cinderella" (Season 1, The Handmaiden's Tale). These metaphors mark Jenny as lacking economic capital ("poor") and in need of social capital (in the form of relationships with powerful elite people ("Daddy Warbucks"). It is also interesting to note that both metaphors position Jenny as an orphan, so although Jenny has a close knit family, the fact that they are middle-class locates her as without the family bloodline necessary for successful navigation of the UES. In "The Handmaiden's Tale," Jenny's construction as subservient to the Queen Bee (and, in turn, members of the elite upper-class) continues when Jenny is labeled as the "handmaiden" to Blair's Queen. Although Jenny tries to spin the term positively, her friend quickly points out that "handmaiden is Jane Austen for slave." In contrast, Blair's upper-class minions are referred to as "Ladies in Waiting," a term that situates them as nobility, although of a lower rank than their Queen. These metaphors work to position Jenny as a servant or slave, necessarily subordinate to all upper-class girls.

Narrating Class on *Gossip Girl*

At the beginning of each episode, Gossip Girl provides a recap of the previous show. Her opening statement is always the same: "Gossip Girl here—your one and only source into the scandalous lives of Manhattan's elite." Through this repeated opening statement, the show is situated as about the upper-class, but the framing of elite society as "scandalous" works to prepare the viewer for plotlines about the upper-class that are shocking and outrageous. In episode after episode, Gossip Girl calls attention to the ways in which the middle-class is different from (and inherently better than) the upper-class. Gossip Girl never refers to the middle-class specifically; instead, by creating an "us (middle-class) versus them (UES)" mentality, she situates the viewer as not part of the UES. For example, Gossip Girl describes Sundays on the UES in comparison to a "normal" Sunday:

> Is there anything better than a lazy Sunday? Reading the paper in bed, scrambling an egg or two…yeah, right. We Upper East Siders don't do lazy. Breakfast is brunch, and it comes with champagne, a dress code, and about 100 of our closest friends. (Season 1, The Wild Brunch)

Through this bait-and-switch technique, the middle-class representation of Sunday is normalized, while the "Upper East-Siders" are made to seem strange, thus maintaining the us versus them mentality so important to the program's narrative. Moreover, when Gossip Girl calls attention to the ways in which the UES is different from the rest of the country, it is typically in some problematic way. For instance, Gossip Girl claims, "On the UES, appearances are often deceiving" (Season 1, The Handmaiden's Tale), suggesting that in the rest of the country, where middle-class values rule, appearances are *not* deceiving, so you can trust the face people show to you. In a similar vein, Gossip Girl claims, "For the rest of the country, Thanksgiving is when families come together to give thanks, but, on the UES, the holiday thankfully returns to its roots: lying, manipulation, and betrayal" (Season 2, The Magnificent Archibalds). Gossip Girl's narration works rhetorically to center the middle-class as "normal" and "average," while encouraging us to think about the elite upper-class as having the potential to corrupt middle-class innocence.

On *Gossip Girl*, viewer sympathies align with Dan and Jenny, as we are introduced to the world of the UES through their perspectives. The series premiere begins in Grand Central Station, with shots of white upper-class "it-girl" Serena juxtaposed with those of Dan and Jenny returning to the city. Gossip Girl's narration focuses on Serena: "Spotted at Grand Central, bags in hand, Serena van der Woodsen. Wasn't it only a year ago our 'it-girl' mysteriously disappeared for boarding school? And, just as suddenly, she's back." Gossip Girl credits her readers for the "tip," while the viewer sees several young women taking pictures of Serena, presumably to send to Gossip Girl. In contrast, Dan and Jenny's return receives far less fanfare and interest. Greeted by their father, trading hugs, they serve as a more normative version of family; it is with them the viewer identifies. From this opening scene, the juxtaposition between the UES teens and the middle-class Humphreys is clear. Viewers connect with the middle-class Humphreys as a "way-in" to the UES, to the upper-class, and to the myth of the American Dream.

The show insists that the Humphreys are middle-class, even though they likely are not really, and, even more so, when they are not at all (for instance, after Rufus marries the uber-wealthy Lily van der Woodsen and the family moves into her penthouse in the UES). No matter where they live, *home* for the Humphreys is always situated as a loft in Brooklyn, which the program constructs through mise-en-scène as decidedly middle-class. The Humphrey's loft is industrial, featuring exposed brick walls, peeling paint, and metal garage doors that separate Jenny and Dan's bedrooms. The décor is shabby chic: fabric covers an old tattered chair; decorative, colorful pillows are scattered over the beds and floor; mismatched lamps stand atop banged up coffee tables; the kitchen has no storage, so the walls are lined with plates and bowls of distinct patterns and colors. The feeling created is messy and lived in; contrastingly, both Serena and white UES bad boy Chuck Bass live in sterile, yet opulent hotel penthouses. As opposed to the bright, playful colors of the Humphrey's loft, the hotel relies on a somber gray and maroon palate. Situating the Humphreys in the Upper West Side, a locale seen as more artistic and liberal and as in direct contrast to the Upper East Side, which is old moneyed and conservative, signifies the Humphreys as a way for presumed middle-class viewers to access this world of extreme wealth and extravagance.

Gossip Girl is ostensibly about the upper-class, yet the show centers the middle-class by fashioning it as good and moral. Although authenticity is arbitrary (Johnson, 2003), *Gossip Girl* discursively positions particular morals and values as "authentic" or "natural" to the middle- or upper-class. For example, the show frames the middle-class, primarily represented by the Humphreys, as valuing hard work, compassion, and self-control. Conversely, the exploits of the UES characters show the upper-class to be depraved, greedy, and excessively materialistic. In turn, these traits characterize individuals as belonging to specific classes, further insisting that these value systems endure across disparate social spaces. For instance, following Blair's graduation from high school, The Girls on the Steps consider making Jenny their Queen Bee, an instance that works to authenticate her middle-classness. Instead of using bullying tactics to maintain her elite social position, Jenny attempts to bring a middle-class sensibility to her leadership, claiming there will be no more "hierarchies or mean girls." Unhappy with Jenny's attempt to end elitism at their school, her minions tell her, "We're going back to the old way: Queens, hierarchies, and no more Brooklyn Wannabes" (Season 3, Dan de Fleurette). Although Jenny's father recently married an extremely wealthy UES socialite, Jenny's middle-classness is static: because she was not born in to the UES, she can never authentically be part of the upper-class. In this way, *Gossip Girl* positions classed subjectivities as based on an imagined authentic morality as opposed to economic reality.

No matter how far the Humphreys rise in the social order, they are always already middle-class and, as such, expected to adhere to, what the show presents as, a middle-class value system. Rufus works to instill middle-class values in Jenny and Dan through what Jenny calls his "anti-capitalist rants" (Season 1, Pilot) and his ongoing insistence that they work hard for what they desire. Despite Rufus's attempts to keep his kids grounded, their gendered roles impact their contrasting abilities to navigate their elite preparatory schools' social systems and preserve their middle-class morality. For instance, in her efforts to penetrate the boundaries of The Girls on the Steps and UES society, Jenny makes choices that place her outside of cultural expectations of white middle-class femininity as responsible, submissive, and refined (Banet-Weiser, 1999). Jenny's big break into the elite social circle comes when she accepts an invitation to Blair's annual slumber party (Season 1, Dare Devil). When the 14-year-old attempts to turn down a martini, Blair says, "It's a party Jenny, either swallow or swipe your metro card back home." Jenny obliges. Instead of staying true to her middle-class values, Jenny is framed as willing to do whatever is necessary to gain Blair's approval, including breaking the law by drinking alcohol. Later in the evening, Dan, disgusted by Jenny's actions (i.e., drinking alcohol, lying, and wearing a skimpy dress), exclaims, "This is not who you are!" In an ongoing theme, behaving badly is conceived of as not in Jenny's nature but a result of the poor choices she makes in her attempts to fit in with her much wealthier classmates.

Just seven episodes later, Dan lands in an illegal situation; however, this narrative does not position Dan as other than whom he authentically is, instead highlighting his middle-class morality. Dan chooses to attend an illegal party at his prep school pool, and, when a student leaves behind a cell phone with incriminating pictures, he and the other students face expulsion. In a group assembly, the head mistress explains that if she does not learn who had the key to open the school, she will expel the entire group. Rufus, seemingly unconcerned that Dan attended the illicit party, encourages Dan to cooperate since "these other kids are going to be looking out for themselves" (Season 1, School Lies). When Serena (the key holder) urges Dan to trust her, he argues, "We're not in the same boat here. I'm on partial scholarship. My parents have no way of buying my way back into school." Unlike Jenny who works to hide her middle-class roots, Dan continually calls attention to what makes him a class outsider. In this sense, he is committed to his middle-class status, a trait that Jenny lacks, positioning her as incapable of meeting the demands of middle-class femininity. Eventually, Serena confesses, relieving Dan of any responsibility. He does not have to prioritize his relationship with Serena, so his middle-class individualism remains intact, as the viewer is left to assume that he would have been willing to tell the truth had Serena not professed her guilt. Dan's middle-class morality redeems him, because, unlike as with Jenny, his foray into criminality is seen as a momentary lapse, a mistake, not an ongoing attempt to fit in where he does not authentically belong.

Gendering Capital

An ongoing theme on *Gossip Girl* concerns the ways in which Rufus sacrifices for his children's education (he pays tens of thousands of dollars each year for tuition, despite the fact that they are on scholarship), while the UES teens are expected to sacrifice for their parents. *Gossip Girl* shows Rufus to be a particularly sound parent who is willing to do whatever is necessary for his children's well-being (for instance, he considers selling his art gallery to pay Dan's college tuition). Conversely, the parents of the UES include a cocaine-addicted, embezzling criminal and a mother so concerned with maintaining her romantic relationships, she allows the doorman of her building to sign her children's school permission slips. Jenny's forays into elite society are often exasperating because she has such a loving and dedicated father in Rufus, who is the most involved of all the parents; he cooks breakfast and dinner for his children and has open conversations with them about school, parties, romance, and sex. Despite his attempts to keep his kids grounded, Jenny cannot escape the lure of popularity and elite society that she accesses through her preparatory school.

According to Bourdieu (1984, 1986, 1990), it is possible for an individual to transcend her lack of economic capital through the accumulation of cultural capital. In *Reproductions*, Bourdieu and Passeron (1990) explore "the extremely sophisticated mechanisms by which the school system *contributes* to reproducing the structure of the distribution of cultural capital" (p. vii, original emphasis). In elite prep schools, students accumulate cultural capital (including credentials, status, symbols, an appreciation for the fine arts, and linguistic skills) that can be used in later life, so prep schools help transmit power and privilege (Cookson & Persell, 1985). On *Gossip Girl*, the prep school environment of Constance Billard, which Dan describes as "populated by mean girls and date rapists" (Season 1, 17 Candles), is distinguished as the biggest threat to Jenny's middle-class morality. Jenny is shown to be most interested in socializing, making connections, and rising in the high school social hierarchy, so she is never framed as having the potential to access what the show situates as the "true" benefits of a prep school education (i.e., cultural capital). *Gossip Girl's* message is inherently regressive—returning to paternalistic ideologies about why girls should not be educated. That is, middle-class girls should avoid elite schools because it is too dangerous for their middle-class moral sensibilities.

As opposed to collecting cultural capital, Jenny pursues social capital, which the program's narrative frames as an inferior form of capital. Bourdieu (1984, 1986) conceived of social capital as relationships that provide access to networks of influence (as opposed to the educational credentials and verbal facility afforded by cultural capital). In feminizing social capital, *Gossip Girl* problematizes the qualities women are most encouraged to display, such as intimacy and nurturing. Jenny attempts to create relationships (building social capital) with The Girls on the Steps because being a part of the ruling elite carries certain rewards (parties, boyfriends, etc.). Jenny's pursuit of social capital, by building relationships with Queen Bee Blair and her minions, is problematized because it is shown as threatening to her middle-class innocence. In the early part of Season 1 of *Gossip Girl*, Jenny's image is innocent and childlike. She wears little to no makeup and her blonde hair falls simply in long locks. Her physical appearance is in line with what Walkerdine (1997) highlights as the blonde-haired girl who needs to be protected by the middle-class. In "The Wild Brunch," one of the first steps Jenny takes to imitate Blair is to mimic the flowers Blair has in her penthouse—hydrangeas. After complimenting Blair on the flowers and learning their name, Jenny asks her father to go with her to the Sunday Market, so she can get some for herself. This scene is purely innocent: a father/daughter trip to the market where Jenny buys flowers.

From these early episodes, as Jenny begins to make her way into The Girls on the Steps, her actions become increasingly troublesome. For instance, when The Girls on the Steps tell Jenny they plan to take her out for her fifteenth birthday, she panics about finding a dress to wear. Jenny is unable to make a dress (as she would have in the past), since she sold her sewing machine, so, when she finds herself in the closet of mean girl Hazel's mother, she is tempted to steal one of the dresses, which she then trades at a consignment shop for another dress to wear to the party. The next day at school, Jenny learns that the dress she stole is actually a $15,000 original Valentino, so she returns to the consignment shop in an attempt to retrieve it. Jenny's lack of cultural capital is made clear when the shop owner refuses to give Jenny the Valentino back, explaining, "Look, it's not my fault you don't know what a Valentino is worth." Desperate, Jenny takes the dress into the dressing room, puts it on under her coat, and walks out of the store, stealing the dress for a second time. When Rufus learns what Jenny has done, he exclaims, "You don't have to do those things Jenny. You're making a choice." Jenny argues the only other choice would be to have no friends, but Rufus maintains, "You've got so much more to offer than those girls have" (Season 1, The Blair Bitch Project). In an ongoing theme, behaving badly (i.e., drinking alcohol and stealing) is constructed as not in Jenny's nature but instead as an aspect of her attempts to fit in with her much wealthier classmates, to become popular. If she would simply be "true to herself," focus on her education and not on building relationships, Dan and Rufus suggest Jenny could succeed on her own. Whereas the upper-class Queen Bee's boundary maintenance, gossiping, and socializing are seen as authentically part of upper-class femininity (the show is ripe with ongoing references to adult upper-class women who behave in a similar manner), when Jenny attempts to rise in the social order, her actions are framed as inauthentic.

Rufus consistently articulates and valorizes middle-class individualism. He tells Dan and Jenny they can do anything they set their minds to and argues that when they take advantage of the connections they make through prep school, they are "using" people, which is against their moral code. In Season 2, burgeoning fashion designer Jenny begins to skip school, removing any chance she once had at gaining cultural capital. Instead, again focused on social capital, Jenny crashes an UES gala (she claims the event will be full of "Fortune 500 owners") with a guerilla fashion show (There Might be Blood). The fashion show is a huge success and is featured on Page Six (the gossip column of *The New York Post*); however, Rufus tells her he has "never been more disappointed" (Season 2, Bonfire of the Vanity). Not only does he attempt to punish Jenny, he even goes so far as to identify her as the person responsible for crashing the gala to the police. Although Jenny escapes legal retribution, her life spins out of control when she runs away from home and finds herself alone, with no place to stay, on the cold Manhattan streets on Thanksgiving. Importantly, Jenny is not framed as incapable of achieving success. Indeed, the fashion show is well-planned, organized, and a true victory. Additionally, when she begins to meet with agents about designing her own fashion line, she expresses knowledge of her clientele and is able to explicate what makes her unique as a designer. As is common with Jenny, she is both empowered and victimized. Despite her success, she is punished for turning her back on her family, lying, skipping school, and using others in pursuit of her dream when her business partner (a 16-year-old model), Agnes, is revealed to be a self-involved, immature, hysterical sociopath. In a dramatic turn, Agnes, angry that Jenny has been seeing agents without her, burns all of Jenny's designs, essentially putting an end to Jenny's dreams.

When Jenny works to build social capital, she is consistently punished, but when Dan does the same, his pursuits are situated as for a worthwhile cause and he is rewarded, pointing to the ways their gendered roles alter their abilities to navigate elite society and maintain their middle-class morality. For instance, Dan's application to Yale University requires a letter of recommendation. He hopes to impress Noah Shapiro, editor of the *Paris Review* (a literary magazine), with a writing sample, so Dan takes Shapiro's advice to "seek out danger" by spending the day with Chuck Bass (Season 2, The Serena also Rises). Unimpressed with the story, Shapiro tells Dan to dig deeper into the "Charlie Trout" (a pseudonym Dan provides for Chuck Bass) character. Dan, staying true to his middle-class individualism, refuses; however, after seeing Jenny's successful fashion show, Dan is inspired, telling Rufus, "Look, the morning after my little sister staged a fashion show that all of New York City will be talking about is not the time for the 'slow and steady' speech. I'm sorry. I tried it your way" (Season 2, There Might be Blood). Shapiro loves the writing sample and agrees to write a recommendation letter. Importantly, Shapiro is so impressed he passes the story on to *New York Magazine*, which wants Dan to use his connections to write a story on Chuck's father, Bart, on the twentieth anniversary of Bass Industries. When Dan uncovers information that could potentially send Bart to prison, he refuses to move forward on the story, instead passing on the piece he wrote about Chuck to Bart, allowing Bart to see that Chuck believes his father blames him for his mother's death during childbirth. After reading the story, in an extremely rare moment of intimacy between the two, Bart apologizes to Chuck. Dan later tells Rufus that he took his advice and killed the story. Rufus responds, "You saved a family" (Season 2, Bonfire of the Vanity). Dan uses Chuck to get what he desires—a recommendation letter to Yale—but, since the story is not made public, he is seen as hurting neither Chuck nor Bart, so his actions are framed as moral. Unlike with Jenny, he is able to rise in the social order by using his connections in a manner that is shown as in line with his authentic middle-class morality.

Despite his warnings about their fellow students, Dan clearly benefits from the cultural capital associated with a prep school education and appears to do so without trying, while also remaining true to his authentic middle-class identity. By graduation, Dan, who has always considered himself an outsider, realizes the cultural capital he accrued has made him an insider. Blair explains, "You're friends with Nate Archibald…you got into Yale…published in the *New Yorker*. You may pretend to not be like us, but you are" (Season 2, The Goodbye Gossip Girl). With ease, Dan gained a significant amount of cultural capital, but he also remained true to his middle-class value system, so his achievements are framed as individual successes resulting from hard work and self-discipline. Indeed, he is the ultimate neoliberal citizen. He shows self-determination and self-empowerment, and he happily endures hardship while showing facility for overcoming class-based disadvantages (Hasinoff, 2008; Joseph, 2009; Ouellette & Hay, 2008). Dan insists that he is happy being a social outsider, he has no desire for popularity, so, unlike as with Jenny, his rise in the social hierarchy is incidental, allowing his middle-class sensibility to remain intact.

Middle-Class Girls Gone Bad

The narrative of *Gossip Girl* frames meanness (as defined by covert forms of aggression) as authentic only to upper-class femininity. In turn, the show suggests that middle-class girls who attempt to play in the social hierarchy of the upper-class become bad as opposed to mean, thereby securing upper-classness as part of the Queen Bee construction and feeding into societal anxiety about middle-class girls and meanness. Blair and her minions are framed as naturally excelling at using covert forms of aggression. For example, in Season 2, Blair's minions begin to bully Jenny. The girls approach Jenny at her locker, tease her about her handbag, which they claim "belongs in the trash," and then empty the contents of the handbag on the floor. Jenny, who appears unimpressed, asks, "Really? That's the best you can do?" Penelope, one of Blair's minions, quickly replies, "Our methods may lack imagination, but they're effective, especially over a long period of time." So effective, in fact, that the insinuation of future bullying is enough to cause Jenny to pack her bag and drop out of school (The Ex-Files).

Although Blair is mean, she is also constructed as good. In the earliest episodes of the first season of *Gossip Girl*, Blair is framed sympathetically. It is a common trope on the series to show Blair as the victim of other people's selfish behavior. For instance, viewers see Blair work hard to please her fashion designer mother who calls Blair her "best advertising" (Season 1, Pilot); at the same time, Blair's mother consistently makes negative comments about the fit of Blair's clothes, her hair, and her food choices, such as when she suggests Blair might "find a low fat yogurt more appealing" than a croissant (Season 1, Bad News Blair). In the first season episode "Blair Waldorf Must Pie!," the viewer learns that Blair has overcome bulimia, but the narrative focus on Blair's mother's ongoing jabs at her appearance suggest her mother is to blame for the eating disorder, framing Blair as a victim to her cruel mother. In this way, although Blair is at times a mean bully, she is also always endearing and her actions forgivable.

While Blair is constructed as mean *and* nice, bad *and* good, Jenny's construction is more rigid. Jenny is good only when authentically situated in the middle-class and bad when she attempts to access the upper-class. As opposed to Blair, whose actions are often presented compassionately, Jenny's desires for social climbing and the choices she makes in order to become popular are consistently framed unsympathetically. For example, when Jenny realizes her egalitarian leadership style is not going to work at Constance Billard, she comes to understand that in order to rule as Queen Bee, she must acquire significant economic capital. Former Queen Blair explains, "A true monarch bestows favors" (Season 2, The Serena Also Rises). Blair's economic capital allowed her to throw extravagant parties for her minions and give them designer clothing. Whereas Blair is rich, Jenny finds increasingly dangerous ways to earn money, such as dealing drugs (Season 3, The Treasure of Serena Madre). By dealing drugs, Jenny makes her own money as well as her own connections. When Rufus discovers a large bag of pills in Jenny's possession, he exclaims, "I look at you, and I don't see my daughter anymore." As Gossip Girl explains, "There comes a time when every father learns you can't keep a *bad* girl down," contributing to a cultural anxiety about meanness run amok. The middle-class Wannabe has become a bad girl who lies, steals, and deals drugs. Jenny's attempts to be Queen Bee are always failures because meanness is framed as authentic to upper-class femininity only; middle-class girls are authentically nice. Her efforts to social climb are constructed as most concerning because instead of being mean, she becomes dangerously bad.

In the third season finale (Last Tango, Then Paris), Jenny's life is out of control: she has stolen from her stepmother, dealt drugs, and lied repeatedly. Her father explains that he has no other option but to send Jenny to live with her mother in Hudson where presumably she can be guided toward appropriate white femininity. Rejecting her father's plan to force her to leave the UES, Jenny enters Chuck's penthouse. Throughout her tenure on the show Jenny has worked to emphasize her autonomy (i.e., she runs away from home and considers being emancipated from her parents), but these actions are made to appear problematic. When Jenny enters Chuck's penthouse, she is again shown enacting her empowerment toward a self-destructive end. Chuck sits alone in the dark, drinking liquor, and nursing a broken heart. His loneliness (true-love Blair rejected him and his father died) makes him more empathetic than Jenny, who seems petulant in her disobedience to her father and refusal to live with her mother. The two kiss briefly before the scene ends, and, in the next shot, Jenny is lying in Chuck's bed in only a black slip, while Chuck stands above her in a bathrobe.

Although it appears as though Jenny initiates sex with Chuck as a final act of defiance against her father's attempts to rehabilitate her, whatever autonomy she demonstrates is entirely denied through Dan and Rufus's insistent claims that Chuck "took advantage" of her. Positioning Jenny as a victim of Chuck's callousness (as opposed to an empowered agent in control of her sexuality) restores her to passive modes of "good" femininity. If Chuck took advantage of Jenny (and not the other way around), then she remains a "good girl" who has been corrupted by her transgression into the UES. Her attempt to adopt the sexual autonomy that her upper-class peers embody is condemned. The lesson she learns is that she should remain true to her authentic middle-class self, which involves a rejection of autonomy, as only harm comes to her when she enacts agency in order to increase her social or economic standing.

Gossip Girl shows the tendency of middle-class girls to become bad instead of mean to be true of not only girls but of middle-class women, emphasizing the dangers of upward mobility to middle-class femininity and morality. In the second season of *Gossip Girl*, a new teacher, Rachel Carr, joins the faculty at Constance Billard. Ms. Carr is originally from Des Moines, Iowa and was working most recently with Teach for America (a nonprofit organization that provides teachers to low income communities). Despite her philanthropic roots, Ms. Carr is constructed as incapable of maintaining her middle-class value system when Blair lures her into a war. In "You've Got Yale," Ms. Carr gives Blair a B on a paper. Blair explains, "You're new here, so you don't know how it works. Second semester seniors get a free pass." Ms. Carr expresses her middle-class sensibility when she replies, "Maybe in time I'll get in trouble for not inflating grades, but until then I'll give them based on merit." When, in retaliation, Blair humiliates Ms. Carr by inviting her to the opera and then stands her up, Ms. Carr reports her for hazing a teacher, risking Blair's admission to Yale.

In hopes of getting even with Ms. Carr, Blair tasks her minions with researching her background in order to dig up dirt; however, Ms. Carr is so good and moral, Hazel calls her the "Midwest Mother Teresa" (Season 2, Carnal Knowledge). Left with nothing to work with, Blair creates a rumor that Ms. Carr engaged in an inappropriate relationship with Dan by sending a picture to the Gossip Girl blog of Dan and Ms. Carr hugging. When Dan learns that Ms. Carr lost her job because of the picture, he goes to visit her at home. Although the school no longer employs her, Ms. Carr's sexual aggressiveness with Dan (she grabs him by his shirt, kisses him, and pulls him inside her apartment) frames her as a bad girl. Moreover, when Constance Billard reinstates Ms. Carr due to a lack of verifiable evidence, her bad girl construction continues when she engages in sex with Dan on school grounds during play rehearsals that the entire senior class attends. She also stoops to the level of Blair when she sends Gossip Girl information about Blair that Dan told her in confidence. Dan admonishes Ms. Carr: "I believed in you, all your talk about integrity and ideals…you're just as bad as (Blair). No, you're worse. Blair's a high schooler; you're an adult." Reprimanded by Dan, Ms. Carr admits, "I don't know what's happened to me. I don't know what I've become" (Season 2, The Age of Dissonance). This storyline cements a running theme on *Gossip Girl* that suggests middle-class girls and women's desire to be part of the upper-class will turn them from authentically good to dangerously bad.

Surveillance and Cyberbullying

Beyond simply serving as a tool for narration, the Gossip Girl blog functions as an instrument for celebrity making (the teens featured most prominently develop a particular level of recognition and fame), surveillance, and bullying. One of the key tactics of social aggression is gossip. "Gossip is one of the fundamental weapons that girls use to humiliate each other and reinforce their own social status" (Wiseman, 2002, p. 122). In many ways, the Gossip Girl blog is the ultimate tool of cyberbullying. The entire purpose of the blog is to spread gossip about the students at Constance Billard and St. Jude's. Who writes the blog remains a mystery for nearly the entire series, so her posts are anonymous. Moreover, the students provide Gossip Girl's tips, so they are all imbricated in the bullying culture the blog perpetuates. While sites of leisure have "typically been places where youth can express themselves outside of surveillance" (Harris, 2004, p. 118), *Gossip Girl* shows the ways in which leisure sites (i.e., restaurants and clubs, boutiques and stores) have been infiltrated by surveillance performed by teens themselves who use information as a sort of currency by sending it to Gossip Girl. Thus, as Foucault (1995) portrayed the role of surveillance, the UES teens have been interpellated into surveillance culture.

The show makes clear that in order to be popular, the UES teens must submit to the surveillance perpetrated by Gossip Girl. For instance, after Jenny's first foray into the UES social scene, at the Kiss on the Lips party, she worries that she will become fodder for the blog. Blair explains, "If you want to be a part of this world Jenny, people will talk," positioning surveillance as a necessary component of mattering in the UES (Season 1, The Wild Brunch). Through this process of surveillance, particular classed identities emerge. When Jenny is featured on the Gossip Girl blog, she accesses celebrity in the UES, which she desperately desires, but her coverage is always focused on behaviors that seemingly go against her middle-class morality, behaviors that Dan and Rufus insist make her other than whom she authentically is. The implications of surveillance factor differently depending on the socio-economic context. For the UES teens, surveillance operates as a form of promotion that helps them develop a celebrity following. For middle-class girls and women, surveillance, in the guise of the Gossip Girl blog, is a disciplinary technology and a tool of bullying. For instance, as discussed in Chapter 3, Jenny's attempt to access popularity through her relationship with prep school hunk Asher is thwarted when Gossip Girl outs Asher for kissing another boy (thanks to a tip from Dan). Gossip Girl goes from congratulating "Queen Wannabe" for finding "her perfect king" (Season 1, Desperately Seeking Serena), to claiming that Asher was "bragging that Little J swiped her V card at his register," to confirming that Jenny "didn't spread her legs after all. She spread lies instead. Asher is gay" (Season 1, All about my Brother). In this case, Jenny loses her social status, her boyfriend, and her friends; she is isolated. While the upper-class teens are also the focus of Gossip Girl, they quickly rebound. Serena explain, "I've been on Gossip Girl plenty of times. Eventually everyone forgets" (Season 2, Carnal Knowledge). In contrast, when Gossip Girl bullies Jenny, she is shown as unable to recover in the same way, highlighting how the consequences of the blog differ depending on the socio-economic context.

Aside from situating the effects of cyberbullying as socio-economically dependent, the Season 2 episode "Carnal Knowledge" additionally highlights the struggle schools face with cyberbullying. As explained by Klein (2012), "While schools have legal rights to prohibit certain language or behaviors on school property or at school-related activities, these rights do not extend to the Internet" (p. 225). Legal experts argue cyberbullying legislation should also limit where and when school administrators discipline student cyberbullying, suggesting administrators should overlook cyberbullying that occurs off-campus, unless the student threatens violence (Beckstrom, 2008). *Gossip Girl* illuminates the difficulty schools face determining when to discipline students' online behavior. As discussed earlier, Blair seeks revenge on Ms. Carr by sending a tip to Gossip Girl that Ms. Carr is having an affair with Dan. When Ms. Carr reports Blair to Headmistress Kweller, the Headmistress admits the Constance Billard administration knew about the Gossip Girl blog for some time, but did not feel the need to intervene as long as the blog focused on students. Because Blair, through the Gossip Girl blog, bullied a teacher, Headmistress Kweller expels her.[3] After Blair assures her father that she was not lying about Ms. Carr's relationship with Dan, he defends Blair to the school administration, arguing this is a "free speech issue. You can't punish kids for posting to a public website" (Season 2, Carnal Knowledge). Eventually, Gossip Girl releases a picture of Dan caressing Ms. Carr's face that appears to substantiate the rumor Blair started, so she is allowed to return to school and Ms. Carr is fired. Blair escapes punishment, and the middle-class Ms. Carr (like Jenny) is driven out of town by cyberbullying.

In the series finale, Dan ultimately reveals that he is Gossip Girl in a story he writes and gives to Nate to publish in his fledgling newspaper, potentially saving the financially troubled tome. In so doing, and through the reactions of the individuals about whom he wrote, the blog, which was originally seen as vindictive and cruel, is reframed as the moral authority on the UES. In this sense, the mechanisms of surveillance operate differently in terms of class *and* gender. Performing surveillance allows Dan to experience social mobility and maintain his middle-class virtue, a privilege associated with his gender. In support of Dan, Serena claims, "He wouldn't have had anything to post if everyone hadn't been sending him tips," reconstituting the blog, through Serena's narration, as a "love letter" to the UES and maintaining Dan's moral authority since he only posted tips that others sent. Dan goes on to marry Serena, achieving his American Dream and becoming a part of the high society he was so quick to critique. Moreover, the show makes clear that the punishing surveillance performed by the blog in no way hurt the UES teens in any significant way, as they are all leading successful lives—Blair a thriving fashion designer, happily married to powerful entrepreneur Chuck, while Nate considers a bid for mayor. In contrast, Jenny, is gone from the UES, her dreams of becoming a fashion designer and increasing her socio-economic status dashed, as her father and brother (Gossip Girl himself) demanded she was far better off away from the UES. Jenny can neither experience the privilege of celebrity that accompanies surveillance (as the UES teens and even Dan do), but she also does not have the moral authority to perform surveillance. She remains forever a Wannabe, always situated in the precarious position of never being upper-class nor fully middle-class.

Raced and Classed Meanness

Along with upper-classness, *Gossip Girl* characterizes whiteness as a necessary component of the Queen Bee construction. The show is notable in that several of the upper-class girls of color are mean, but the ultimate mean girl and the leader of the clique is always white. This postracial ethos functions to center whiteness in a context in which race is seemingly configured as irrelevant (Dubrofsky & Ryalls, 2014). Ostensibly, in the context of Jenny and Dan's private schools, people of all races are equally privileged—white, Black, Asian, and Latino students populate the halls of the schools. Despite the suggestion that race is immaterial in the UES, when a character of color is not upper-class, she is doubly marginalized. The only prominent secondary character on the show who is not white is Vanessa. Although not explicitly identified racially, the show signifies Vanessa as mixed race. She has curly hair and expresses a hippie aesthetic through her "ethnic" way of dressing (long colorful skirts, scarves, plastic and beaded jewelry). At a Polo match, Vanessa's boyfriend comments that everything is "so white." Vanessa replies, "Welcome to my world" (Season 3, Reversals of Fortune). Although Jenny and Vanessa are both middle-class, Vanessa's mixed-race construction marks her as different from Jenny. *Gossip Girl* shows Jenny's virtue and innocence, traits culturally assumed to be associated with whiteness (Dyer, 1997), as in constant need of protection. Jenny's representation as pure and naive is juxtaposed with that of Vanessa, who seems more experienced, hardened, and able to take care of herself. The only adolescent character to hold a job, Vanessa does not attend a preparatory school and expresses disgust with the upper-class, including Jenny and Dan's classmates whom she calls "over-privileged, under-parented, trust fund brats" (Season 1, The Handmaiden's Tale). As a result, Vanessa does not figure in to the show's class narrative, as she seemingly eschews any desire for social mobility.

When both Jenny and Vanessa develop crushes on UES golden boy Nate, the normally incredibly supportive Vanessa treads into mean girl territory when she finds a letter Nate sent to Jenny expressing his romantic feelings for her (Season 2, It's a Wonderful Lie). Contributing to the theme of toxic female friendships prevalent on the show, Vanessa hides Nate's letter from Jenny in the hopes that she can romance him instead. Although Vanessa hopes to keep her relationship with Nate a secret, a Gossip Girl blast makes their clandestine romance public. Jenny is furious that Vanessa has been dating Nate behind her back, so The Girls on the Steps (who are upset that Nate is dating below his socio-economic status) are able to easily persuade Jenny to retaliate. Jenny delivers Vanessa a dress for the Snowflake Ball (Nate is Vanessa's date) that, unbeknownst to Vanessa, is transparent in the light. When Vanessa arrives to the Ball, the crowd erupts with laughter when a spotlight shines on her. In her attempt to be deceitful, Vanessa is publically humiliated.

Vanessa's mixed-race, middle class construction situates her as unable to be mean. In contrast, although Jenny is middle-class, her whiteness does allow for her to (albeit briefly) fulfill the duties of Queen Bee (as discussed earlier), marking whiteness as essential (and more important than socio-economic standing) to the Queen Bee. The majority of Blair's upper-class minions are raced other than white (e.g., Latina, Black, and Asian), yet none is mentioned as a potential Queen Bee. The girls are relegated to the margins of the show's plotlines, often used for comedic effect, excluding them from the important world of the other (white) girls on the show (Ross 2008). This narrative turn polices racial boundaries by reproducing a social hierarchy in which girls of color are limited to subordinate positions. Although girls of color have access to the social spaces of both The Girls on the Steps and the UES, they do so only as minions who serve to protect and enforce the power of the Queen Bee who is always white. Despite being upper-class, they are not considered for the role of Queen Bee. In this way, *Gossip Girl* acknowledges girls of color as mean girls, but the ultimate mean girl and the leader of the clique is always white, centering whiteness in a context in which race is seemingly configured as irrelevant.

Saving the Middle-Class Wannabe

Gossip Girl contributes to and updates the contemporary mean girl narrative. In line with girls' studies scholars who have noted the mean girl image is white (Behm-Morawitz & Mastro, 2008; Chesney-Lind & Irwin, 2008; Kelly & Pomerantz, 2009; Ringrose, 2006; Ryalls, 2012), *Gossip Girl* confirms whiteness as an aspect specific to the Queen Bee. The show acknowledges Blair's minions (most of whom are girls of color) as mean girls, yet only white girls are considered for the role of Queen Bee. Upper-classness is also offered as a necessary component of the Queen Bee image. When Blair and her minions are mean, they conform to social expectations of appropriate upper-class behavior, while Jenny and Vanessa's attempts to be like them signify that they are defying normative ideals of middle-class femininity. In constituting the role of Queen Bee as authentically upper-class, *Gossip Girl* relegates middle-class girls to the margins of the upper-class, decreasing their ability to access social power and acceptance, the same power and privileges that remain available to middle-class boys and men. In so doing, *Gossip Girl* upholds cultural expectations of white middle-class girls as moral, self-sacrificing, noncompetitive, and unambitious. The story line of Jenny Humphrey is ultimately a warning about what can happen when a middle-class girl desires to be part of a class to which she does not authentically belong. Jenny's attempts at upward mobility are framed as corrupting the middle-class values of self-control, integrity, family loyalty, and sexual purity. Jenny's forays into wealthy society are shown to cause her to become dishonest, cruel, and bad; on the other hand, Vanessa, a middle-class girl of color, is presented as strong enough to stand against the pull of eliteness. She is in many ways more honorable than the white characters, yet (or perhaps as a result of) she is of no consequence. Instead, the program's focus remains on saving middle-class white girls, like Jenny.

The ways *Gossip Girl* frames Jenny as desiring, gaining, and maintaining popularity are reflective of a social anxiety regarding girls and elitism. Because Jenny is seen as rebelling against her middle-class morality when accumulating social and cultural capital, she is punished for her overt desire to be popular and rise in the hierarchy of The Girls on the Steps and the elite social structure of the UES. As a result, middle-classness is promoted as the baseline of what a nice girl should be. Jenny's brother Dan floats easily through his time at St. Jude's preparatory school, amassing cultural capital and eventually an acceptance to Yale. In line with his middle-class authenticity, Dan turns down Yale because the tuition is too expensive, choosing instead to go to New York University and live at home in Brooklyn. Because Dan is framed as not caring about being popular, unlike Jenny, he is marked by the most "upright and valued motives in the American mythos of upward mobility: hard work, perseverance, and moral uprightness" (Winn, 2000, p. 44). In contrast, Jenny is shown as incapable of using cultural capital and, instead, her forays into elite society are situated as causing her to become dishonest, cruel, and bad. Overwhelmingly, the prep school environment is seen as a dangerous place for white middle-class girls. In the first three seasons of *Gossip Girl*, Jenny's relationships with young women are dominated by fear, control, and aggression.

The Gossip Girl blog constructs class as an identity based on moral value systems as opposed to socio-economic standing, suggesting middle-class girls are incapable of maintaining their morality in an upper-class environment. Unlike her upper-class classmates, eventually the cyberbullying Jenny faces causes her to leave the UES. Removing Jenny from the upper-class lessens her access to greater social power, material benefits, and social privileges that could potentially help her to increase her socio-economic standing. At the end of Season 3, Jenny leaves Manhattan to live with her mother in Hudson, where her father claims there are no "mean girls or drug dealing boyfriends" (Last Tango, Then Paris). Jenny makes her final appearance in the series finale as a guest at Dan and Serena's wedding. When she encounters her ex-stepmother Lily, she smiles and says "last minute inspiration," as she climbs the stairs to the bride. Importantly, the bag she carries, which she indicates with a nod of her head as the "inspiration," is labeled "Waldorf Designs." This moment, in which Jenny's fashion design dreams are dashed and she serves as a courier for her nemesis's fashion line (Blair never expressed any desire to be a fashion designer in the early seasons of the show in which Jenny featured prominently), serves as her ultimate humiliation. Although Rufus claims that leaving town was "the best thing that ever happened to Jenny," we receive no context for what this means. Rufus has deemed her a success, but we are left to assume that success, in his mind, is a return to passive, docile, white, middle-class femininity. Here, again, Jenny's narrative is situated in ambivalence: her moral character remains intact, while her drive and dreams are diminished. She is no longer at-risk, but she also no longer has long-term access to the UES.

Notes

1. This chapter is derived, in part, from an article I published in *Communication and Critical/Cultural Studies* on January 14, 2016, available online: http://dx.doi.org/10.1080/1479142 0.2015.1122200
2. In the season two finale, several of the main characters graduate from high school and attend Manhattan based colleges, such as New York University.
3. Gossip Girl posts her tips anonymously, but, in this case, one of Blair's minions, Nelly Yuki, reports Blair to Headmistress Kweller.

References

Aapola, S., Gonick, M., & Harris, A. (2005). *Young femininity; Girlhood, power, and social change*. New York: Palgrave Macmillan.

Banet-Weiser, S. (1999). *The most beautiful girl in the world: Beauty pageants and national identity*. Berkeley: University of California Press.

Beckstrom, D. C. (2008). State legislation mandating school cyberbullying policies and the potential threat to students' free speech rights. *Vermont Law Review, 33*(283), 283–321.

Behm-Morawitz, E., & Mastro, D. E. (2008). Mean girls? The influence of gender portrayals in teen movies on emerging adults' gender-based attitudes and beliefs. *J & MC Quarterly, 85*(1), 131–146.

Bourdieu, P. (1984). *Distinctions* (R. Nice, Trans.). Cambridge, MA: Harvard University Press.

Bourdieu, P. (1986). The forms of capital. In J. G. Richardson (Ed.), *Handbook of theory and research for the sociology of education* (pp. 241–158). New York: Greenwood Press.

Bourdieu, P. (1990). Academic order and social order: Preface to the 1990 edition. In P. Bourdieu & J.-C. Passeron (Eds.), *Reproduction in education, society and culture* (pp. vii–xiii). London: Sage.

Bourdieu, P., & Passeron, J. (1990). *Reproduction in education, society, and culture*. London: Sage.

Chesney-Lind, M., & Irwin, K. (2008). *Beyond bad girls: Gender, violence and hype*. New York: Routledge.

Cookson, P. W. J., & Persell, C. H. (1985). *Preparing for power: America's elite boarding schools.* New York: Basic Books.

Dubrofsky, R. E., & Ryalls, E. D. (2014). *The Hunger Games:* Performing not-performing to authenticate femininity and whiteness. *Critical Studies in Media Communication, 31*(5), 395–409.

Dyer, R. (1997). *White.* New York: Routledge.

Foster, G. A. (2010). *Class-passing: Social mobility in film and popular culture.* Carbondale: Southern Illinois University Press.

Foucault, M. (1995). *Discipline & punish: The birth of the prison.* New York: Vintage Books.

Franklin, N. (2007, November 26). High-school onfidential. *The New Yorker.* Retrieved from http://www.newyorker.com/magazine/2007/11/26/high-school-confidential-2

Gonick, M. (2004). The 'mean girl' crisis: Problematizing representations of girls' friendships. *Feminism & Psychology, 14*(3), 395–400.

Harris, A. (2004). *Future girl: Young women in the twenty-first century.* New York: Routledge.

Hasinoff, A. A. (2008). Fashioning race for the free market on *America's Next Top Model. Critical Studies in Media Communication, 25*(3), 324–343.

hooks, b. (2000). *Where we stand: Class matters.* New York: Routledge.

Johnson, P. E. (2003). *Appropriating blackness: Performance and the politics of authenticity.* Durham, NC: Duke University Press.

Joseph, R. L. (2009). "Tyra Banks is fat": Reading (post-)racism and (post-)feminism in the new millennium. *Critical Studies in Media Communication, 26*(3), 237–254.

Kelly, D. M., & Pomerantz, S. (2009). Mean, wild, and alienated: Girls and the state of feminism in popular culture. *Girlhood Studies, 2*(1), 1–19.

Kendall, D. (2010). Class: still alive and reproducing in the United States. In M. S. Kimmel & A. L. Ferber (Eds.), *Privilege: A reader* (2nd ed., pp. 145–152). Boulder, CO: Westview.

Klein, J. (2012). *The bully society: School shootings and the crisis of bullying in America's schools.* New York University Press.

Mantsios, G. (2000a). Class in America: Myths and realities. In T. E. Ore (Ed.), *The social construction of difference and inequality: Race, class, gender, and sexuality* (pp. 512–526). London: Mayfield Publishing Company.

Mantsios, G. (2000b). Media magic: Making class invisible. In T. E. Ore (Ed.), *The social construction of difference and inequality: Race, class, gender, and sexuality* (pp. 512–526). London: Mayfield Publishing Company.

Ouellette, L., & Hay, J. (2008). *Better living through reality TV: Television and post-welfare citizenship* Malden, MA: Blackwell Publishing.

Ringrose, J. (2006). A new universal mean girl: Examining the discursive construction and social regulation of a new feminine pathology. *Feminism & Psychology, 16*(4), 405–424.

Ross, S. (2008). Dormant dormitory friendships: Race and gender in *Felicity*." In G. Davis & K. Dickinson (Eds.), *Teen TV: Genre, consumption and identity* (pp. 141–150). British Film Institute.

Ryalls, E. D. (2012). Demonizing "mean girls" in the news: Was Phoebe Prince "bullied to death?" *Communication, Culture, & Critique, 5,* 463–481.

Ryalls, E. D. (2016). Ambivalent aspirationalism in millennial postfeminist culture on *Gossip Girl*. *Communication and Critical/Cultural Studies, 5*, 463–481.

Schwartz, J. (2007–2012). *Gossip girl* [Television series]. Burbank, CA: Warner Brothers Television.

Simmons, R. (2002). *Odd girl out: The hidden culture of aggression in girls*. New York: Harcourt.

Walkerdine, V. (1997). *Daddy's girl: Young girls and popular culture*. Cambridge, MA: Harvard University Press.

Winn, J. E. (2007). *The American dream and contemporary Hollywood cinema*. New York: Continuum.

Wiseman, R. (2002). *Queen bees & wannabes*. New York: Three Rivers Press.

CONCLUSION

Trumping the Myths of Bullying

It has been 18 years since the Columbine massacre rocked the U.S. public conscious and, as a result of Simmons and Wiseman's books, 15 years since "mean girls" entered (and were forefronted in) the bullying lexicon. During this period, schools and lawmakers have spent a great deal of time and energy attempting to put an end to the problem of bullying, but little has changed. As discussed in Chapter 1, while there has been a decline in reports of bullying in schools, anti-bullying curriculum has been shown to be largely ineffective. What's more, for nearly two decades U.S. culture has been telling kids to be "nice," because bullies are truly terrible people who get nowhere in life, yet in 2016, this same culture elected Donald Trump president of the United States. To say that Trump ran his campaign, and now the country, as a bully is an understatement. Trump "gleefully flouts all of the usual rules of political and social decorum, constantly launching attacks—many of them rather offensive—against both his political rivals and members of the media he believes have treated him unfairly" (Singal, 2015). Given the anti-bullying movement, Trump, who openly mocked the disabled and women and who has shown unadulterated hostility toward Muslims, Latinx immigrants, and Black Americans is seemingly a paradox (Bouie, 2017; Curry, 2016). In a cultural context where kids are told over and over again that bullies never win, the country elected a man who has already eroded "the moral values that schools and parents have been helping to instill in young people—empathy and 'upstanding,' a term schools use that means looking out for fellow students who are being mistreated" (Bazelon, 2016). Since his election, "the Southern Poverty Law Center has received more than 430 reports of bullying, harassment and racist displays around the country" (Bazelon, 2016).

To call Trump a bully seems obvious; perhaps less obvious is that he more specifically fits many of the qualities of the Queen Bee as she has been constructed in popular media. His tendency to roll his eyes, make negative facial expressions, and verbally reject others is in line with the tactics of relational aggression. More precisely, the Queen Bee is able to intimidate and terrorize others while simultaneously manipulating her minions to carry out her commands. Trump has mastered these tactics; the majority of the Republican party seems "terrified of arousing the ire of (its) tempestuous new leader" (Bade, 2016). In most cases, Trump does not have to "speak or tweet himself. Plenty of others are willing to do it for him" (Bade, 2016). When Trump does tweet, he use his Twitter account repeatedly to shame anyone who dares to disagree with him, and, during the campaign, "he regularly took shots at adversaries, including Marco Rubio ("Little Marco"), Ted Cruz ("Lyin' Ted"), and Speaker Paul Ryan (a "very weak and ineffective leader")" (Bade, 2016).

While in popular media sites, hierarchy, methods of relational aggression, sexism, and racism are framed as intrinsic to Girl World, these issues are endemic to U.S. culture. As Hadley (2003) explains, the tactics of relational aggression are not new:

> They include calling people names, such as "the axis of evil;" refusing to let people into your group, often part of racism, anti-Semitism and playground games; threatening to cut off relations or resources, such as embargoes, ending diplomatic ties, and divorce; practicing the elitism and exclusion emblematic of caste systems or the social register. (pp. 376–377)

In their short time in the White House, Trump and his minions have shown themselves to be experts at these tactics (i.e., name-calling, ostracizing, marginalizing, and excluding). Michael Anton, Jeff Sessions, Stephen Miller, and Stephen Bannon occupy prominent positions in Trump's administration. Under a pseudonym, Anton wrote that Islam is an inherently violent religion, "defended the World War II-era America First Committee, which included anti-Semites, as 'unfairly maligned,' and called diversity 'a source of weakness, tension and disunion'" (Schulberg, 2017). According to the NAACP Legal

Defense Fund, "Sessions showed 'an unrelenting hostility toward civil rights and racial justice'" (Bouie, 2017). Miller's high school classmates remember him as a bigot, xenophobe, and homophobe. A Duke University (Miller is an alumnus) administrator calls Miller "incredibly intolerant" (King, 2017). Bannon "made a single hop from the leader of Breitbart, the nation's most bigoted mainstream website, to bullying his way into the highest office in the land" (King, 2017). These men are "the architects of Trump's policy, the executors of a frighteningly coherent political ideology…of unvarnished nativism and prejudice" (Bouie, 2017).

The ascension of Trump and his minions speaks to many of the myths of youth bullying that I have outlined in this book. First, social and relational aggression have been cemented in the public consciousness as a biologically determined feminine way to bully. As I discussed in Chapter 3, while there are images of "mean boys" in popular culture, they are queered and situated as feminine, further bolstering this myth. Trump and his minions' identities as heterosexual men who manipulate, gossip, and exclude shatter this illusion. Not only do boys use covert forms of aggression, adult men do as well, which destroys a second myth of youth bullying. Narratives of bullying seem insistent that bullying is a youth problem and that no longer being a victim (and presumably a bully) is as simple as growing up. For instance, Dan Savage's It Gets Better project has been roundly critiqued for suggesting that LGBTQ teens "just wait it out" (Majkowski, 2011, p. 164) and "endure suffering in the interest of inevitable happiness" (Grzanka & Mann, 2014, p. 369). The Trump administration is indicative of the ways in which bullying is widespread among adults.

Third, while the bullying discourse works to individualize racism, sexism, and homophobia as bullying behaviors carried out by "mean" teens, the Trump administration reveals the systemic nature of these oppressive structures. Not only are Trump and his minions bullies, but their policies work to marginalize women, LGBTQ individuals, and people of color. According to American Civil Liberties Union LGBT project director James Esseks, Trump "has surrounded himself with a vice president and Cabinet members who have repeatedly sought to sanction discrimination against LGBT people in the name of religion" (Boyer, 2017). For example, in February 2017, Trump and the Departments of Justice and Education bullied transgender kids by rescinding "instructions that schools nationwide must respect the gender identities of transgender students, allowing them access to bathrooms and other facilities or single-sex programs that align with their sense of self" (Steinmetz, 2017).

Fourth, cultural anxiety about cyberbullying is reflective of adult fear of the ways in which youth use new communication technologies, situating bullying online as something only young people do. Indeed, First Lady Melania Trump has "called for a gentler and kinder America…where children can spend time on social media without fear of harassment" (Gambino, 2016). Given her husband's use of Twitter where he regularly mocks and degrades his critics and shares "posts from sources with a history of spreading racism, antisemitism or white supremacy" (Gambino, 2016), Melania's insistence that cyberbullying is the purview of young people is laughable. Indeed, as Shariff and Gouin (2006) point out, "Not only is cyber-bullying prevalent among adolescents, but it also occurs among adults" (p. 34). Of course, it is only among teens that cyberbullying is represented as a tool for murder.

A final myth of the contemporary bullying discourse (not connected to Trump's presidency) is the causal link between bullying and suicide, most clearly exhibited through the term "bullycide." Bazelon (2012) quotes Ann Haas, a senior project specialist for the American Foundation for Suicide Prevention, as saying that one problematic message embedded in "bullycide" is that "bullying kills—as if it's a normal response to kill yourself, when of course most people who are bullied *don't* do that." In the tragic case of the suicide pact between 14-year-old best friends Paige and Haylee, media repeatedly report that the cause of their pact was the bullying they faced (Hopper, 2011; Prois, 2011; Quigley, 2011). The insistence that bullying triggered Paige and Haylee to kill themselves continues, despite the fact that their mothers explained that both girls were being treated for depression (Quigley, 2011). As opposed to constructing teens, like Haylee, Paige, Phoebe Prince, and Tyler Clementi as facing several challenges that were very hard for them to manage, the bullying narrative represents teens who bully online as wholly unredeemable murderers, deserving of legal retribution.

Where Do We Go From Here?

My interest in this project was piqued when I saw the intense media scrutiny being paid to mean girls. Like many others, I was 10 the first time I was stung by a Queen Bee. My last year in elementary school began like any other. I was thrilled to leave for school, but, as soon as I reached the playground, I knew something was amiss. Instead of being greeted by my friends warmly, I faced nastiness, manipulation, and exclusion, all key traits of what we now understand to be relational aggression. During the next two months, my one-time friends giggled when I walked by, called me names behind my back, created and perpetuated a number of rumors about me, and maintained control over the rest of my classmates, who also ignored me. At the end of the two months, the isolation abruptly ended when the person who perpetrated the socially aggressive attack approached me to apologize. His name was Jack. Although Jack was the first Queen Bee to victimize me, he was certainly not the last. Who that person was varied over the years—sometimes I was the victim; on other occasions, I behaved in relationally aggressive ways, creating new victims. My own experiences led me to believe that the fixed racialized and gendered binaries created in media with regard to bullying were far too simplistic.

In the 15 years since the publication of Simmons and Wiseman's books, representations of vulnerable victims and mean bullies in several sites of media, including books, newspaper and magazine articles, television shows, and films have proliferated. The media sites I explored in this book, while not exhaustive, are illustrative of a pattern of representation of the victim/bully dichotomy in popular culture. While I have argued against the totalizing image of the always selfish, always cruel, and always evil bully, I do not mean to suggest that bullying is not a serious cultural problem. However, the myths perpetuated by media regarding bullying lead to a cultural milieu focused on the wrong issues (i.e., cyberbullying and bullycide) and nearly fanatical about arresting mean kids. While we may hear more about cyberbullying, there is currently no evidence that online bullying has increased or occurs more often than traditional face-to-face bullying (boyd & Palfrey, 2013; Meredith, 2012). Moreover, although bullying occurs among both boys and girls, the focus in popular culture on girls' aggression characterizes girl bullying as different from and, in most cases, more dangerous than physical violence. This illusion works to uphold a dichotomy in which boys only bully other boys, while girls seemingly bully only girls, erasing the bullying and harassment girls face from boys.

The myths and misinformation that circulate within the bullying discourse are widely believed by those who have substantial power over youth, which "makes the need to get the record straight all the more apparent" (Chesney-Lind & Irwin, 2008, p. 2). As I have discussed, "zero-tolerance policies aimed at stopping bullying may actually backfire" (Fox, 2016) and should be eliminated. As mentioned earlier, all 50 states now have bullying laws; of those 50, 23 include "cyberbullying" as part of the law, and of those, 14 include off-campus behaviors (Hinduja & Patchin, 2016). Most bullying laws see cyberbullying as a problem that should be dealt with at the school level, leaving it to the up to the school to discipline students in cases of cyberbullying (Warren, 2014). As it stands now, these statutes are incredibly vague, so when, where, and for what students should be punished is also ambiguous. Troublingly, it seems more often than not schools, in an attempt to teach kids a lesson, are quick to discipline, a zero sum game that does nothing to actually eliminate bullying from academic culture. Cyberbullying legislation should allow "school administrators to discipline students for on-campus cyberbullying but not off-campus conduct, unless the off-campus bullying constitutes an objective threat of violence to students, teachers, or school administrators" (Beckstrom, 2008, p. 320). In Chapter 4, I quoted documentarian Michael Moore as saying, "Anything that might help end the problem of bullying can't be seen as a negative." This statement is reflective of so many people's views of bullying. Of course, bullying is bad; of course, bullies are terrible people, so we should do *whatever it takes*.

We need to be much more creative with how we address bullying. Schools "must balance *legal* constraints such as equality and freedom of expression through innovative, *educational responses* to address bullying" (Shariff & Gouin, 2006, p. 31, original emphasis). According to a panel of experts commissioned by the National Academy of Sciences, "The programs that appear most effective are those that promote a positive school environment and combine social and emotional skill building for all students, with targeted interventions for those at greatest risk for being involved in bullying" (Fox, 2016). Anti-bullying curriculum is often focused on empowering the bystander to intervene on behalf of the victim; however, research shows that less overt forms of intervention, those that do not require directly addressing the bully, may be more productive (Dillon & Bushman, 2015). For instance, in October 2015, the Ad Council and a coalition of media, corporate, and non-profit partners launched the "I Am a Witness" campaign. The campaign's logo—an open eye within a speech bubble—was made in to an emoji. Using the emoji, kids can "call out bullying in text messages or online communications" (Beres, 2015).

I know that in being critical of our cultural response to bullying, cyberbullying, and, most significantly, bullycide, I run the risk of being seen as callous and heartless. In fact, I see my approach to this project as being exactly the opposite. I take very seriously the damage that bullying can cause to both the victim and the bully; however, I take issue with the simplistic way in which bullying has been structured in the public discourse. The myths of this narrative at face value are illogical (i.e., girls' verbal communication is *more* damaging than boys' physical violence), yet they seem to have taken hold to such an extent that they are largely unquestioned. When journalists and filmmakers tell stories about bullycide, as opposed to explaining the multiple reasons as to why teens take their lives, they represent the same particular story in which an individual's (or individuals') bullying behaviors murdered the vulnerable victim. This trope mistakenly leads to the conclusion that sending mean teens to jail will stop other potential victims—mainly white girls and gay boys (or those perceived as gay)—from killing themselves. Moreover, as I have shown, the erasure of certain identities from the coverage of victims, namely lesbians, and girls and boys of color, aligns representations of bullying with long established discourses about white youth while repackaging them for a new audience under the guise of "bullying." It is my hope that in raising these critiques of the bullying discourse, we can take more seriously the effects that structural sexism, racism, classism, and homophobia have on young people, looking broadly at culture as opposed to individual youth.

References

Bade, R. (2016, December 21). Trump posse browbeats hill Republicans. *Politico*. Retrieved from http://www.politico.com/story/2016/12/donald-trump-congress-republicans-232800

Bazelon, E. (2012, March 29). The problem with *Bully*. *Slate Magazine*. Retrieved from http://www.slate.com/articles/news_and_politics/bulle/2012/03/bully_documentary_lee_hirsch_s_film_dangerously_oversimplifies_the_connection_between_bullying_and_suicide_.html

Bazelon, E. (2016, November 16). Bullying in the age of Trump. *The New York Times*. Retrieved from https://www.nytimes.com/2016/11/16/opinion/bullying-in-the-age-of-trump.html?_r=0

Beckstrom, D. C. (2008). State legislation mandating school cyberbullying policies and the potential threat to students' free speech rights. *Vermont Law Review, 33*(283), 283–321.

Beres, D. (2015, November 4). How a powerful anti-bullying message became one simple emoji. *The Huffington Post*. Retrieved from http://www.huffingtonpost.com/entry/i-am-a-witness-emoji-anti-bullying_us_56376cbce4b063179912de88

Bouie, J. (2017, February 6). Government by white nationalism is upon us. *Slate*. Retrieved from http://www.slate.com/articles/news_and_politics/cover_story/2017/02/government_by_white_nationalism_is_upon_us.html

boyd, d., & Palfrey, J. (2013). What you must know to help combat youth bullying, meanness, and cruelty. *Kinder & Braver World Project* (Vol. 2013–5). Cambridge, MA: The Berkman Center for Internet & Society.

Boyer, D. (2017, January 31). Trump will preserve Obama's order to protect LGBT workers under federal contract. *The Washington Times*. Retrieved from http://www.washingtontimes.com/news/2017/jan/31/white-house-tries-calm-fears-gay-rights-rollback/

Chesney-Lind, M., Irwin, K. (2008). *Beyond bad girls: Gender, violence and hype*. New York: Routledge.

Curry, A. (2016, June 9). What does the success of Trump's campaign say to our kids…and future bullies? *The Huffington Post*. Retrieved from http://www.huffingtonpost.com/andi-curry/what-does-the-success-of-_b_10323720.html

Dillon, K. P., & Bushman, B. J. (2015, April). Unresponsive or un-noticed?: Cyberbystander intervention in an experimental cyberbullying context. *Computers in Human Behavior, 45*, 144–150.

Fox, M. (2016, May 10). Zero-tolerance for bullying doesn't work, experts say. *NBC News*. Retrieved from http://www.nbcnews.com/health/kids-health/zero-tolerance-bullying-doesn-t-work-experts-say-n571326

Gambino, L. (2016, November 3). Melania Trump takes on cyberbullying. *The Guardian*. Retrieved from https://www.theguardian.com/us-news/2016/nov/03/melania-trump-cyberbullying-campaign-speech

Grzanka, P. R., & Mann, E. S. (2014). Queer youth suicide and the psychopolitics of "it gets better." *Sexualities, 17*(4), 369–393.

Hadley, M. (2003). Relational, indirect, adaptive or just mean: Recent work on aggression in adolescent girls—Part 1. *Studies in Gender and Sexuality, 4*(4), 367–394.

Hinduja, S., & Patchin, J. W. (2009). *Bullying beyond the schoolyard: Preventing and responding to cyberbullying*. Thousand Oaks, CA: Corwin Press.

Hopper, J. (2011, April 20). Suicide pact: Minnesota teens Haylee Fentress and Paige Moravetz commit suicide at slumber party. *ABC News*. Retrieved from http://abcnews.go.com/US/suicide-pact-minnesota-eighth-graders-haylee-fentress-paige/story?id=13411751

King, S. (2017, February 13). Stephen Miller is the latest insufferable liar and bigot on Team Trump. *Daily News*. Retrieved from http://www.nydailynews.com/news/politics/king-stephen-miller-latest-liar-bigot-team-trump-article-1.2971639

Majkowski, T. (2011, March). The "it gets better campaign": An unfortunate use of queer futurity. *Women & Performance: A Journal of Feminist Theory, 21*(1), 163–165.

Meredith, L. (2012, August 7). Cyberbullying claims exaggerated. *Laptop Mag*. Retrieved from http://www.laptopmag.com/articles/cyberbullying-claims-exaggerated

Prois, J. (2011, April 21). Bullied middle schoolers, Paige Moravetz and Haylee Fentress, take lives in suicide pact. *The Huffington Post*. Retrieved from http://www.huffingtonpost.com/2011/04/21/marshall-middle-school-suicide_n_852252.html

Quigley, R. (2011, April 26). 'Never let a day go by when you don't say I love you': Mothers of suicide pact teens reveal agony of their daughters' deaths. *The Daily Mail*. Retrieved from http://www.dailymail.co.uk/news/article-1380771/Devastated-mothers-Minnesota-suicide-pact-teens-emotional-interview.html

Schulberg, J. (2017, February 8). Trump aide derided Islam, immigration and diversity, embraced an anti-semitic past. *The Huffington Post*. Retrieved from http://www.huffingtonpost.com/entry/michael-anton-trump-essay-publius-decius-mus_us_589ba947e4b09bd304bff3c8

Shariff, S., & Gouin, R. (2006). Cyber-dilemmas: Gendered hierarchies, free expression and cyber-safety in schools. *Atlantis, 31*(1), 27–37.

Singal, J. (2015, September 10). An expert on bullying explains Donald Trump's mean, consequence-free rise. *Science of Us*. Retrieved from http://nymag.com/scienceofus/2015/09/bullying-researcher-explains-donald-trump.html?mid=huffpost_parents-pubexchange_article

Steinmetz, K. (2017, February 23). President Trump just rolled back guidelines that protected transgender students. *Time*. Retrieved from http://time.com/4679063/donald-trump-transgender-bathroom/

Warren, A. (2014, July 1). 49 states have cyberbullying laws: Is your state one of them? *Crimewire*. Retrieved from https://www.instantcheckmate.com/crimewire/post/cyberbullying-laws-by-state/

INDEX

Sharon R. Mazzarella
General Editor

Grounded in cultural studies, books in this series will study the cultures, artifacts, and media of children, tweens, teens, and college-aged youth. Whether studying television, popular music, fashion, sports, toys, the Internet, self-publishing, leisure, clubs, school, cultures/activities, film, dance, language, tie-in merchandising, concerts, subcultures, or other forms of popular culture, books in this series go beyond the dominant paradigm of traditional scholarship on the effects of media/culture on youth. Instead, authors endeavor to understand the complex relationship between youth and popular culture. Relevant studies would include, but are not limited to studies of how youth negotiate their way through the maze of corporately-produced mass culture; how they themselves have become cultural producers; how youth create "safe spaces" for themselves within the broader culture; the political economy of youth culture industries; the representational politics inherent in mediated coverage and portrayals of youth; and so on. Books that provide a forum for the "voices" of the young are particularly encouraged. The source of such voices can range from in-depth interviews and other ethnographic studies to textual analyses of cultural artifacts created by youth.

For further information about the series and submitting manuscripts, please contact:

SHARON R. MAZZARELLA
School of Communication Studies
James Madison University
Harrisonburg, VA 22807

To order other books in this series, please contact our Customer Service Department at:

(800) 770-LANG (within the U.S.)
(212) 647-7706 (outside the U.S.)
(212) 647-7707 FAX

Or browse online by series at WWW.PETERLANG.COM